SHEATHING THE SWORD

Recent Titles in
Contributions in Political Science

Ethics for Policymaking: A Methodological Analysis
Eugene J. Meehan

Foreign Policy and Ethnic Groups: American and Canadian Jews Lobby for Israel
David Howard Goldberg

U.S. Senate Decision-Making: The Trade Agreements Act of 1979
Robert W. Jerome

Policy Theory and Policy Evaluation: Concepts, Knowledge, Causes, and Norms
Stuart S. Nagel, editor

The Nixon Presidency: Power and Politics in Turbulent Times
Michael A. Genovese

Cautious Revolution: The European Community Arrives
Clifford Hackett

Biotechnology: Assessing Social Impacts and Policy Implications
David J. Webber, editor

Carl Schmitt: Politics and Theory
Paul Edward Gottfried

Outdoor Recreation Policy: Pleasure and Preservation
John D. Hutcheson, Jr., Francis P. Noe, and Robert E. Snow, editors

Governors, Legislatures, and Budgets: Diversity across the American States
Edward J. Clynch and Thomas P. Laugh, editors

Conflict Resolution and Public Policy
Miriam K. Mills, editor

Surveillance in the Stacks: The FBI's Library Awareness Program
Herbert N. Foerstel

SHEATHING THE SWORD

The U.N. Secretary-General
and the Prevention of
International Conflict

THOMAS E. BOUDREAU

Foreword by James S. Sutterlin

Contributions in Political Science, Number 273

GREENWOOD PRESS

New York • Westport, Connecticut • London

Library of Congress Cataloging-in-Publication Data

Boudreau, Tom.
    Sheathing the sword : the UN Secretary-General and the prevention
of international conflict / Thomas E. Boudreau ; foreword by James
S. Sutterlin.
        p.   cm. — (Contributions in political science, ISSN 0147-1066 ;
no. 273)
    Includes bibliographical references and index.
    ISBN 0-313-26109-1 (alk. paper)
    1. United Nations. Secretary-General. 2. Peaceful change
(International relations) 3. Pacific settlement of international
disputes. I. Title. II. Series.
JX1977.A362B68   1991
327.1'7–dc20   90-47520

British Library Cataloguing in Publication Data is available.

Library of Congress Catalog Card Number: 90-47520
ISBN: 0-313-26109-1
ISSN: 0147-1066

First published in 1991

Greenwood Press, 88 Post Road West, Westport, CT 06881
An imprint of Greenwood Publishing Group, Inc.

Printed in the United States of America

(∞)

The paper used in this book complies with the
Permanent Paper Standard issued by the National
Information Standards Organization (Z39.48-1984).

10 9 8 7 6 5 4 3 2 1

Copyright Acknowledgments

The author and publisher thank the following for permission to use extracts of their
work:

*The Quiet Approach: A Study of the Good Offices Exercised by the United Nations
Secretary-General in the Cause of Peace* by Vlatislav Pechota, sales no.
E.75.XV.PS/6, copyright UNITAR, published by United Nations Institute for
Training and Research, New York, 1972;

Whole-Earth Security: A Geopolitics of Peace by Dan Deudney, World Watch
Institute, Washington, D.C.;

Protecting the Innocent (1983) and *The Secretary-General and Satellite Diplomacy*
(1984) by Tom Boudreau, Carnegie Council on Ethics and International Affairs,
New York;

The Secretary-General of the United Nations: His Political Powers and Practice by
Stephen M. Schwebel, published by Harvard University Press, Cambridge, Mass.,
copyright © 1952 by the President and Fellows of Harvard College, reprinted by
permission.

Dedicated to *Private Joe Polowsky,*

who first gave life to the

"spirit of the Elbe," and who

did not let the dream die

There was a tremendous burst of lilacs as we approached the Elbe River. This exaltation of being alive.... There were even jokes that we were approaching the River Jordan, crossing into Canaan.... We also knew that the United Nations was being born in San Francisco on the very same day, twenty-fifth of April. Can you imagine? The very day we linked up with the Russians at the Elbe River.

— Private Joe Polowsky

CONTENTS

FOREWORD

It is a good and propitious time to consider in depth the political role of the Secretary-General of the United Nations in the prevention and resolution of conflict. The drafters of the UN Charter accorded to the Secretary-General a political mandate advisedly, with a clear purpose in mind: to strengthen the capacity of the new world organization to maintain peace. It was one of their wisest innovations. There have been times when some Member-States of the United Nations have clearly regretted the mandate given, taking umbrage at the resolve of Secretaries-General to act in the interest of peace rather than the interest of one or another country. But the Secretaries-General have prevailed, deeply convinced of the importance of their freedom to act independently of the pressure or influence of any government or ideology when they have seen peace and international security threatened.

The wording of the Charter is sparse in defining the political role of the Secretary-General. To do the bidding of the principal organs of the United Nations as provided in Article 98 would seem at first glance more a task than a privilege. To bring to the attention of the Security Council any perceived threat to international peace and security as provided in Article 99 would seem a power seldom to be applicable in a literal sense and, indeed, it has been only rarely invoked in the early years of the United Nations' existence. Yet it is from these Articles that the global political role played by successive Secretaries-General derives. For by extension they require that a Secretary-General be informed of circumstances and conditions that may lead to conflict, that he reach conclusions on faults and intentions, and that he act as necessary in his judgment to fulfill the ultimate intentions of these Articles, which is to make of the Secretary-General a unique instrument for preventing war.

When the Charter was agreed to in San Francisco these crucial Articles were the subject of little debate. Field Marshal Jan Christian Smuts said later there was general agreement that the position of the Secretary-General "should be of the highest importance and for this reason a large measure of initiative was expressly conferred." With the notable changes in Soviet foreign policy — not least with regard to the United Nations — since Mikhail Gorbachev assumed leadership in Moscow, this early agreement seems to have been restored. Just as the improved relationship between the Soviet Union and the United States has increased the present and potential effectiveness of the Security Council, so, too, has the restored consensus on the political role of the Secretary-General both facilitated and enhanced his ability to act to prevent conflict, an objective to which the present Secretary-General has attributed the highest importance since his first day in office.

Under these encouraging circumstances, it is compellingly logical that the Secretary-General be equipped with all the means needed to take advantage of the opportunities that exist in larger measure than in the past to contribute to peace. In the present book, Dr. Boudreau has put forward serious and original suggestions concerning what is required, drawing on the experience of five Secretaries-General and on a profound understanding of the significance of the relevant Articles of the Charter and of the global reach of the Secretary-General's preventive responsibilities. This can contribute substantially to a very immediate need. For now is the time to ensure that the Secretary-General of the United Nations has the resources — human, technological, and financial — that will permit him to play his intended political role in preventing those conflicts by which a world still rent by racial hostility, social tensions, and grave economic want will long be threatened.

James S. Sutterlin, Visiting Fellow
Institution for Social and Policy Studies, Yale University
Former Director in the Executive Office of the Secretary-General
November 1989

PREFACE

While conducting research on the United Nations over the past several years (1982–1988), I have been fortunate to have the help of many people. Yet, regretfully, I cannot thank or acknowledge all of them here; some have requested confidentiality, others have moved on, and one, Wilfred Mercer, Chief of the UN Communications Service, died unexpectedly in 1984. Mr. Mercer provided invaluable assistance in helping me understand UN communications.

The idea for this book began as I worked as Project Director of the UN and Crisis Management Research Projects (1982–1984) at the Carnegie Council on Ethics and International Affairs in New York City (then called the Council on Religion and International Affairs). Working there was an extremely rewarding experience. I want to give a special thanks to Robert J. Myers, President of the Carnegie Council; I would also like to thank Ulrike Klopfer, Susan Wolfson, and John Tessitore (the latter two are now at the United Nations Association of the U.S.A.) for their help and editorial assistance during my time at the Carnegie Council (1982–1984). Furthermore, this book would never have been written without the original inspiration and support of L. F. Goldie, Director of the International Legal Studies Program at the Syracuse University's Ernest I. White College of Law. He served as legal advisor to my research projects at the Carnegie Council. Many UN diplomats and Secretariat officials provided insights and assistance as well. I want to thank James O. C. Jonah, Assistant Secretary-General and head of the Secretary-General's new Office of Research and Collection of Information (ORCI). I also want to thank Tapio Kanninen, Timour Dmitrichev, Juergin Dedring, and David Biggs of ORCI for their help and constructive criticisms. I would especially like to thank James

Sutterlin, former Director, in the Executive Office of the Secretary-General, now a visiting fellow at the Institution for Social and Policy Studies at Yale University. His wise advice has been invaluable over the past several years.

Finally, I would like to thank Brian Urquhart, formerly the Under-Secretary-General for Special Political Affairs and now Scholar-in-Residence at the Ford Foundation; Mr. Urquhart kindly allowed me to quote extensively, in Chapters 3 and 4 below, from his book *Hammarskjöld*.

The research for this book was done during a difficult time for the United Nations. During the early 1980s, the United Nations seemed to be an "orphan child" in U.S. academia and seemed largely ignored as a serious scholarly subject. (This has, of course, belatedly changed with the recent successes of UN diplomacy throughout the world.) Fortunately, scholars at Yale University proved to be an outstanding exception to this "benign neglect." In particular, Paul Bracken, Bruce M. Russett, and William Foltz provided constant encouragement. In view of this, I would like to thank them for their support. With their help, a UN/Yale War Prevention Diplomacy Project was organized in the spring of 1985. Since then, a number of conferences have been sponsored by this joint project to investigate the possibilities and problems of a war prevention diplomacy in a multinuclear world. Several sections of this book were presented as papers at these conferences and are appropriately cited in the following text.

For instance, an updated version of Chapter 11 was presented to the Warsaw Seminar on War-Risk Reduction held in late April 1989. This seminar consisted of 16 scholars and diplomats from the United States, Europe, and the Soviet Union. The seminar was co-sponsored by the Yale Program for International Security and Arms Control, the United Nations Secretariat, and the Polish Peace Research Council. Secretary-General Pérez de Cuéllar met with us in the Warsaw Castle during the last day of this seminar.

Earlier parts of Part I and Chapter 10 were published in the Carnegie Council Reports: *Protecting the Innocent* (1983) and *The Secretary-General and Satellite Diplomacy* (1984). The key ideas concerning UN negotiating teams, discussed in Chapter 9, were published in *WORLDVIEW* in November 1983. The idea for such teams originally comes from a negotiating technique developed by the Iroquois Indians, governed by the "Great Law of Peace," who still reside in upstate New York.

Among those who commented on parts of the final draft of this book were Gordon Thompson, Director of the Institute for Resource and Security Studies in Cambridge, Massachusetts (and valued colleague in the PRISM Project), Daniel Deudney at Princeton University, Seymour Maxwell Finger at the Ralph Bunche Institute at the City University of New York, Marc Catudel at St. John's University, and Teresa Rae Farley, Esq., in Minneapolis.

I would also like to acknowledge the faculty research grant that I received from St. John's University for the summer of 1989 that enabled me to complete this book.

These funds enabled me to hire Ann Temple and Mary Melfi as research assistants; they provided invaluable editorial assistance during the last stages of writing this book. I would especially like to thank Martha Melfi who has typed innumerable drafts of this book.

Finally, I would like to thank my wife, Mary, for her patience, humor, and perseverance during my absences on research trips and during the many weekends that I have worked on this book.

The assistance, insights, and criticisms of such people have helped shape *Sheathing the Sword*. Nevertheless, final responsibility for the recommendations and any error contained within is mine alone.

SHEATHING THE SWORD

I

A PARADOXICAL PEACE

We are living in an age of apparent extremes; while the Cold War seems to be abating, violence and bloodshed seem to be the daily fare of Cambodia, Central America, the Middle East, and southern Africa. Europe is tearing down old walls, and a new political rapprochement seems to be emerging between the East and West; yet, at the same time, long neglected and enduring ethnic conflicts increasingly threaten to rend the social fabric within eastern Europe and even the Soviet Union.

At the same time, the political and economic differences between the North and the South are becoming more pronounced. Extraordinary population growth coupled with extreme poverty creates a powder keg of rising expectations among the poorest peoples and states in the world. There is a growing danger of conflict in sub-Sahara Africa and South America caused by resource scarcity or massive social dislocation because of environmental degradation. The problems of inflation, debt, hunger, AIDS, oil dependence and depletion, and narcotics are increasingly threatening entire societies. The gap between the rich and poor continues to widen throughout the world. Thus, the current era seems to be a curious combination of intensified expectations of peace coupled with new and increasing dangers of social upheavals, regional ethnic conflicts, and even war. In such times, the hope of lasting international peace seems, at the very least, premature despite some promising short-term trends.

Furthermore, dangerous contradictions continue to plague the growing political and economic relationships between the United States and the Soviet Union. While both sides profess peaceful intentions toward one another, each side apparently continues to build new nuclear weapons.[1] Despite the START negotiations, both sides also continue to modernize their strategic nuclear delivery systems, leading the world deeper into the dreaded era of counterforce weaponry. For instance, only a few days after the Malta summit between Presidents Bush and Gorbachev, the U.S. Navy tested its new D-5 or Trident II missile — arguably the most dangerous counterforce weapon yet developed. At the same time, nuclear, chemical, and missile proliferation continues throughout the world as other nation-states, such as Brazil, South Africa, Pakistan, and Iraq, come closer to developing, or actually producing, the atomic bomb.[2] Because of these paradoxical political developments, it is not clear whether this is a new age of peace, or whether nations simply continue, as Shakespeare states, to commit "the oldest sins the newest kind of ways."

In view of these disturbing realities, it makes simple sense to examine carefully and critically the practical prospects of finding peaceful solutions to potential — or actual — international conflicts. In particular, institutions or individuals who can effectively intervene in a political crisis deserve special attention; they are a rare and precious international resource that should not be casually dismissed as being irrelevant to the realpolitik of international affairs. One such individual is the Secretary-General of the United Nations.

Although the political influence of the UN Secretary-General may seem at times marginal, and even insignificant, his office has proven to be in the past a key focal point of international efforts to prevent war. For instance, largely through the preventive efforts of Hammarskjöld, the danger of war between the United States and the People's Republic of China was averted in the mid-1950s.[3] The intervention of Secretary-General Thant in the 1962 Cuban crisis bought time for both the Soviets and Americans.[4] The determined and distinguished efforts of Pérez de Cuéllar nearly succeeded in preventing the Falkland/Malvinas War — even though he intervened at the last minute after U.S. Secretary-of-State Haig's shuttle diplomacy ended in stalemate.[5] Despite the often legitimate criticisms of the UN General Assembly or the UN Security Council, the office of the UN Secretary-General has proven to be a valuable international asset in crisis diplomacy and conflict prevention.

Yet, as Secretary-General Pérez de Cuéllar noted in the early 1980s, the "diplomatic means" at his disposal are "quite limited."[6] This is a revealing statement. The Secretary-General is, in effect, admitting that he is inhibited by a lack of resources and political support from asserting his preventive role — even though numerous resources, both men and material, are still devoted to preparing for war.[7]

In view of this, the purpose of this book is to examine and evaluate the present, and potential, "diplomatic means" available to the office of the Secretary-General to prevent conflict. Special attention will be devoted to the constitutional powers and responsibilities of the Secretary-General under Article 99 of the Charter of the United Nations.

ARTICLE 99 OF THE UN CHARTER

Article 99 of the UN Charter states, "The Secretary-General may bring to the attention of the Security Council any matter which in his opinion may threaten the maintenance of international peace and security."[8] This short Article is commonly regarded as providing the political basis for the Secretary-General's preventive role.[9] As Stephen Schwebel states:

Article 99 is more important as the prime and unmistakable affirmation of the political character of the Secretary General. The power it confers, taken together with his strategic world position as the chief permanent officer of the United Nations . . . constitutes, particularly when blended with Article 98, the broad legal base for the Secretary-General's political personality.[10]

In his first Annual Report (1982), current UN Secretary-General Javier Pérez de Cuéllar acknowledged his constitutional obligation under Article 99. He stated that in order "to avoid the Security Council [from] becoming involved too late in critical situations, it may well be that the Secretary-General should play a more forthright role in bringing potentially dangerous situations to the attention of the Council within the general framework of Article 99 of the Charter."[11] In order to do this, he stated that it was crucial to enhance his office's ability to anticipate and help resolve "incipient disputes by peaceful means." He explains how this could be done in a key section of his report: "In order to carry out effectively the preventive role foreseen for the Secretary-General under Article 99, I intend to develop a wider and more systematic capacity for fact-finding in potential conflict areas."[12]

This key section immediately became caught up in political controversy as a major power — the Soviet Union — objected at the time to its intent.[13] The negative response proved, if nothing else, that the legal interpretation of this Article is still controversial — even though it has been nearly 40 years since the Charter was written.

Under the leadership of Gorbachev, the Soviet Union has done a complete turn at the United Nations; yet, their earlier objections to the Secretaries-General's preventive powers proves, if nothing else, that there is not yet an enduring consensus over the constitutional interpretation of Article 99. In view of this, there is a need to explore its origins and implementation throughout the history of the United Nations, and, in particular, to examine how previous Secretaries-General have viewed their "preventive role" under the Charter.[14] There is also a need to examine the future promise of preventive action by the Secretary-General. The sad but simple truth is, as Secretary-General Pérez de Cuéllar readily admits, that the measures used by the UN Secretariat to anticipate and prevent conflicts are institutionally inadequate; regional wars continue to erupt between UN members as unspoken truces collapse or negotiations fail. Thus, there is an obvious need to rethink and evaluate how to improve the Secretary-General's preventive powers under Article 99 of the Charter.

CONFLICT PREVENTION: EMERGING SUCCESSES

Thus, the precise focus of this book is on conflict prevention, not on the often more dramatic UN efforts to terminate fighting through negotiations, Security Council action, or peacekeeping.[15] Specifically, I examine the UN Secretaries-General's efforts under Article 99 in conflict prevention from 1945 to the beginning of 1987 — the end of Pérez de Cuéllar's first term.

Of course, during the first part of his second term, Secretary-General Pérez de Cuéllar — working closely with key aides and members of the Security Council — has achieved significant, and often spectacular, results in several regional conflicts: Soviet troops have withdrawn from Afghanistan under a UN agreement that took several years to negotiate, and the bloody fighting between Iran and Iraq ended after both sides accepted a UN cease-fire.

Yet, these successes did not suddenly emerge from an institutional or political void; much of the diplomatic planning and preparation for these regional settlements took place during Pérez de Cuéllar's first term as Secretary-General. In particular, his strong and persistent leadership from 1982 to 1987 in urging reforms and structural strengthening of the Secretary-General's preventive role has gone largely unreported in the Western, and even the world, press. So, we will examine many of these reforms and initiatives here.

The final outcomes to several of these dramatic developments are not yet fully apparent. Because of this, the story of the unique UN role in ending the fighting between Iran and Iraq or in Afghanistan and Cambodia will have to be written in the future — when the end results are clear and current diplomatic efforts are not jeopardized by premature disclosures. In short, the following analysis will be limited to an explanation of the history, current status, and future possibilities of the Secretary-General's preventive role.

This book does not attempt to develop a defense of the UN system as a whole, nor does it aspire to a comprehensive description of every UN Secretary-General and his varied responsibilities. The goal of this book is simple and limited. Specifically, I examine the preventive role and discretionary powers of the UN Secretary-General in order to determine how he might become a more effective third party in international affairs. As Edward De Bono points out, this third-party function of the Secretary-General can be, to some extent, separated from the organization itself.[16] The United Nations is often criticized for being a "talk shop" and thus ineffective, especially in the crucial area of preserving international peace. Yet, those that criticize the diplomats' penchant for seemingly endless discussion should remember Winston Churchill's simple reminder that "jaw-jaw is better than war-war."

Even so, intervention by the Secretary-General is no panacea for peace; his influence is small upon the world stage, his political power almost nonexistent, and his value as a spokesman in international affairs has eroded in past years. Despite this, however, the office of the Secretary-General has a remarkable vitality and potential. For all its weaknesses and faults, the office of the Secretary-General is a recognized and often — depending on the skills that the individual brings to the office — a highly respected third party. In a world of still-increasing nuclear, chemical, and conventional arsenals, there are ample reasons for strengthening the Secretary-General's preventive role; hence, the reason for writing this book.

ORGANIZATION

We begin this task by examining, in Chapter 1, the legal and political basis of the UN Secretary-General's preventive role. In Chapters 2 through 5 we examine how all five UN Secretaries-General have understood their preventive role and responsibilities. It is important to understand what this role is and how past Secretaries-General have fought to assert the influence of their office in order to prevent potential or actual conflict. As we see in Part I, it has been a long, and often lonely, struggle. Part I ends with an analysis of the organizational reforms and constitutional innovations during the first term of the current Secretary-General, Javier Pérez de Cuéllar. At the very end of his first term, he organized a new office — the Office of Research and the Collection of Information (ORCI) — to help him assert his preventive role.

In Part II, I examine the organizational and operational reforms of the Secretary-General's preventive efforts in some detail.

Specifically, I attempt to demonstrate how the constitutional responsibilities of the Secretary-General under Article 99 should be developed within a global framework for conflict identification and prevention. In short, the "systematic capacity" that the current Secretary-General seeks under Article 99 must be developed in relation to the entire Earth. Therefore, I argue that the Secretary-General's preventive role should be supported by a global system of conflict identification, analysis, and telecommunications. Current reforms in these areas are also evaluated. I end the book by summarizing the relevance of my analysis for the Secretary-General's preventive role and discretionary powers for the future.

NOTES

1. See Ruth Leger Sivard, *World Military and Social Expenditures 1987–1988* (Washington, D.C.: World Priorities, 1987).

2. See Leonard Spector's series of books on global proliferation dangers (Cambridge: Ballinger Press). Also see my essay "Broken Promises and Vertical Proliferation: The Case for Reform of the Non-Proliferation Treaty" (Cambridge: Institute for Security and Arms Control, Briefing Paper prepared for 1990 NPT Review Conference, December 1989).

3. See Joseph P. Lash, "Dag Hammarskjöld's Conception of His Office," *International Organization 16* (1962). See also Mark W. Zacher, *Dag Hammarskjöld's United Nations* (New York: Columbia University Press, 1970), and Brian Urquhart, *Hammarskjöld* (New York: Alfred A. Knopf, 1973), pp. 99–101.

4. Dean Rusk disclosed only in the summer of 1987 that President Kennedy planned, if all else failed, to make a secret initiative through Secretary-General Thant's office. See "Class Reunion," *New York Times Magazine,* August 1987. This has been generally ignored by scholars, especially in the West, who seem to focus on the substance of the negotiations during the 1962 crisis, instead of the diplomatic channels employed. See Boudreau, "Buying Time in a Crisis," *WORLDVIEW,* November 1983.

5. Even though the Secretary-General became directly involved in the negotiations after the sinking of the *General Belgrano* and of *HMS Sheffield,* he very nearly succeeded in arranging a solution. See, for example, Ambassador Anthony Parsons, "The Falkland Crisis in the United Nations, 31 March–14 June 1982," *International Affairs 59,* 2 (Spring 1983).

6. He stated this in his 1983 Annual Report. See Javier Pérez de Cuéllar, *Report of the Secretary-General on the Work of the Organization 1982* (New York: The United Nations).

7. The communication capability of the Secretary-General is especially inadequate; see Chapter 10.

8. Article 99, UN Charter. For a study on the drafting history of the Charter, as well as commentary on the individual articles, see Leland M. Goodrich and Edvard Hambro (eds.), *Charter of the United Nations: Commentary and Documents* (Boston: World Peace Foundation, 1946). For the definitive analysis of the drafting history of Article 99, see Stephen M. Schwebel, "The Origins and Development of Article 99 of the Charter," *The British Year-Book of International Law, 1951,* p. 371.

9. Stephen M. Schwebel, *The Secretary-General of the United Nations: His Political Powers and Practice* (New York: Greenwood Press, 1952), p. 24.

10. Schwebel, *Secretary-General of the United Nations,* p. 24. Article 98 of the Charter, which Schwebel quotes here states, "The Secretary-General shall act in that capacity in all meetings of the General Assembly, of the Security Council, of the Economic and Social Council, and of the Trusteeship Council, and *shall perform such other functions as are entrusted to him by these organs.* The Secretary-General shall make an annual report to the General Assembly on the work of the Organization." Schwebel is referring in this passage to the power of UN organs to assign "such other functions" to the Secretary-General.

11. The term "preventive role" comes from de Cuéllar's first *Annual Report.* See Javier Pérez de Cuéllar, *Report of the Secretary-General on the Work of the Organization* (New York: The United Nations, 1982).

12. Secretary-General de Cuéllar makes this point in his 1982 *Annual Report,* p. 8. As we shall see in Chapters 2 and 3, his view of his "preventive role" under Article 99 was shared by his early predecessors. The Preparatory Commission, established by the San Francisco Conference (1945), stated only in a general way the potential powers of the Secretary-General under this Article, explaining, "It is impossible to foresee how this Article will be applied; but the responsibility it confers upon the Secretary-General will require the exercise of the highest qualities of political judgement, tact and integrity." See the *Journal of the Preparatory Commission* (London, 1945) and the document series bearing symbol PC/EX/SEC/, Preparatory Commission, Documents, Committee 6.

13. Confidential Interview, Secretariat Official, spring 1983. Before recent reforms, the Soviets claimed that collective security is the primary responsibility of the Security Council, especially when "enforcement" actions are contemplated.

14. As mentioned in note 6, the definitive analysis of the drafting of Article 99 is provided by Schwebel, both in his article "The Origins and Development of Article 99," and his book, *The Secretary-General of the United Nations.* My analysis in Chapter 1 builds upon, but does not duplicate, Schwebel's definitive work.

15. Unfortunately, it is very hard to measure successful conflict prevention since "nothing" happens — there is no change in the status quo. Even so, it is arguably the most important aspect of diplomacy.

16. Edward De Bono, *Conflicts: A Better Way to Resolve Them* (London: Harrap, 1985), p. 173.

1
ARTICLE 99: THE OPTION AND THE OBLIGATION

BACKGROUND: THE SECURITY COUNCIL AND THE SECRETARY-GENERAL: THE ODD COUPLE

A close and cooperative relationship between the UN Secretary-General and the Security Council is essential to the United Nations' effectiveness and success. Yet, rather than act as a preventive partnership, the Security Council and Secretary-General often seem to be the odd couple of international affairs — they always work together, but they never seem to be a close or comfortable fit. As we shall see, this relationship has been marked by periods of diplomatic disagreement, open contention, and — especially in the early days of the United Nations — benign neglect.

Furthermore, until now, the Security Council has not worked very well throughout much of the UN's history. The permanent members of the first Security Council represented the most powerful states among the allies during World War II; the founding fathers of the United Nations obviously hoped that the wartime alliance that successfully waged war against fascism would continue and help preserve the peace in the postwar world. Yet, the Cold War — which resulted from the political, social, and economic conflicts between the United States and the Soviet Union — fractured the very core of the United Nations and often prevented the political consensus between the great powers that is needed to progress toward an enduring peace. So, not surprisingly, deeply divided by disagreements, and often paralyzed by the veto of a permanent member, the Security Council has not operated, during its first 40 years, according to the hopes of the drafters of the UN Charter. In view of this, the question has to be asked: Why study Article 99, which gives the Secretary-General the power to convene the Council, at all?

The answer to this question is simply that Article 99 is the constitutional source of significant preventive and discretionary powers for the Secretary-General. In a world of often warring nation-states, this Article provides an individual with the discretionary and preventive powers to analyze and — if need be — actively intervene in an incipient conflict involving nation-states or, even, ethnic representatives. This is a unique, if often overlooked, arrangement in international affairs. In short, convening the Council is only one of the Secretary-General's potential responsibilities under Article 99. He also derives, in large part, his third-party preventive role from this Article.

Specifically, the Secretary-General can, via Article 99, play a role in keeping communications and (at least) the appearance of conditional cooperation between two sides locked together in a confrontation. Because of this, the office of the Secretary-General can help promote the perception — based upon his preventive role — of continued cooperation among potential or actual adversaries. He can be especially helpful in soliciting and obtaining concessions and "understanding" that facilitate an enduring agreement or simply a cease-fire *in situ*. He can do this in a public way in order to build "golden bridges" behind each party and thus help to "save face"; or, he can help to promote behind-the-scenes, covert cooperation and thus contribute to the confidence of senior leaders that the other side continues to be interested in a diplomatic, not military, solution. However marginal the Secretary-General's probable impact is in this area, it is a potentially invaluable contribution in a world of threatening regional conflicts, nuclear proliferation, and growing chemical weapons arsenals.

Furthermore, the Secretary-General has the right and responsibility because of Article 99 to call upon the permanent powers of the Council and keep them fully informed and involved — either on a formal or informal level — in impending third-party negotiations. This can often be critical to the success of a diplomatic initiative — as illustrated by the cease-fire arranged between Iran and Iraq.

Accordingly, in this chapter, we examine this Article in greater detail in order to determine, if possible, the precise legal, preventive, and discretionary powers possessed by the Secretary-General. Specifically, we focus on what the Secretary-General does, or is allowed to do, before invoking Article 99. If and when he invokes Article 99, his preventive role under the Charter ends — at least in regard to the specific issue that he raises by invoking the Article. Any action after becomes, for better or worse, the responsibility of the Council, who can then delegate specific tasks to the Secretary-General under Article 98 of the Charter. (See Appendix I for a list of the key Articles — 97–101 — concerning the powers of the Secretary-General.)

ANALYSIS OF ARTICLE 99

Despite its constitutional significance, Article 99 itself is deceptively short and seemingly simple. It merely states, "The Secretary-General may bring to the attention of the Security Council any matter which in his opinion may threaten the maintenance of international peace and security."

At first glance, the language of Article 99 seems precise and straightforward.[1] It simply gives the Secretary-General the option to report before the Security Council upon any matter that in his judgment may threaten international peace and security. It does not require him to report to the Council. The Article merely provides him with the legal authority and opportunity to do so if he believes that circumstances warrant review by the Security Council, the UN organ that has primary responsibility for preserving peace.

Yet, as Leon Gordenker states, "The seemingly simple language of Article 99 becomes complex when it must serve as a guide to action."[2] If we take a second glance, the wording of Article 99 seems peculiar, especially the part that allows the Secretary-General to bring any matter that *in his opinion* may threaten international peace and security. Obviously, the use of "opinion" here implies the Secretary-General's own judgment. Yet, it seems strange to emphasize the mere opinion of one man in an organization of nation-states. Even so, this ambiguous word in the UN Charter recognizes the importance of the Secretary-General's judgments about threats to the peace in the world.

The complexity of this seemingly simple Article intensifies when the indeterminacy of the word "may" becomes fully apparent. The word "may" appears in two different contexts within the same short sentence. When used the first time, it seems to provide the Secretary-General with a certain discretion to decide whether he should invoke the Council. The debate at the San Francisco conference where the Charter was drafted in 1945 supports this discretionary definition of the word;[3] there was a motion at the conference to change the wording of the Article from "may bring" to "shall bring."[4] However, the motion was defeated because the majority of states "appeared to lean in the direction of the exercise of Article 99 as a matter of the Secretary-General's discretion," and the motion was withdrawn.[5]

Yet, this is not necessarily a passive discretionary power; the French use the verb *"pouvoir"* to translate "may."[6] *"Pouvoir"* can be defined as "to be able." The noun form of *"pouvoir"* is "power," as in "I have the power" or "I have the authority." Thus, in the French version of the Charter, Article 99 implies that the Secretary-General has the discretionary power or authority to convene the Council. This meaning is in contrast to the weaker, more ambiguous English word "may," which simply suggests that he "can convene the Council if he wants to." The use of the verb *"pouvoir"* is more precise since it suggests that there is nothing casual about the Secretary-General's discretionary responsibilities and powers under this Article.

The word "may" is used in a very different context the second time it appears in Article 99; this time, the word seems to emphasize, not the Secretary-General's discretionary role, but the uncertainty of events that may threaten international peace and security. In this context "may" is conditioned by the words that immediately precede, and follow, its placement in the Article. The first key phrase that conditions this word is "any matter." It is significant that Article 99 does not use here the language that is commonly found elsewhere in the Charter. It does not say "any dispute or situation."[7] Instead, the broader word "matter" is used. The language used here provides a liberal — and not limited — scope to the Secretary-General's discretionary powers. Furthermore, the matter in question does not need to unquestionably threaten, beyond a reasonable doubt, the maintenance of international peace. Using his own judgment, or "opinion," the Secretary-General "may" simply believe or suspect or fear that a specific matter, incident, or situation threatens the "maintenance of international peace and security."

In short, there does not have to be a definitive determination that a clear threat exists. Thus, the use of the word "may" in this second context implies that the Secretary-General has a broad discretionary power because of the uncertainty of events.

Furthermore, the very general phrase "any matter" is obviously not limited to military movements, diplomatic developments, or strictly political affairs. Matters such as economic recession, social unrest, or even environmental degradation that creates vast refugee flows — as well as international tensions — can contribute to threats to the peace.[8] Hence, the phrase "any matter" must have an expansive meaning that includes a wide variety of political, economic, social, humanitarian, and environmental factors.

This expanded definition enables the Secretary-General to make strategic forecasts of global trends that may threaten international security. In a very real sense, he must provide a strategic vision of the future and be a spokesperson for the international community's continuing interest in maintaining international peace.[9] To a certain extent, the Secretary-General already does this through his *Annual Report*. Yet, in view of the encompassing meaning of "any matter," he need not limit expressions of his interest or concern to a report made only once a year. This preventive role includes anticipatory analysis of potential issues and events on a global scale; as such, he is one of the few figures in international affairs that can provide a positive vision of the future, as well as a warning when required. For instance, he could — on a regular, procedural basis — provide the Security Council with reports of areas and issues that he is monitoring under Article 99. For instance, this could be done on a monthly basis when a new President (a position that is rotated monthly among members of the Security Council) takes up his official duties.

ARTICLE 99: THE SOURCE OF THE SECRETARY-GENERAL'S PREVENTIVE ROLE

The phrase "the maintenance of international peace and security," which appears elsewhere in the Charter, orients Article 99 in a very specific direction. The word "maintenance" implies that the purpose of the Article is preventive; the emphasis is on preserving international peace and security.[10] The Charter makes a clear distinction between "to maintain" and "to restore" international peace.[11] Each is governed by an appropriate section in the Charter, and, sometimes, within a single Article.[12] Article 99 says nothing about the Secretary-General having the authority to bring to the attention of the Security Council a matter that may "restore" international peace and security. In short, Article 99 clearly does not give the Secretary-General any rights or responsibilities to take steps to enforce international peace and security; this is the explicit role of the Security Council under Chapter VII of the Charter. His authority in this area is carefully constrained and limited to functions that the Security Council might explicitly give him under Article 98 in enforcement actions that it must initiate. Thus, Article 99 defines and limits the Secretary-General's role to conflict prevention. Because of this Article, the Secretary-General is, in a very real sense, an international watchman of the peace.

Secretary-General Pérez de Cuéllar is quite explicit about the importance of Article 99 to his preventive role. He stated in a speech at Sorbonne University in April 1985:

> It is quite clear from the wording of Article 99 itself — and this is borne out by the deliberations of the Preparatory Commission — that the Charter regards the Secretary-General, in addition to his other functions, as an instrument of multilateral diplomacy at the anticipatory or preventive level. The words "in his opinion" and "may threaten the maintenance of international peace and security" clearly indicate: (1) that he may bring to the attention of the Security Council not only actual but also potential causes of conflict; and (2) that he must constantly and independently monitor developments in all matters which have a bearing on international peace and security.[13]

As we shall see, his conviction that Article 99 is a key source of his discretionary power and preventive role has been supported by all of his predecessors.

ARTICLE 99: THE OBLIGATION

Article 99 implies an obligation. In order to determine whether he should exercise his powers under Article 99, the Secretary-General must keep himself fully informed about matters that may threaten international peace and security.[14] It is inconceivable that the framers of the UN Charter gave the Secretary-General an important role under Article 99 in the "maintenance of international peace and security" without the requisite responsibility to keep himself fully apprised of world events.

In view of the Secretary-General's obligation in this area, there is a problem concerning the means he uses to inform himself of impending conflicts. Simply put, the means used by the Secretary-General to gather information must enable him to make intelligent and informed judgments. To suggest that the Secretary-General collect information relevant to this responsibility by reading the newspapers on his way to work or by watching the nightly news is to condemn him to political irrelevance. An ideal arrangement would be that information gathering by the Secretary-General is worldwide, multicultural, continuous, and procedural. Such a system must effectively enable the Secretary-General to fulfill his obligation to inform himself about developing trends. Because the means to be used to gather information are not explicitly stated in Article 99, they must be implied.

THE IMPLIED POWERS DOCTRINE

A review of the wording of Article 99 is important because it reveals the imprecision and ambiguity of certain key terms and words; these words are meant to be carefully defined and analyzed. Yet, it is equally important, if not more so, to note what the Article does not mention or imply and seems to exclude. Most important, Article 99 makes no mention of how the Secretary-General is to ascertain whether a matter may threaten the maintenance of international peace and security.[15] Specifically, Article 99 is silent on how the Secretary-General is to gather information relevant to the prevention of conflict. Because of these omissions, several legal authorities argue that Article 99 gives the Secretary-General, by necessary implication, the right and responsibility to gather information that is relevant to the maintenance of international peace and security.[16]

According to the doctrine of implied powers, the Secretary-General possesses the implied powers, stemming from Arti le 99, to conduct independent investigations and to gather informa ion.[17] Thus, the argument for the implied powers of the Secretary-General under Article 99 is analogous to a key argument developed in U.S. jurisprudence by Chief Justice Marshall in *McCulloch v. Maryland*. In that case, Marshall declared, "Let the end be legitimate, let it be within the scope of the constitution, and all means which are appropriate, which are plainly adapted to that end, which are not prohibited, but consistent with the letter and spirit of the constitution, are constitutional."[18]

Based upon Marshall's reasoning, one legal commentator, Wasif F. Abboushi, argues that the Charter contains similar implied powers that are necessary if the ends of the United Nations are to be achieved. Abboushi takes a unique position:

> It is immaterial to investigate the intentions of the framers of the Charter since Article 99 cannot be useful and purposeful without the power of investigation being possessed by the Secretary-General. The investigatory powers of the Secretary-General are constitutional authority vested in him. Means of implementing Article 99 should be within his discretion, for, without those means, the provisions of Article 99 become ineffective. The power of the Secretary-General to conduct investigations is an implied power within the scope of the Charter.[19]

While supporting the implied powers of the Secretary-General under Article 99, legal scholar Stephen Schwebel (now on the International Court of Justice) takes a less radical position than Abboushi.[20] Specifically, he concludes that a careful analysis of the framers' intentions supports the implied powers of the Secretary-General under Article 99. After reviewing the drafting history of the Article, Schwebel states, "It is not unreasonable to suppose that . . . the framers foresaw that the Secretary-General would wish to take so profound a step as invoking Article 99 only upon the basis of complete and objective data gathered, if need be through his own investigation."[21]

Yet, neither Schwebel nor Abboushi suggest that the means that the Secretary-General chooses to inform himself to fulfill his responsibility under Article 99 are unlimited. Obviously, the means of information gathering must be consistent with the UN Charter, which contains some important limitations.[22] However, as I will argue shortly, the proper legal test applied to these means must be an effectiveness as well as the functional test, or the Secretary-General is not fulfilling his obligation under the Charter to maintain international peace.

THE "CHAIN OF EVENTS" DECLARATION: A KEY LIMIT OF IMPLIED POWER?

An inherent limit to the Secretary-General's implied powers is often thought to be contained in the 1945 "Chain of Events" Declaration; yet, as we shall see below, this declaration applies only to fact-finding by the Security Council. Even so, it has confused the precise legal and discretionary powers of the Secretary-General over the past 40 years.

The issues of investigations and fact-finding were carefully considered at the San Francisco drafting convention of the Charter in 1945. As a result of these deliberations, a declaration was issued by the then four great powers concerning independent investigations by the Security Council. Specifically, the great powers — the United States, the Soviet Union, China, and the United Kingdom — sought to exert political control over possible future consequences of Security Council actions.[23] Thus, they jointly issued a clarification of the Charter that specified what issues required a procedural vote within the Council and what issues involved a substantive decision subject to the veto.[24] In the now well-known "Chain of Events" Declaration, the four sponsoring governments stated,

> Decisions and actions by the Security Council may well have major political consequences and may even initiate a chain of events which might, in the end, require the Council under its responsibilities to invoke measures of enforcement under section B, Chapter VIII. This chain of events begins when the Council decides to make an investigation, or determine that the time has come to call upon states to settle their differences, or to make recommendations to the parties. It is to such decisions and actions that unanimity of the permanent members applies, with the important proviso, referred to above, for abstention from voting by parties to a dispute.[25]

In short, one of the great fears of the four sponsoring governments was that an investigation by the Council might initiate a chain of events leading to enforcement measures. Thus, the four jointly issued this statement in order to ensure that each government justify and maintain its veto power over any Council action that might eventually lead to the mobilization of military forces by Security Council action.

Yet, there are constitutional safeguards that protect against the feared chain of events. A key safeguard is the veto power of the permanent members on the Security Council. Article 27 of the Charter requires the concurring votes of all the permanent members of the Council concerning substantive decisions. Since its insertion into the draft of the Charter, Article 27 has proved to be a controversial and often divisive issue; for instance, some critics claim that the veto power inhibits significant decisions and needed policy or military action by the Security Council.[26]

Yet, as Inis Claude points out, the veto is a "deliberately contrived circuit breaker in the decision-making process of the Security Council, designed to prevent the commitment of the Council to a position or a course of action in opposition to the expressed will of a great power."[27] He states that, although some critics of the United Nations lament the existence of this circuit breaker, the veto ensures that the supreme interests of such a permanent power will not be jeopardized by any Council action.[28] This in turn assures the great powers that the Council will not initiate a chain of events resulting in military action unless they all agree. Such a safeguard, Claude argues, was essential to the creation of the Security Council — and, indeed, to the United Nations — because it ensured that the permanent powers would participate in the new organization.[29]

The importance of the veto to the permanent powers is illustrated by the 1950 decision of the Soviet Union to boycott the Security Council. The absence of the Soviet Union enabled the rest of the Security Council to authorize the initial deployment of UN military forces to South Korea in response to the North Koreans' invasion during June of that year.[30] Soon after this, the Soviets returned to the Council and vetoed any further authorizations of military action.

Because of this experience, it is unlikely that any permanent power will boycott or remove itself from the Council in the future. In an ironic and unintended way, the Soviet absence during the Korean invasion — and the subsequent Council decision to field UN military forces — demonstrated the importance of the veto power in order to prevent action by the United Nations.

In other words, the veto power of the permanent powers ensures an important form of negative control in Council deliberations by assuring that no action will be taken unless all the permanent powers agree. Thus, the veto power provides a safeguard that protects the status quo. This is similar to the rule in Quaker consensus decision making that, unless there is unanimity, there is no action and, hence, the status quo is preserved.

This form of protecting the status quo through the potential power of the veto has important implications for a possible expansion of Security Council powers in the future. For instance, in view of this safeguard, Security Council regulation of strategic trusts areas

(Article 82 of the Charter) should be considered. Such regulation could be expanded to include disputed boundaries or territories such as the Falkland/Malvinas Islands, the polar caps, and the inland seas. This might help ensure that nothing is done to change the status quo of legally ambiguous areas of the world, without the concurring vote of the permanent powers of the Security Council. Or, what if the sole power to threaten, or sanction, the use of nuclear weapons was given to the Security Council?[31] This might ensure that such a power would never be used, especially in view of the Council's often chronic inaction as a decision-making body. Although these possibilities may seem very remote, given today's political realities, they illustrate the value of the veto in preventing a decision, and a subsequent chain of events caused by Security Council action. In short, the political guarantee via the veto that nothing will be done — that no feared chain of events will ensue — can be as important as a promise that action will be taken to restore the *status quo ante.*

The safeguard of the veto is especially important when the preventive powers of the Secretary-General are considered before his invocation of Article 99. Specifically, there is a need to distinguish the duties of the Secretary-General under Article 99 to inform himself fully about world events and the investigative powers of the Security Council. Only the latter can precipitate a chain of events leading to enforcement action (or a veto). In view of this, there is an obvious legal distinction between the means of information gathering that are relevant before and after the invocation of Article 99. Vratislav Pechota makes such a useful distinction when he discusses the difference between "enquiry" and "fact-finding."

ENQUIRY VS. FACT-FINDING

Dr. Pechota once served as chairman of the General Assembly's Legal Committee. In view of his experience at the United Nations, he makes a valuable distinction between fact-finding, which is often regulated by the Security Council, and enquiry.[32] He defines enquiry as a "procedure which is ancillary in character and limited in its purpose. In the exercise of the Secretary-General's good offices, it usually precedes or accompanies other actions designed to bring about a settlement and reinforce those actions by providing an objective basis for decision."[33] Fact-finding, by contrast, has become a relatively independent procedure.[34] Pechota defines it as either "a main component of the Secretary-General's involvement in a particular case or as one phase in a series of tasks."[35] For instance, an official fact-finding mission by the Secretary-General usually follows from a specific order or request from a main UN organ, such as the Security Council exercising its powers under Article 98 of the Charter.

This distinction is valuable because all too often fact-finding is thoroughly confused with enquiry.[36] Such imprecision eventually results in the loss of procedural options and alternatives because the identity of two distinct methods of information management and peaceful settlement become merged.

In particular, Pechota's distinction between the two methods of information gathering is very useful in the context of Article 99. Before the formal invocation of the Article, the gathering of information through enquiry by the Secretary-General is systematic, although unfocused, and ancillary to his overall responsibility to help maintain international peace and security. In short, before the invocation of Article 99 by the Secretary-General, it is legally impossible and politically premature to assert that the procedural gathering of information by enquiry can trigger the much feared chain of events (in the Council) that so worried the great powers at San Francisco.

Information gathered by enquiry may trigger Article 99, which places the matter before the Security Council. Once this happens — after Article 99 is invoked — information gathering will undoubtedly be strictly supervised by the Security Council. Under these circumstances, the phrase "fact-finding" — as a main component of the Security Council's action in the matter — may be the best way to define the gathering of information. At this point, the Council must decide if further information regarding the matter under review is warranted.

Of course, this distinction between enquiry and fact-finding cannot be rigorously maintained in the real world. For instance, there might be information that is relevant to both the prevention of conflict and to the restoration of international peace and security. Even so, the distinction does correspond to the obvious legal change and transformation that occurs in UN practice and procedure when Article 99 is formally invoked. By invoking this Article, the Secretary-General is, in effect, stating that a matter, which may threaten international peace and security, is no longer a procedural matter and that Council consideration is now warranted. The transition in the nature of information gathering by the Secretary-General from enquiry to fact-finding is clearly marked by the invocation of Article 99.[37]

Once the Council is convened, the chain of events becomes a possibility. This transition demonstrates the seriousness and significance of the Secretary-General's power under Article 99 to convene the Council. It permits one man's opinion to be the basis for mobilizing international attention and concern, via the Security Council, upon any matter that may threaten international peace and security. If it so decides, the Council can take significant steps, including enforcement actions, to maintain international peace and security.

Yet the possibility of Council action should not be used as a procedural or substantive restraint upon the Secretary-General's responsibility to inform himself about a potential conflict. The very purpose of Article 99 is to provide for the possibility of Council action. It is incongruous to argue — as some member-states have done in the past — that, because of the potent chain of events that may result from information gathering, only the Security Council has a role within the United Nations concerning the maintenance of international peace and security.[38] Such a viewpoint is blatantly contradicted by Article 99 of the UN Charter, which gives an important preventive role and responsibility to the Secretary-General as well. It is legally correct to assert that the Security Council has a unique and exclusive role in the restoration of international peace and security via possible enforcement actions.[39] But to overgeneralize upon this role and claim exclusive jurisdiction over any matter that may threaten the maintenance of international peace and security is to contradict the UN Charter and act as though Article 99 does not exist.

The Charter does not admit to partial or selective application of its Articles.[40] This does not mean that important distinctions can be glossed over by a general, vague appeal to the authority of the Charter. As we shall see, this is what Hammarskjöld did to justify "executive action" by his office.[41] Neither does it mean that the explicit intentions of the framers of the Charter can be cavalierly ignored. The Charter was clearly framed with the intent to give the Secretary-General an important role, via Article 99, in maintaining international peace and security. To contend otherwise is to obliterate a crucial Article of the Charter that deals with an issue of potentially vital importance to the preservation of peace.

THE EFFECTIVENESS OF THE SECRETARY-GENERAL'S PREVENTIVE ROLE

The UN Charter was drafted, not by scholars sitting in an ivory tower, but by practicing statesmen whose nations had just survived a savage war. Fully aware of the imperfections of political life, the drafters of the Charter created a document that reflected the wartime and prewar experiences they had recently endured. They obviously did not create an organization designed to fail. Thus, an implicit working assumption of the drafters — made explicit in Article 1 of the Charter — is that the United Nations must be effective. Of course, effectiveness is a fundamental — although implicit — purpose of any organization.[42] The institution must work, or changes must be made.

One can readily apply an effectiveness test to any organization by asking if its standard operating procedures are successful.[43] If they are not, their very ineffectiveness implies an agenda for reform. In the context of Article 99, the effectiveness test suggests that if the current means the Secretary-General employs to gather information are not effective — that is, he is unable to identify and prevent potential conflicts — then this inadequacy requires institutional adjustment until the purposes of the Article are achieved. In short, the ineffective UN efforts in this area — cited by both the Secretary-General and by critics — imply their own agenda for reform.[44]

There are many means of gathering information, some more effective than others. The task then is to find the means by which the Secretary-General can best fulfill his constitutional obligation to aid in the maintenance of international peace and security.

A central thesis of the following chapters is that Article 99 of the UN Charter, which gives the Secretary-General an explicit role in the maintenance of international peace and security, obligates and entitles him to use the most effective measures possible to gather information about potential conflicts so that he can exercise his preventive role and determine whether to convene the Security Council.

Furthermore, the Secretary-General's preventive role applies to any area, including the global commons — the high seas, the polar caps, and even near outer space — where a potential conflict can occur involving one or more of the UN members. Viewed in this way, Article 99 obligates the Secretary-General to develop a truly global early warning and information system that enables him to anticipate, ascertain, and analyze "any matter that may threaten the maintenance of international peace and security." Only with such a system can he make an intelligent and informed determination that a threat does, in fact, exist. Otherwise, he simply cannot fulfill his duties under the Charter to "bring to the attention of the Security Council any matter which in his opinion may threaten the maintenance of international peace and security." Various interventionary methods and strategies used by the Secretary-General in the past — such as a "U.N. presence," "preventive diplomacy," or "good offices" — can also be construed as information-gathering procedures that enable him to fulfill his constitutional obligation under Article 99 of the UN Charter.[45] As we shall see, the current information-gathering techniques used by the UN Secretariat are quite primitive, although reforms are currently being implemented.

A GLOBAL CAPACITY FOR CONFLICT IDENTIFICATION: THE LEGAL FRAMEWORK

Obviously, an effective global capacity for conflict identification is a tall order — some might say it is utopian and impossible. Yet, the precise issue, from a constitutional point of view, is not whether such a system is currently feasible or even politically practical for the time being. The point is that the Secretary-General has the constitutional power, under Article 99 of the UN Charter, to develop a wider and more systematic capacity for information-gathering that encompasses the entire earth.

In short, the geographical shape of the globe itself, including the global commons, provides the controlling legal framework for subsequent institutional development of his powers under Article 99. These powers may be latent, unused, and held in reserve, depending upon fluctuating financial or political conditions. All too often, the waxing and waning of daily political sparring has defined the powers of Article 99. This has obviously happened periodically throughout the history of the United Nations. Because these powers of the Secretary-General are so often left unused, there is a danger that the legal foundations for these powers will always be overlooked, ignored — or even doubted and denied. Yet, the legal powers implied by Article 99 still exist even if a Secretary-General is unable, or unwilling, to exercise them.

It would make an interesting study to examine the political reasons why the Secretary-General's preventive powers are not always fully exercised.[46] However, such a study would be premature without first defining and developing the full legal scope of the Secretary-General's discretionary and preventive powers. Accordingly, we limit ourselves in the chapters ahead, especially in Part I, to examining the legal development and scope of the constitutional powers of the Secretary-General under Article 99 of the Charter.

THE EARLY STRUGGLES OVER ARTICLE 99

Since the founding of the United Nations, there has been considerable energy expended by the Secretariat officials — including the Secretary-General himself — in order to ensure that his legal powers, options, and obligations under Article 99 are fully recognized and respected by the Security Council. In the early years of the United Nations, Secretary-General Lie fought and won several "bitter fights" to gain recognition of his "preventive role."[47] Capitalizing upon Lie's successes in this area, Hammarskjöld proceeded to develop a very broad definition of the Secretary-General's constitutional powers to prevent conflict. As we shall see, Hammarskjöld's definition of "executive action" is, perhaps, an overly broad and injurious construction of the Secretary-General's role under Article 99. His successor Secretary-General Thant continued to develop the Secretary-General's role in conflict prevention. Under Thant, humanitarian issues were added to the list of any matter that might affect the maintenance of international peace and security. Under Waldheim, the United Nations suffered from an unparalleled period of listlessness and loss of public support. Fortunately, the first Annual Report (1982) and subsequent reforms by the current Secretary-General, Javier Pérez de Cuéllar, have brought this issue of the Secretary-General's preventive powers back into the forefront at the United Nations.[48]

NOTES

1. Leon Gordenker, *The U.N. Secretary-General and the maintenance of peace* (New York: Columbia University Press, 1967), pp. 137–38.

2. Ibid., p. 137.

3. UNCIO, Report of Rapporteur of Committee I/2 on Chapter X (The Secretariat), Doc. 1155, I/2/74 (2), p. 7. See also, Summary Report of Seventeenth Meeting of Committee I/2, June 1, 1945, Doc. 732, I/2/50, and Summary Report of Eighteenth Meeting of Committee, I/2, June 2, 1945, Doc. 762, I/2/53. Also Leland M. Goodrich and Edvard Hambro (eds.), *Charter of the United Nations Commentary and Documents* (Boston: World Peace Foundation, 1946), pp. 271–72.

4. Goodrich and Hambro, *Charter of the United Nations,* pp. 271–72.

5. Ibid.

6. *Charte des Nations Unites et Statut de la Cour Internationale de Justice,* Service de l'information des Nations Unites, Nations Unites, New York.

7. Gordenker, p. 137.

8. Tapio Kanninen, "Towards Effective War Risk Reduction within the United Nations Framework," a paper delivered at the Conference on the Reduction of the Risk of War through Multilateral Means, Kingston, Ontario, October 7–8, 1988.

9. Ibid.

10. I am suggesting here that the word "maintenance" is used in connection with efforts to achieve a pacific settlement under Chapter VI whereas the word "restore" refers to enforcement actions by the Security Council under Chapter VII. Of course, the words "maintain" and "restore" are both used in Article 39, which is the first Article in Chapter VII. Yet, as Goodrich and Hambro point out, this Article was the source of "considerable confusion," which led to a very thorough reconsideration of the relevant paragraphs at the United Nations Conference on International Organization (UNCIO). See Goodrich and Hambro, *Charter,* pp. 157–58 for an elaborate discussion of the drafting history of Article 39.

11. See Article 39, UN Charter. Also see UNCIO, Report of Paul-Boncour, Rapporteur, on Chapter VIII, Section B, Doc. 881, III/3/46, p. 4. Finally, also see Goodrich and Hambro, pp. 155–59.

12. Broadly speaking, the word "maintenance" refers to efforts under Chapter VI of the Charter, and "restore" refers to enforcement actions under Chapter VII. See note 8.

13. UN Secretary-General Pérez de Cuéllar addresses Sorbonne University, April 1985. Copy of speech available through UN Office of Public Information or his office.

14. Hammarskjöld, for instance, justified his trip to Laos on the basis that he had to "inform myself about the present problems of the country." See Brian Urquhart, *Hammarskjöld* (New York: Alfred A. Knopf, 1973), p. 352. Javier Pérez de Cuéllar also shares the opinion that he is obligated to inform himself, under Article 99 of the UN Charter, of any event that may threaten international peace and security. See his first Annual Report (1982), *Report of the Secretary-General on the Work of the Organization.*

15. This is a curious omission in view of the importance of the issues raised in Article 99. Gordenker suggests that Article 99 "exists primarily for use in a crisis," when (presumably) the danger is obvious to all, yet no state is willing to take the initiative of convening the Council. See Gordenker, p. 139.

16. For instance, both Schwebel and W. F. Abboushi ascribe to this view. See Stephen M. Schwebel, *The Secretary-General of the United Nations: His Political Powers and Practice* (New York: Greenwood Press, 1952). Also see his article, which is a definitive analysis of the drafting history of Article 99, "The Origins and Development of Article 99 of the Charter," *The British Year-Book of International Law, 1951,* p. 371, and W. F. Abboushi, *The Secretary-General of the United Nations: Constitutional Powers and Developments,* University of Cincinnati, Ph.D. 1959 (unpublished — a copy is available in the UN library.) Also, Hammarskjöld, a noted scholar of international law, shared this view as well. See Mark Zacher, *Dag Hammarskjöld's United Nations* (New York: Columbia University Press, 1970), pp. 35–39.

17. Wasif F. Abboushi, pp. 63–66, treats this doctrine extensively in the context of the UN Charter.

18. *McCulloch v. Maryland.* Supreme Court of the United States, 1819. 4 Wheat. 316 4L.Ed. 579.

19. Abboushi, *The Secretary-General of the United Nations,* p. 64.

20. Schwebel, *British Year-Book of International Law, 1951,* p. 390.

21. Ibid.

22. One important limitation is Article 2, Paragraph 7, which states: "Nothing contained in the present Charter shall authorize the United Nations to intervene in matters which are essentially within the domestic jurisdiction of any state."

23. For an excellent summary and critique of the "chain of events" statement, see Ernest L. Kerley, "The Powers of Investigation of the United Nations Security Council," *American Journal of International Law 55* (1961), 892. The "chain of events" statement by the four great powers reflects the fear that each would be subject to UN action unless they exercised a veto power over *all* important Security Council decisions.

24. Goodrich and Hambro, *Charter of the United Nations,* 330–33. They reprint the statement.

25. Ibid., p. 331.

26. This issue is explored by Inis L. Claude, *Swords into Plowshares,* 4th ed. (New York: Random House, 1971), pp. 141–62.

27. Ibid.

28. Ibid.

29. Ibid.

30. Schwebel, *The Secretary-General of the United Nations,* pp. 103–12.

31. I first pointed out and discussed this possibility with Dan Deudney of Princeton during the summer of 1985; he encouraged me to develop this idea in further depth — even though we both realize that the political realization of this is very remote, given today's international climate.

32. See Vratislav Pechota, *The Quiet Approach: A Study in the Good Offices Exercised by the United Nations Secretary-General in the Cause of Peace* (New York: UNITAR, 1972), pp. 64 and 65. Also see my own distinction between "humanitarian fact-finding" and "humanitarian enquiry" in *Protecting the Innocent* (New York: Council on Religion and International Affairs, 1983), pp. 7–11. Also see Chapter 5 in this volume.

33. Pechota, *The Quiet Approach,* p. 64. Influenced by Pechota's distinction between fact-finding and enquiry, I think it is useful to note the different methods of information gathering that each entails. The distinction is especially important

in terms of the institutional origins of each method, that is, whether it requires prior approval by the Security Council or whether it can be used by the Secretary-General without the prior permission of the Council. See *Protecting the Innocent,* pp. 7–11.

34. Pechota, *The Quiet Approach,* pp. 64–65.

35. Ibid.

36. Different scholars give sometimes widely varying definitions of the term "fact-finding." See Edward Plunkett, Jr., "Fact-Finding as a Means of Settling a Dispute," *Virginia Journal of International Law 9* (1969), 154. For a variety of methods of fact-finding, used by separate international organizations and nation-states in differing contexts to clarify compliance with international treaties, see *Consideration of Principles of International Law Concerning Friendly Relations and Cooperation among States in Accordance with the Charter of the United Nations,* study prepared by the Secretary-General in pursuance of General Assembly Resolution 2104 (XX) A/6228, April 22, 1966.

37. Of course, the transition may not be so clear-cut; the Council could, while placing the matter on its provisional agenda, refuse to consider the matter further. This possibility is explored by Schwebel, "The Origins and Development of Article 99," p. 337.

38. This has been the position of the Soviet Union in particular; see its response to a request by the Secretary-General pursuant to General Assembly Resolution 2864 (XXVI) as reported in Davidson Nicol, *The United Nations Security Council: Towards Greater Effectiveness* (New York: UNITAR, 1982), pp. 268–71.

39. See Chapter VII, the UN Charter.

40. According to well-established rules of legal construction, the Charter must be read in its entirety, including Article 99. For an interesting and brilliant example of Charter exegesis, see Myres S. McDougal and W. Michael Reisman, "Rhodesia and the United Nations: The Lawfulness of International Concern," *American Journal of International Law 62* (1969), 1.

41. We cover this topic extensively in Chapter 3 of this book.

42. The principle of institutional effectiveness was first enunciated by L. F. Goldie, Director of the International Legal Studies Program at the Syracuse University College of Law and advisor to my UN research project.

43. This test is my development of Goldie's principle (above). The test is based upon a truism that borders on a tautology: no organization is created to be "ineffective"; one must assume that the founders of the United Nations intended it to work, and to work well. Ineffectiveness implies its own agenda for change until the purposes of the organization — any organization — are achieved. This gives a very dynamic and experimental interpretation to the Charter of the United Nations.

44. Secretary-General Pérez de Cuéllar discusses the weaknesses of the United Nations in this area in his 1982 Annual Report, passim. Criticisms of the United Nations are legion; see, for example, Richard Bernstein, "The United Nations vs. the United States," *The New York Times Magazine,* January 22, 1984.

45. We shall review these procedures in Chapters 2 through 4.

46. This study, especially in Part I of the book, is largely limited to examining the constitutional powers and scope of Article 99.

47. This struggle is fully described in Schwebel, *The Secretary-General of the United Nations,* and in Chapter 2.

48. We review these changes in Chapter 5.

2

THE STRUGGLE TO KNOW
AND TO SAY: TRYGVE LIE

The office of the Secretary-General is, potentially, a significant center for mobilizing political power and public opinion. By virtue of his position as head of the United Nations, the Secretary-General enjoys a saliency in international affairs that enables him to gain immediate — if limited — access into the inner sanctums of governmental decision making as well as the editorial offices of major news agencies around the world.[1] If armed with relevant and timely information concerning a potential conflict, the Secretary-General could conceivably take immediate steps to end the conflict before the outbreak of war.

Yet, a politically powerful Secretary-General is a two-edged sword: the same information used by the Secretary-General to forestall a conflict could also embarrass the governments who favor and support a conflict over the status quo — governments who most likely sit as member-states of the organization over which the Secretary-General presides. Thus, the limited political power of the Secretary-General is based on a paradox: if the Secretary-General is too weak, he cannot be employed by governments to bail themselves out of unexpected difficulties; if he is too strong, he may assert his position and perspective over the will and way of governments reluctant to surrender any sovereignty — even if it means violence and war. Thus, the Secretary-General must walk a narrow and crooked path between political influence and political irrelevance.

The ambivalence of governments toward his office may explain why some member-states of the United Nations want the Secretary-General to "know little and say even less."

This tendency became especially apparent during the early days of the United Nations when the first Secretary-General, Trygve Lie, raced and fought a bitter behind-the-scenes battle in order to secure the right to report, upon a procedural basis, before the Security Council.[2] He also struggled to enhance his ability to gather information that might be relevant to the maintenance of international peace and security.[3] Jealously guarding what they perceived as their prerogatives of power, some members of the Security Council challenged the first Secretary-General's attempts to assert his preventive role. In short, during the first days of the United Nations, there was clearly confusion within the Security Council concerning Article 99 and the preventive role of the Secretary-General. Because of this, the prospect of the Secretary-General's intervening in Council proceedings was regarded as an ambiguous blessing by some members. Even so, Lie was, at first, somewhat successful in asserting the powers of his office. The legacy of Lie's early struggles to "know and to say" lives on and exerts a subtle though pervasive influence on UN proceedings today.

TRYGVE LIE: PROCEDURAL POWERS

Trygve Lie of Norway was an unlikely first Secretary-General. A labor leader in Norway, he had gone into exile in England as foreign minister with King Haakar when the Germans invaded his country in 1940. He helped the Allied cause by ordering ships of the Norwegian merchant marine then at sea in 1940 to British ports. Yet, despite these efforts, there was little evidence of executive ability in his record. Furthermore, he was a man with a volatile temper and was sensitive to his image in the public eye. Critics suggest that he was out of his league as UN Secretary-General. His private outbursts of anger directed toward diplomats and Secretariat staff are still legendary at the United Nations.[4]

Yet, although there are legitimate criticisms of the first Secretary-General, it is indisputable that he established — often against great opposition — a firm foundation for his office's participation in General Assembly and Security Council proceedings. He had the foresight to fight key battles and to establish critical procedural precedents that enabled the Secretary-General to speak before the main organs of the United Nations. In a very real sense, he gave a voice to his office.

Because the full story of Lie's procedural innovations is told in Stephen Schwebel's book *The Secretary-General of the United Nations,* I shall only briefly recount it here.[5] Unlike Schwebel, who focuses upon the overall political role of the Secretary-General, I shall concentrate specifically upon the evolution of the preventive role and responsibilities of the Secretary-General under Article 99.

THE STRUGGLE TO SAY: OPENING THE DOOR

Lie was in office only two months when he had his first opportunity to make an important procedural intervention before the Security Council. The method he used was a legal memorandum concerning the right of Iran to withdraw its complaint concerning Soviet troops within its borders from the agenda of the Security Council.[6] Iran wished to delete the issue from Security Council proceedings because substantial negotiations with the Soviet Union had been initiated. The Soviets, wishing the matter to be removed from the Security Council's considerations, supported the Iranian position.

Secretary-General Lie and his legal counsel Abraham Feller drew up a legal memorandum that, in essence, supported the Soviet position.[7] Lie explained his reasons for the memorandum, stating, "I saw no point in keeping the question on the agenda. The United Nations, I felt, should aim to settle disputes, not to inflame them."[8]

Lie was also aware that the submission of the legal memorandum might be an important precedent in terms of establishing the right of his office to participate in Council proceedings; unfortunately, the President of the Security Council at the time, Quo Tai-Chi of China, took a dimmer view of the Secretary-General's intervention.[9] Irritated that he had not been consulted beforehand by the Secretary-General about his "unprecedented decision to intervene on [a] controversial issue" he was "ready to ignore" the legal memo and proceed directly to a vote on the Soviet resolution, which called for a "deletion of the Iranian item from the agenda."[10] There were immediate objections from several Council members, as the following transcript reveals:

Dr. Lange: (Poland)

The Secretary-General has submitted to us a legal opinion . . . and then we went on discussing as if the Secretary-General's opinion did not exist. I submit . . . that the Secretary-General is an important official of the United Nations, invested with special and important powers by the Charter, and that we cannot vote now as if his opinion did not count or exist.

The President:

I am quite agreeable to the suggestion that we cannot vote upon the Soviet representative's motion until we have heard from the Committee of Experts . . . in regard to the observation by my Polish colleague that the Secretary-General is a very important official of the Secretariat, in that there is no disagreement, no difference on my part. But I would like to point out to him that in Chapter XV, Article 97, it is expressly stated that "He shall be the chief administrative officer of the Organization." So, whatever observations we may receive from him, and I am sure the Council will wish to give due weight and due consideration to his observations, the decision remains with the Council.

Mr. Gromyko: (USSR)

Since we have decided that the Secretary-General's memorandum must be referred to the Committee of Experts, how can we immediately vote or make a decision? As regards the function of the Secretary-General, the question which arose here was incidental. Of course, these functions are more serious and more responsible than has been suggested just now. It is sufficient to refer to one Article of the Charter in order to come precisely to this conclusion regarding the very great responsibility incumbent upon the Secretary-General. Article 99 ... "The Secretary-General has all the more right, and moreover the duty, to submit reports on the various aspects of questions that are being considered by the Security Council."[11]

Gromyko's last statement is of particular interest; it is a very strong endorsement of the reportorial role — "duty" — of the Secretary-General under Article 99. At the time (1946) Gromyko and the Soviets obviously thought that Secretary-General Lie's position was fully consistent with the UN Charter. It is perhaps gratuitous to point out that, although the UN Charter has not changed, the Soviet position concerning the duties of the Secretary-General has.[12] The 180-degree shift of the Soviet position suggests that their objections are based upon political, not legal, considerations. Only recently, under the leadership of Gorbachev, have the Soviets returned somewhat to their original position in the late 1940s.

The Security Council's debate on the Secretary-General's legal memorandum, and the Soviet objections to the President's actions had their effect.[13] Sydney Bailey explains what happened next:

On the proposal of the President of the Council, the Secretary-General's memorandum was referred to the Committee of Experts. The Committee duly met the next day and agreed "in principle that when a matter has been submitted to the Security Council by a party, it cannot be withdrawn ... without a decision by the Security Council."

But there agreement ended, and the Committee had no option but to report to its parent body (which had the same membership as itself) that it had not been able to formulate a common opinion.[14]

It is interesting to note that, although the Security Council Committee did not agree or act upon the contents of the Secretary-General's legal memo, they did implicitly recognize his right to make a statement concerning an issue actively before Council members. As Schwebel notes, "The Council failed to agree on Mr. Lie's view, but the Secretary-General won something of a victory nevertheless."[15]

This victory concerning the Secretary-General's right was confirmed nine months later when Lie submitted another legal memo concerning the Security Council consideration of the Trieste Statute.[16] This time, "Nothing was said of the propriety or the impropriety of the Secretary-General's submitting a statement — it seemed to be taken for granted."[17]

The Secretary-General's intervention during the Council's debate on the Iranian situation had the political effect of supporting the Soviet position. Encouraged by Lie's innovations and activism, the Soviet Union supported the Secretary-General's right to intervene and participate in Council proceedings in the next "bitter fight" over his right to "know and to say."[18]

THE SECRETARY-GENERAL AND THE SECURITY COUNCIL: RULES OF PROCEDURE

One of the weaknesses of the Security Council's rules of procedure, when they were first written, was that the role of the Secretary-General was indeterminate. As Schwebel points out, "The provisional rules of procedure prepared for the Security Council by the Preparatory Commission lacked provision for the Secretary-General's addressing written or oral communications to the Council."[19]

Article 99 gives the Secretary-General the right to convene the Security Council, but the Charter is silent about the Secretary-General's right to say anything in Council proceedings. In short, the Secretary-General is given an important preventive responsibility via the Council without the concomitant right to address the issue that he has raised. It is as though the Secretary-General can (via the Security Council President) convene the Council but then is expected to sit silently as the members of the Council struggle with a possible solution.

This prompted the Security Council's Committee of Experts to meet in May of 1946 to "remedy the deficiency."[20] The Committee held a series of meetings for the purpose of codifying the Council's Rules of Procedure.

The Secretary-General was represented at the first session of the Committee by Arkady A. Sobolev, the Assistant Secretary-General for Security Council Affairs.[21] Schwebel points out, "The point at issue was whether his [the Secretary-General] rights of communication would be restricted or unrestricted, a question which resolved itself largely into whether his interventions would be at the pleasure of the President of the Security Council or at the discretion of the Secretary-General."[22]

Several meetings of the Committee were held where this issue was debated.[23] Interestingly enough, the Soviet delegation urged that the Secretary-General be given an unrestricted right to intervene and to make statements before the Security Council. The Australian delegation strongly supported the Soviet position.[24] However, the United States opposed this position. The U.S. representative, Joseph E. Johnson, questioned whether the "Charter could be interpreted as giving the Secretary-General an 'absolute and unlimited right of intervention.'"[25] Taking a position that has been echoed, ironically, by the Soviet Union in later years, Johnson stated that he was "not at all sure that the Charter can be construed as authorizing the Secretary-General to make comments on political and substantive matters."[26] The Secretary-General's representative, Sobolev, had instructions to take a position that was in the middle of these extremes; he was instructed to press for the adoption of a rule similar to that of the Economic and Social Committee, which stated that the Secretary-General may intervene and speak "upon the invitation of the President."[27] The British, meanwhile, were silent. As Schwebel states, "The British delegate, true to national form, was for deleting nothing and defining nothing, but advocated that the Committee 'let experience show how the powers of the Secretary-General should be put into practice.'"[28]

When the issue was put to a vote, the Soviet and Australian position lost, Sobolev's proposal was provisionally adopted, and the Secretary-General was given the right to speak before the Council "upon invitation of the President."[29] But the British delegate arrived shortly after the vote with new instructions to support the Soviet and Australian position.[30] As Schwebel explains:

> The British shift apparently was sufficient to tip the balance in the direction of deleting the "invitation" phrase. For Brazil, Mexico and Poland quickly fell in line, and Mr. Sobolev then promptly came forward to suggest the immediate drafting of a new text, which, adopted the same day, reads: "The Secretary-General, or his deputy acting on his behalf, may make either oral or written statements concerning any question under consideration by the Security Council."[31]

This rule is embodied in Rule 22 of the current Provisional Rules of the Security Council, which gives the Secretary-General a broad power to participate in Council Proceedings. The last phrase "under consideration by the Security Council" has important implications, as we shall see in Hammarskjöld's report to the Council on the situation in Laos.

Schwebel notes, "The role which the Secretary-General played in acquiring his rights of Security Council intervention appears from the record to have been a passive one. The record in this regard is deceptive."[32] Although he does not explicitly say so, Schwebel strongly hints that Secretary-General Lie played an important role in the British shift. He notes, "The British shift, in particular, seems in response to an unusual pressure from somewhere, for it does not conform to the general pattern of British thought respecting the Secretary-General."[33] Since he interviewed Lie several times, Schwebel was in a unique position to ascertain the importance of this issue for the new Secretary-General. Schwebel does not specifically quote the Secretary-General on any aspect of these early crucial debates, although he does quote the "words of a supremely informed and reliable source" that the Secretary-General was in fact engaged in a "bitter fight" to assert and "win his communication rights in the Council."[34] Schwebel also suggests, "Whatever the reason for the British shift, in the affair as a whole the Secretary-General played a more active role than appearances indicate."[35]

This early debate and decision by the Committee of Experts of the Security Council were critically important to the subsequent institutional development of the office of the Secretary-General. The adopted rule gave the Secretary-General procedural access to the Security Council proceedings and debates. As Schwebel states, "It was in this [debate] that the Secretary-General won the right to speak freely to the U.N. organ charged with 'primary responsibility for the maintenance of international peace and security.'"[36]

PROCEDURAL CORNERSTONES

Having won the important right to intervene directly in Security Council proceedings, Lie established a firm legal and procedural basis for the Secretary-General's preventive role, especially in terms of his responsibilities under Article 99 of the Charter. Armed and equipped with the procedural right to participate in important discussions and debates, the Secretary-General can interject his own perspective and provide the Council with relevant reports or legal memoranda prepared by the Secretariat. As we shall see, these procedural rights have been elaborated upon and developed by Lie's successors, particularly Dag Hammarskjöld. Also, the acquisition of these rights created the procedural cornerstone of the Secretary-General's "early warning system." We define and elaborate this system in Part II. For now, however, it is important to note how the Secretary-General's right to report to the Security Council historically and legally evolved from these first bureaucratic battles over the Secretary-General's right to "speak out."

THE STRUGGLE TO KNOW

The Secretary-General's struggle to say something before the Security Council on a procedural basis was only half the problem; the other half was his need to know, in a timely and relevant fashion, what was going on in the world. Without knowing what was occurring in the world, the Secretary-General could have little to say, especially about the prevention of an incipient conflict. Hence, Secretary-General Lie (and his successors) devoted considerable energies to improving the United Nations' ability to gather information and to send out investigative missions.

As already mentioned, the UN Charter says nothing about the Secretary-General's right to know, that is, his right to make independent enquiries or investigations concerning incipient disputes or conflicts; the Charter, however, does contain Article 99.

As we have seen, Article 99 does not specify exactly how the Secretary-General is to ascertain whether a conflict threatens international peace, nor does it state how the Secretary-General is to obtain relevant information that would allow him to make this judgment. Clearly, the power to obtain such information is implied as a means of achieving the explicit purpose or end of the Article — namely, the possible invocation of the Council.

Yet, any investigations, or "information searches" by the Secretary-General present serious problems of definition. First, it is not at all clear what type of information is relevant to the Secretary-General's judgment that a situation threatens international peace and security. Second, even if the type of information that is relevant is carefully specified, it is not at all clear how this information is to be gathered in a timely fashion. Third, even if relevant and timely information is gathered, a matter may not be of such a serious nature as to require that the Secretary-General invoke the Security Council. In other words, the Secretary-General may make an extensive investigative effort in a situation that seems to threaten international peace, only to discover as more facts are gathered, that no threat exists. In short, there is no clear and automatic relationship between the Secretary-General's gathering information and invoking Article 99; hence, it may be hard to justify certain instances of enquiry in hindsight, especially when no action seems to result.[37] Finally, some Member-States of the United Nations act as if

Article 99 of the Charter simply does not exist and believe the Secretary-General has no implied powers to gather facts and make enquiries concerning potential conflicts.

GREECE: 1946

The question of the scope of the Secretary-General's information-gathering capability first appeared during the Security Council's debate concerning the Greek frontier in 1946. There was a shortage of relevant information concerning the situation there, so U.S. Ambassador Herschel Johnson proposed a resolution asking that "the Security Council . . . establish a Commission of three individuals to be nominated by the Secretary-General, to represent the Security Council."[38]

These individuals were then to report to the Council. Secretary-General Lie then interjected the following comments:

Just a few words to make clear my own position as Secretary-General and the rights of this office under the Charter. Should the proposal of the United States not be carried, I hope the Council will understand that the Secretary-General must reserve his right to make such enquiries or investigations as he may think necessary, in order to determine whether or not he should consider bringing any aspect of this matter to the attention of the Council under the provisions of the Charter.[39]

In his comments the Secretary-General explicitly invoked the language of Article 99 "whether or not he should consider bringing any aspect of this matter to the attention of the Security Council in order to justify his right to make such enquiries or investigations as he may think necessary." Lie was asserting in Council chambers the right of the Secretary-General to inform himself about a potential conflict. Moreover, shrewdly broadening the scope of the already liberal phrase "any matter" (Article 99), Lie interpreted his right to include "any aspect of this matter." This provided even greater latitude to Article 99, especially in view of its constrained scope at the time.

This generous interpretation of his right to inform himself under Article 99 was not challenged by any member-state on the Council. In fact, his assertion drew surprising support when the President of the Security Council, Andrei A. Gromyko, stated in response to Lie's assertion,

As the representative of the Union of the Soviet Socialist Republics, I would like to say the following in connection with the statement made by the Secretary-General. I think that Mr. Lie was right in raising the question of his rights. It seems to me that in this case, as in all other cases, the Secretary-General must act. I have no doubt that he will do so in accordance with the rights and powers of the Secretary-General as defined in the Charter of the United Nations.[40]

There was no further discussion of the Secretary-General's comment, and the Council went on to other business.[41]

SOUTH KOREA: 1950

The invasion of South Korea by North Korean forces in June of 1950 provided the pretext for the Secretary-General's next formal citation of Article 99. The Security Council met on June 25, 1950, to consider the Korean attack. Lie later claimed that, at this meeting, "for the first time . . . I invoked Article 99 of the Charter."[42] He claims he did so based on information he had received from the UN Commission to Korea, which had sent an urgent communiqué to the Secretary-General informing him of the invasion.

Yet, before Lie received the Commission's report, the Americans had already requested an urgent meeting of the Security Council.[43] Even so, the President of the Council permitted the Secretary-General to speak first,[44] and Lie presented the cablegram from the Commission, as well as his own opinion that "the present situation was serious . . . and a threat to international peace."[45] As already mentioned, the Soviets were abstaining from Security Council proceedings; this was an obvious mistake on their part because it subsequently enabled the United States to mobilize the entire United Nations against the North Korean invasion.

An interesting — and little noticed — aspect of this affair was the reporting role of the Secretary-General at the Security Council's meeting on Korea. The Secretary-General was responding to a report from the field, that is, the Korean Commission, and he duly reported upon the Commission's communiqué to the Council. His right to receive information from a UN field mission concerning a matter that may threaten international peace and security was never disputed. This has important implications when we consider the establishment of permanent and procedural inputs for the Secretary-General's reporting system in Part II.

Lie's claim that he invoked Article 99 to convene the Council is, in historical perspective, sharply debated and disputed. Critical commentators on the United Nations quickly dismiss the Secretary-General's claim that "for the first time, I invoked Article 99."[46] The simple fact is that the U.S. delegation had first requested an emergency meeting. The first formal invocation of Article 99 is commonly attributed to Hammarskjöld during the Congo crisis.[47]

AFTERMATH OF UN ACTION IN KOREA

The Korean War seriously weakened political support for the first Secretary-General of the United Nations. Because of his active involvement in, and support for, the UN military operations against North Korea, Lie was quickly viewed by the Soviets and their allies as a pawn of the United States and Western powers.

Because of the Cold War paralysis of the Security Council, caused by the very hot and bloody fighting in the Korean peninsula, there was no agreement by the great powers on the Secretary-General's second term. In an unusual step, in 1950 his term was provisionally extended by the General Assembly (without a recommendation by the Security Council) for three more years.[48] Even so, his effectiveness was diminished by the Soviet Union's constant attacks upon him.[49] During these three years, he stoically led the United Nations' efforts during the Korean War.

Near the end of his term, Lie reflected upon the nature and powers of his office. He stated,

> I think the Office of the Secretary-General should be clearly defined . . . the Charter should actually say that he is more than the Chief Administrator. I think the experience gained now, the Secretary-General's right to state his opinion, should be clearly stated in the Charter. Article 99 should be detailed, its implications written out . . . Article 99 is an atomic bomb, or at least a 32-inch gun. . . . Why can't I use the smaller rifles? Why just on world peace?[50]

As we shall see, Article 99 does allow for precise and very specific initiatives by the Secretary-General — despite Lie's protests to the contrary. Critics could easily point out that Lie was a "loose cannon" at the United Nations and simply lacked the diplomatic finesse to use Article 99 in a subtle or effective way.

Even so, Lie raises a good point. The Secretary-General must be cautious about actually convening the Council under the Article. Also, the procedural powers that are implied by Article 99 — as well as by other key Articles — could be strengthened by explicit mention in the Charter. As Schwebel notes, "Unquestionably, the definition in the Charter of the political powers which a liberal interpretation would give to Articles 97, 98, and 99 would greatly strengthen the Secretary-General's hand. Such a clarification could prove of particular value in time of challenge of the Secretary-General's initiative."[51] (See Appendix II for list of relevant articles from UN

Charter.) As we shall see, Schwebel's 1952 statement proved prophetic during the Hammarskjöld era.

Lie was succeeded as Secretary-General by Dag Hammarskjöld in 1953. Lie had apparently gained a reputation for being a bumbling "global activist," and many originally thought (and hoped) that the Swede, Hammarskjöld, would be content to be a "global clerk."[52] Yet, Hammarskjöld proved to be, perhaps, the most dynamic and innovative Secretary-General to date. Building upon the precedents established by Lie, Hammarskjöld developed the powers of his office, especially in the context of Article 99. His legacy is still cherished — although controversial — at the United Nations today. In the next chapter, we examine in greater depth his constitutional innovations and controversial actions concerning the Secretary-General's preventive role.

NOTES

1. Oran Young uses the term "saliency" to describe the possible influence of the Secretary-General. See Oran R. Young, *The Intermediaries: Third Parties in International Crises* (Princeton: Princeton University Press, 1967), pp. 83–84, 264–65.

2. Schwebel uses this term "bitter fight" to describe the early struggles of the Secretary-General to assert his "voice" in the Security Council. See Stephen M. Schwebel, *The Secretary-General of the United Nations: His Political Power and Practice* (New York: Greenwood Press, 1952), pp. 86–87.

3. For instance, Schwebel discusses how Lie defended his right of enquiry in the Greek frontier case. See Schwebel, *Political Power and Practice,* p. 90.

4. Although most criticisms are muted, the first Secretary-General does not seem to be highly regarded by many commentators. See, for example, Sydney D. Bailey's discussion of Lie's "intervention" in the Iranian question: *The Procedure of the UN Security Council* (Oxford: Clarendon Press, 1975), pp. 44–46. Bailey focuses upon Lie's legal arguments and concludes, "With the advantage of hindsight, one must conclude that this was not one of Lie's happier efforts." Bailey seems to be overlooking the political and procedural precedent established by Lie's submission of a legal memorandum to the Council. For an alternative view, see Schwebel, *Political Power and Practice,* pp. 49–59. I am also in debt for this description of Lie to Brian Urquhart, *A Life in War and Peace* (New York: Harper & Row, 1987), pp. 102–24.

5. Schwebel, *Political Power and Practice,* passim.

6. Both Schwebel and Bailey discuss this memorandum. See Schwebel, *Political Power and Practice,* pp. 92–96, and Bailey, *The Procedure of the U.N.,* pp. 44–46. Also see UN Doc. S/39.

7. Bailey, *The Procedure of the U.N.,* p. 44.

8. Ibid.

9. Schwebel, *Political Power and Practice,* p. 93.

10. New York *Times,* April 17, 1946. Also see Schwebel, *Political Power and Practice,* p. 93.

11. This entire quotation can be found both in Schwebel, *Political Power and Practice,* pp. 93–94, and in the verbatim text of the Security Council's 33rd meeting, UN Doc. S/P.V./33.

12. For a subsequent statement of the Soviet position, see Davidson Nicol, *The United Nations Security Council: Towards Greater Effectiveness* (New York: UNITAR, 1982), pp. 268–71. We will review the impact of Gorbachev's new approach below in Part II.

13. Bailey, *The Procedure of the U.N.,* p. 45.

14. Ibid.

15. Schwebel, *Political Power and Practice,* p. 94.

16. Ibid., p. 96. I am heavily in debt to Schwebel in the following section.

17. Ibid.

18. Ibid., pp. 94–95.

19. Ibid., p. 84.

20. Ibid.

21. Ibid., pp. 84–85.

22. Ibid., p. 85.

23. Ibid.

24. Ibid.

25. Ibid.

26. Ibid.

27. Ibid.

28. Ibid.

29. Ibid., p. 86.

30. Ibid.

31. Ibid.

32. Ibid.

33. Ibid., p 87.

34. Ibid., pp. 86–87.

35. Ibid. It should be emphasized, once again, that because Schwebel interviewed Lie on this matter, he may have insights into the proceedings and, specifically, the "British shift" that must be kept confidential.

36. Ibid., p. 87.

37. Not every enquiry by the Secretary-General is going to strike "paydirt," that is, provide greater political insight and information about a potential conflict situation. This is illustrated by Hammarskjöld's "U.N. presence" in Laos, which was circumvented by Cold War politics. We shall discuss this example in the next chapter.

38. Schwebel, *Political Power and Practice,* pp. 89–90.

39. Quoted in Schwebel, *Political Power and Practice,* p. 90.

40. Ibid.

41. Ibid.

42. Address to the General Assembly of September 28, 1950, press release SG/121, p. 1. Also see Schwebel, *Political Power and Practice,* p. 90.

43. Lie's claim that he invoked the Council via Article 99 is criticized by both Schwebel and Bailey; see Schwebel, *Political Power and Practice,* pp. 90–91, and Bailey, *The Procedure of the U.N.,* p. 74.

44. Schwebel, *Political Power and Practice,* pp. 90–91.

45. Ibid., p. 91.

46. Bailey, *The Procedure of the U.N.,* p. 74. Also see Schwebel, *Political Power and Practice,* p. 90.

47. See Chapter 3 below on *Hammarskjöld.*

48. Schwebel fully explains the unusual circumstances surrounding this three-year extension of Lie's term. See Schwebel, *Political Power and Practice,* Chapter 8, especially, pp. 187–204.

49. Ibid. See especially pp. 189–91.

50. Ibid., p. 205.

51. Ibid., p. 206.

52. Brian Urquhart describes, in his biography of Hammarskjöld, how and why the great powers settled upon him as the second Secretary-General. See Brian Urquhart, *Hammarskjöld* (New York: Alfred A. Knopf, 1973), p. 15.

3
THE STRUGGLE CONTINUES: DAG HAMMARSKJÖLD

INTRODUCTION

At age 47, Dag Hammarskjöld came to the United Nations after a very distinguished government career in Sweden. The son of a Swedish minister and diplomat, Hammarskjöld developed, early in life, a reputation for being a brilliant student and scholar. After he acquired his Ph.D. from Upsala University in 1933, he quickly rose in the ranks of government service. During World War II, Sweden was officially neutral, yet the government covertly did what it could to help Norway. Hammarskjöld was involved in these efforts, which included planning Norway's postwar economic arrangements and, for his services, was awarded by the Norwegians the *Grand Cross of the Order of St. Olav*.[1]

After the war, Hammarskjöld helped implement the Marshall Plan in Europe, and his administrative talents gained the notice of leading European and U.S. policy makers.[2] He then served as Sweden's Vice Minister of Foreign Affairs. While in this position, he enhanced his reputation among international diplomats, who increasingly appreciated his skills in negotiating, especially behind the scenes.

Hammarskjöld's reputation for administrative skill was undoubtedly one of the reasons he was nominated for Secretary-General; the great powers wanted a man who would run the United Nations smoothly, but not "rock the boat." In this regard, Hammarskjöld surprised his great power supporters by asserting, from the very beginning of his service as Secretary-General, an active and independent position for the United Nations.

Dag Hammarskjöld specifically used Article 99 as one of the main constitutional foundations for a broad development of his office's powers and role in international affairs.[3] Citing the preventive and political powers implied by Article 99, Hammarskjöld instituted a series of legal innovations that substantially contributed to the institutional development and significance of the Secretary-General's preventive role. These innovations proved to be quite controversial during his tenure and continue to be so. Yet, despite the debate surrounding his legacy, it is indisputable that he provided important new practices and concepts — such as a "UN presence" and preventive diplomacy — in international politics. He became, perhaps, the most articulate advocate of the Secretary-General's political powers in the history of the United Nations. To understand the strengths and weaknesses of the Secretary-General's office today, we need to review the constitutional developments that took place during Hammarskjöld's tenure, especially in the area of conflict prevention.

HAMMARSKJÖLD AND ARTICLE 99

Hammarskjöld believed that Article 99 provided his office with an "explicit political responsibility"; in the last year of his life in an Oxford University speech, Hammarskjöld provided his most comprehensive statement concerning this Article:

> It is Article 99 more than any other which was considered by the drafters of the Charter to have transformed the Secretary-General of the United Nations from a purely administrative official to one with an explicit political responsibility. Considering its importance, it is perhaps surprising that Article 99 was hardly debated; most delegates appeared to share Smuts' opinion that the position of the Secretary-General "should be of the highest importance and for this reason a large measure of initiative was expressly conferred." Legal scholars have observed that Article 99 not only confers upon the Secretary-General a right to bring matters to the attention of the Security Council but that this right carries with it, by necessary implication, a broad discretion to conduct inquiries and to engage in informal diplomatic activity in regard to matters which "may threaten the maintenance of international peace and security."[4]

Hammarskjöld's statement reiterates and elaborates upon Lie's contention that the Secretary-General has the right to conduct independent enquiries in order to ascertain whether or not a matter threatens international peace and security.[5] Such a claim provides an important sense of consistency and clarity concerning the powers of the Secretary-General's preventive role — as seen by the Secretaries-General themselves.

Hammarskjöld also cited the importance of evaluating the impact of Article 99 in conjunction with other Articles of the Charter, especially those dealing with the role and responsibilities of the Secretary-General.[6] He stated in the same speech,

> Article 98 entitled the General Assembly and the Security Council to entrust the Secretary-General with tasks going beyond the *verbal formalia* of Article 97 — with its emphasis on the administrative function — thus opening the door to a measure of political responsibility which is distinct from the authority explicitly accorded to the Secretary-General under Article 99 but in keeping with the spirit of that Article.[7]

This is a curious although important statement; Hammarskjöld's interpretation integrates the responsibilities given to him under Article 99 with those given to him by Article 98. (See Appendix II for a list of relevant Articles.) This is a useful perspective that seems to broaden the overall discretionary and executive powers of his office.

Even so, Hammarskjöld is on weaker ground when he invokes the "spirit" of Article 99 to justify the "political responsibility" that might be granted to the Secretary-General under Article 98. Specifically, there is no spirit of Article 99 that can justify executive action by the Secretary-General especially after the Article is invoked. Yet, this is exactly what Hammarskjöld claimed in the Congo crisis, giving the constitutional meaning of Article 99 a broader and more controversial scope.[8]

THE PEKING FORMULA: CONFLICT PREVENTION

Hammarskjöld's first opportunity to exercise the political responsibility of his office came in 1954. His effort to free the U.S. fliers held by the People's Republic of China was also his first major attempt at conflict prevention. The success of his novel efforts in Peking portended much of his dynamic style and flair for action.[9] It was also his first step in the long road to his concept of executive action, which he fully articulated during the Congo crisis.

Hammarskjöld's involvement in this issue formally began when the General Assembly adopted a resolution on December 10, 1954, condemning the People's Republic of China's continual imprisonment of U.S. airmen captured during the Korean War.[10] The resolution stated that the detention and imprisonment of the 11 U.S.

airmen and the detention of all captured UN personnel desiring repatriation were violations of the Korean Armistice Agreement. It requested the Secretary-General in the name of the United Nations to seek the release of the 11 airmen and all other captured UN personnel. The resolution then called upon the Secretary-General to seek the release of the 11 airmen *"by the means most appropriate in his judgment."*[11] [Emphasis added.]

Because of its explicit condemnation of the Chinese, the General Assembly resolution placed the Secretary-General in a tricky position. Hammarskjöld assumed (correctly, as it turned out) that the government of the People's Republic of China would refuse to negotiate with him based on the General Assembly's action. (Also, only a year earlier, the Chinese, who were not members of the United Nations at the time, were locked in bitter and bloody combat with UN forces, and only a precarious armistice preserved the peace in the Korean peninsula.) Because of the condemnatory aspect of the General Assembly resolution, some other grounds had to be found to establish and maintain contact with the Chinese on this matter.

To overcome the political impasse, Hammarskjöld decided to go to Peking and talk directly with the Chinese government about the imprisoned airmen. In a confidential cable to Chou En-lai, the Chinese foreign minister, Hammarskjöld made it clear that he was contacting the Chinese government on the basis of his authority as Secretary-General, not simply on the basis of the General Assembly's resolution.[12] This working arrangement, which provided a way for the Chinese government to receive Hammarskjöld without recognizing the condemnatory General Assembly resolution, became known as the "Peking Formula."[13]

The formula worked; the Chinese government invited Hammarskjöld to come to Peking. When he arrived in the Chinese capital in early January 1955, Hammarskjöld explained his position in his first formal discussion with Chou En-lai.[14]

Hammarskjöld later commented upon his own understanding of the Peking Formula, stating, "The Peking Formula meant that if an organ of the United Nations asks the Secretary-General to do something and does so without delegating its authority, he has only the authority vested in him under the Charter, although he is, of course, guided by the 'Resolution.'"[15]

As author Mark Zacher points out, Hammarskjöld "went on to note that this legal position allowed the Chinese to say. . . . 'We don't care a damn about your instructions, but we do recognize your authority. You are an independent organ of the United Nations. What your relationship is to the Security Council or the General Assembly is your business.'"[16]

It is important to note both the legal source, and political purpose of the Peking Formula.[17] The source of the Secretary-General's authority to conduct negotiations is cited by Hammarskjöld himself as the UN Charter.[18] As we have seen, the only Article that gives the Secretary-General an explicit political personality and role is Article 99.

Beyond this Article, however, are the overall purposes of the United Nations, as cited in Article 1 of the Charter. Both Hammarskjöld and Lash specifically cite the "General Purposes" of the Charter as a further basis for the Peking formula.[19]

Finally, there is Article 98, which states, the "Secretary-General shall perform such other functions as are entrusted to him." Although he was reluctant to admit it, Hammarskjöld was going to Peking, in part, in response to a political function entrusted to him by the General Assembly.

It is important to note that the political purpose of Hammarskjöld's Peking trip was preventive. He was gravely concerned that the continual imprisonment of the U.S. airmen by the Chinese might lead to an escalation of the crisis, even to war.[20] He made this concern explicit in his discussions with Chou. He reiterated upon this concern when he later recounted his conversations with Chou:

> When the Secretary-General of the United Nations has engaged himself and his office, with all the weight it carries in world opinion, for the fate of the prisoners . . . it does not mean that I *appeal* to you or that I *ask you* [his emphasis] for their release. It means that — inspired also by my faith in your wisdom and in your wish to promote peace — I have considered it my duty as forcefully as I can, and with deep conviction, to draw your attention to the vital importance of their fate to the cause of peace.[21]

As we have already seen, the Secretary-General's explicit concern about the prevention of conflict is fully consistent with his responsibilities under Article 99. Because the purpose of his trip was to help preserve the peace, his actions did not intrude into the unique enforcement responsibility of the Security Council. If war had already begun over the issue — and rumors of war were in the air[22] — or if UN troops were continuing to fight the Chinese in Korea, it is unlikely that Hammarskjöld could, or would, have made his trip to Peking.[23] Yet, in the absence of overt hostilities, Hammarskjöld's interest in maintaining international peace and security was fully justified.

As it turned out, Hammarskjöld's preventive efforts were eventually successful. The Chinese released the airmen as a "present" to Hammarskjöld in honor of his birthday, and thus the danger of a major clash between the People's Republic and the

United States was averted. Hammarskjöld's use of the Peking Formula was vindicated by events. The entire episode illustrates Hammarskjöld's ability to develop through the United Nations unique legal/political solutions to the pressing problems of peace in the world. The incident also provided the first significant demonstration of the preventive possibilities of the Secretary-General's office.

ARTICLE 99 AND THE GATHERING OF INFORMATION: THE UN PRESENCE

Hammarskjöld believed that one of his most important responsibilities under Article 99 was to inform himself of potential conflicts and to keep a political pulse on any situation that may threaten the maintenance of international peace and security.[24] To keep himself fully informed, he developed several unique procedures and institutional innovations that enabled him to keep abreast of political developments in troubled parts of the world. His most interesting innovation in this area is the concept of a "UN presence."[25]

The "new and somewhat elusive concept" of a UN presence grew out of a General Assembly resolution on the Middle East that in August of 1958 gave Hammarskjöld new mediatory duties in the area.[26] After returning from a personal visit to the Middle East in early September, Hammarskjöld reported to the General Assembly that the Jordanians had agreed to a UN presence that could continuously monitor the application of the General Assembly's resolution in the region.[27] Urquhart reports that when a German correspondent asked Hammarskjöld to be more specific about his concept of a UN presence, Hammarskjöld replied (in German): *"Name ist schall und Rauch."* (A name is noise and smoke.)[28]

Fortunately Ralph Bunche was more specific about the purpose of a UN presence in Amman. Dr. Bunche described its functions:

> The important aim of the UN "presence" is the establishment of some sort of UN arrangement on the spot with a purpose of watching local developments, holding a finger on the pulse and keeping UN headquarters fully informed about the developments in that area. . . . For the most part those who constitute and lead the "presence" operation, whatever its form, are expected to play their role pretty much by ear, to give well-considered advice where needed and requested, to intervene as necessary but always delicately and diplomatically, and to keep constantly in consultation with the Secretary-General for advice and guidance.[29]

Bunche's comments are insightful. He clearly suggests that one of the main purposes of the UN presence is to keep "UN headquarters fully informed about developments in that area." And "to keep constantly in consultation with the Secretary-General for advice and guidance." Obviously, the UN presence in Amman had other functions and responsibilities as well. Yet, it is significant to note that the idea of a UN presence was directly linked to information gathering by the Secretary-General's office.

The UN presence in Amman proved, in large part, to be a successful means of gathering information and of keeping the Secretary-General fully informed about developments in the area. Furthermore, the head of the UN mission in Jordan, Piero Spinelli, became a trusted and close advisor to the Secretary-General.[30] Because of the success of his efforts, as well as the improving political climate in the Middle East, Jordan agreed in the spring of 1959 that the UN presence in Amman eventually should be phased out.[31]

THE UN PRESENCE: LAOS

Hammarskjöld employed the concept of a UN presence again in Laos in late 1959. On November 6, 1959, Hammarskjöld received an invitation from the government of Laos to visit Vientiane.[32] He stated to members of the Security Council,

> In considering the invitation, I have taken into account my obligations under the Charter and all the information at present available regarding the difficulties facing Laos. . . . I have therefore decided to go to Laos within the next few days for a short visit *in order to inform myself* about the present problems of the country. Were my experiences to indicate that such an arrangement would be warranted — and this seems probable — I would, with the consent of the government, temporarily station a personal representative in Vientiane through whom I could maintain contact after my departure. . . . It may be noted that an individual stationed in Vientiane as my personal representative would be under the exclusive authority of the Secretary-General.[33]

The wording of Hammarskjöld's statement is significant; he stresses that it is his duty to accept the invitation from the government of Laos in order to "inform myself" about the situation in Laos. He then goes on to state his intention "if [it is] . . . warranted" to station a "personal representative in Vientiane through which I could maintain contact after my departure." He then makes a constitutional distinction between a personal and special representative. The former, he states, is under the "exclusive authority" of the Secretary-General whereas the latter is mandated by a UN organ — such as in the Amman UN presence that was established in response to a General Assembly resolution.

Vratislav Pechota, once a research fellow at UNITAR, elaborates upon this distinction between the two types of representatives, noting:

> In the case of Special Representatives, those assigned to tasks formally requested or authorized by the Security Council, the Secretary-General will normally seek, either formally or through informal consultation, prior approval by the Council. He may not regard it necessary when sending his Personal Representative to carry out his good offices.[34]

As we shall see in Part II, the example of a personal representative may have special significance during times of international crisis.[35]

Unfortunately, events in Laos overtook UN efforts to find a peaceful solution to that country's internal difficulties. A series of coups disrupted the government in Vientiane.[36] At the same time, Pathet Lao forces increased their control over much of the countryside. The UN representative could do little else than report that the situation was rapidly deteriorating.[37] Eventually, after new fighting between Pathet Lao and pro-Western forces, a cease-fire was declared, and the superpowers agreed — outside the UN context — to convene a Geneva Conference to consider Laos neutrality. With the convening of the conference in the summer of 1962, the purposes justifying a UN presence in Laos came to an end.[38]

Despite its lack of success, the UN presence in Laos had proved to be an interesting application of the Secretary-General's responsibility to inform himself of matters that may threaten international peace and security. In 1960, while defending the UN presence in Laos against Soviet criticism, Hammarskjöld concluded,

> If the Secretary-General is entitled to draw the attention of the Security Council to threats to the peace and security, has he to rely on reports in the press or from this or that government? Has he to take the word of Moscow or Washington? No, certainly not. He has to find out for himself and that may mean, as in the case of the criticized journey to Laos last November, that he has to go himself. . . . The mission to Laos of the Personal Representative of the Secretary-General, charged him with the coordination of widespread and important practical activities in the social and economic fields, was arranged at the request of the Chief of State and his legitimate government. It has been endorsed by succeeding governments, including the present one. Obviously, the criticism means that the Secretary-General

would not be allowed to respond to a practical request of a government ... unless such a move had the approval of the Security Council, under the unanimity rule, or by the General Assembly, which may not be in session when the need arises. Those countries who wish to have the independent assistance of the United Nations, in the modest forms possible for the Secretary-General and without running into the stormy weather of a major international political debate, will certainly be interested in this attitude of the delegate of the Soviet Union.[39]

HAMMARSKJÖLD: DEVELOPING THE SECRETARY-GENERAL'S REPORTING ROLE

As already mentioned, Article 99 provides the Secretary with the opportunity to report to the Security Council on events that may threaten international peace and security. This, in turn, implies that the Secretary-General has enough information to form an opinion that a specific matter may threaten the peace. In a brilliant procedural innovation, Hammarskjöld examined and elaborated upon this discretionary power, thus giving new meaning and scope to the Secretary-General's preventive role under the Charter.

In early September 1959, Hammarskjöld received a letter from the Royal Government of Laos alleging North Vietnamese aggression and requesting the dispatch of a UN peacekeeping force.[40] Hammarskjöld recognized that, although the letter was addressed to him, it concerned a matter that invoked Security Council responsibility.[41] He therefore requested — without specifically invoking Article 99 — that the President of the Security Council convene a meeting.

As the distinguished international civil servant and author Brian Urquhart points out, Hammarskjöld's innovative request was a calculated risk.[42] To formally convene the Council might be construed, especially by the North Vietnamese, as an explicit recognition of the Laotian charges. So, by "insisting on the procedural nature of his approach, he (Hammarskjöld) hoped to emphasize that his knowledge of the real situation in Laos was insufficient to judge the validity of the Laotian request for UN action."[43] Unfortunately, the ensuing debate quickly enveloped Hammarskjöld's procedural approach in the issues of the Cold War.

The President of the Security Council, Ambassador Ortona of Italy, convened a meeting on September 7, 1959, and called upon Hammarskjöld to speak first.[44] Taking the floor, Hammarskjöld made the following remarks:

In asking for the inscription on the agenda of the item entitled "Report by the Secretary-General on the letter received from the Minister for Foreign Affairs of the Royal Government of Laos . . . to the United Nations," . . . I have based my action on a practice which has developed over the years in the Security Council. According to this practice, the Secretary-General, when he requests it, is granted the floor in the Council in order to make such statements on subjects within the range of the responsibility of the Council as he considers called for under the terms of his own responsibilities. Just as the Council, I feel that he is entitled to request an opportunity to address the Council publicly on a matter which he considers necessary personally to put before the Council. In doing so within the framework to which I have just referred, the Secretary-General does not introduce formally on the agenda of the Council anything beyond his own wish to report to the Council. Naturally, the Council retains the same rights in relation to such initiative of the Secretary-General as it has regarding any request of his to address the Council. What I said should be enough to clarify the Constitutional situation when, in this case, I have asked for an opportunity to report to the Council. It should, thus, be clear that the request is not based on the explicit rights granted to the Secretary-General under Article 99 of the Charter. If it had been so based, the Council, under Rule 3 of the Provisional Rules of Procedure, would not have been free to refuse the Secretary-General to address it — as it is now free to do — and it would have meant the inscription by the Secretary-General of a substantive issue on the agenda. *In this latter respect it would necessarily also have involved a judgment as to facts for which, in the present situation, I have not a sufficient basis.*[45] [Emphasis added.]

This was, needless to say, an unusual and innovative procedure, and the Soviet representative, Ambassador Sobolev (the same Sobolev who served in the early years of the United Nations as an Assistant Secretary-General) was quick to catch its significance. In a lengthy reply to Hammarskjöld's statement, he asked for clarification of the Secretary-General's procedures, stating at one point,

I am forced to state that this meeting of the Security Council has been convened in violation of the Rules of Procedure. The Soviet Delegation does not understand why this had to be done. It does not see why it was necessary to call a meeting of the Security Council in violation of the Rules of Procedure.[46]

Sobolev specifically challenged Hammarskjöld's right — in the absence of invoking Article 99 of the Charter — to report to the

Council under Rule 6 or 22 of the Council's Provisional Rules of Procedure. Concerning Rule 6, Sobolev stated:

[U]nder Rule 6, the Secretary-General shall bring to the attention of all representative matters for the consideration of the Security Council. But if we read the relevant note of 4 September 1959 from . . . Laos, which has been circulated to us, we find no indication that the Government of Laos is submitting the matter for the consideration of the Security Council. Therefore, the Secretary-General's letter would not seem to be covered by the procedure laid down in Rule 6.[47]

Here, Sobolev seems to be stretching a procedural point. It is true that the Laotian letter did not specifically request consideration by the Council, but it did request that the Secretary-General apply the appropriate procedures to the Laotian government's request. The request for the UN troops is clearly within the primary jurisdiction of the Council. To illustrate this point, if Hammarskjöld had asked for a special session of the General Assembly to consider the Laotian request for a peacekeeping force, the Soviets may well have been the first to object.

Furthermore, Sobolev failed to address the central issue the Secretary-General had raised. The confusion surrounding the Laotian letter reveals, in part, the paradoxical position of the Secretary-General who must respond to unfolding events with incomplete information. To remedy this situation, the Security Council must either reflect its appreciation for the Secretary-General's dilemma by allowing him more procedural flexibility in an ambiguous situation or by improving his information-gathering abilities. To suggest that, in effect, the Secretary-General do nothing or, more drastically, cannot do anything while requests from UN Member-States for UN military aid reach his desk is to make a mockery not only of UN procedures but also of the United Nations itself.

Thus, it is not surprising that Hammarskjöld defended his right to bring the matter before the Council without formally invoking Article 99. As already seen, he emphasized, in an elegant explanation, that he did not invoke Article 99 because "it would necessarily have invoked a judgment as to facts for which, in the present situation, I do not have sufficient basis."[48] In short, he was keenly aware of his paradoxical position. On the one hand, he lacked the facts necessary to make an intelligent decision; yet, on the other hand, he most clearly had a duty to process a serious request from a recognized government for UN military assistance.

He resolved this paradoxical position by asking the Council to consider accepting a provisional agenda, which included his report on the Laotian situation. He summarized his position in the brilliant statement (some might say ploy) with, "As I think is clear from my initial statement, I do not request the right to make a statement to the Security Council *until and unless* the Security Council has decided to take up the question *I have raised* for consideration."[49]

After further remarks were heard from Sobolev, President Ortona put the provisional agenda to a vote and it was accepted (with the Soviets voting not to accept the agenda).[50] Although this was a controversial procedure, the Council then went on to consider the Laotian question.[51] Leon Gordenker states that Andrew Cordier, the knowledgeable former Executive Assistant to the Secretary-General, thought that this procedural innovation had "top significance" in terms of developing the Secretary-General's role within Council proceedings.[52]

The Council's debate over Hammarskjöld's action reveals the weakness of the Secretary-General's position when he must sometimes report to the Council without adequate information. As we shall see, this problem of securing enough information in order to act has plagued every subsequent Secretary-General and continues to be a controversial issue at the United Nations today.

The Council's consideration of the Laotian question had unfortunate political implications. Because of the importance of the issue for the Soviet Union and the Western powers, the Laotian question became embroiled in political posturing that left a bitter aftertaste in the minds of many concerning some of the procedural tactics used by the Western powers during this debate. Brian Urquhart fully describes the consequences of the Security Council's debate on Laos in his book, *Hammarskjöld*.[53] Even so, the innovative procedural approach developed by Hammarskjöld during this debate highlights for future reference the preventive possibilities of Article 99.

GATHERING INFORMATION AND PREVENTIVE DIPLOMACY

One of Hammarskjöld's most original constitutional innovations was his concept of "preventive diplomacy."[54] Hammarskjöld believed that the United Nations could be used to fill a political void in a regional conflict that otherwise might tempt superpower intervention and, thus, run the risk of a wider war. As Inis Claude explains: "Hammarskjöld defined it [preventive diplomacy] as United Nations intervention in an area of conflict outside of, or marginal to, the sphere dominated by Cold War struggles, designed to forestall the competitive intrusion of the rival power blocs into that area."[55]

Leon Gordenker of Princeton University (now retired) believes that the defining characteristic of preventive diplomacy is that it involves an exercise of the Secretary-General's powers under Article 99 of the Charter. As Gordenker explains:

> Because the Secretary-General's "Preventive Diplomacy" relates to specific situations and is *not the subject of instructions by the Security Council or the General Assembly,* no single statement accurately defines it. But all approaches to a definition are based on the doctrine that the Secretary-General has a generalized responsibility emanating from Article 99. In addition, the fact that he has been given vaguely defined administrative tasks of high political content, which must be carried out on the basis of a personal interpretation of the terms of reference, has encouraged "Preventive Diplomacy."[56]

Gordenker states that the exercise of preventive diplomacy by the Secretary-General "is not the subject of instructions by the Security Council or the General Assembly."[57] Based upon this definition, Gordenker tentatively distinguishes between preventive diplomacy and peacekeeping. For the purpose of the following discussion, I have adopted Gordenker's distinction. Part of my reasons for doing so are practical. The literature on UN peacekeeping operations is voluminous, and I see no need to add to it here.[58] The former involves independent actions by the Secretary-General or his representatives based on Article 99; the latter involves UN actions emanating from the Secretary-General's office in close consultation and cooperation with a UN organ.[59] Yet, the most important reason for adopting this distinction is that it allows us to focus on preventive diplomacy as a specific application of the Secretary-General's preventive role under Article 99.

Furthermore, Gordenker cites a later date (1958) than most commentators concerning the genesis of preventive diplomacy.[60] He states, "A series of specific developments, beginning in 1958, furnish the basis for Hammarskjöld's theory of Preventive Diplomacy."[61] The first case he cites involved a dispute between Thailand and Cambodia concerning the ownership of the Temple of Preah Vihear. Gordenker summarizes what occurred.

> Hammarskjöld discussed the dispute separately with representatives of the two governments and consulted members of the Security Council. He was then invited, no doubt in part at least on his own suggestion, to send a representative to help them with conciliation. He named Ambassador Johan Beck-Friis of Sweden as his Special Representative. The latter was eventually successful in

easing the tension between the two governments, to the extent that they resumed diplomatic relations.[62]

The interesting aspect of this case is the use of a special representative by the Secretary-General. Gordenker notes, "In the 'Beck-Friis' appointment, Hammarskjöld himself determined the terms of representation, and sent him on a mission involving not direction of the work of the Secretariat but a dispute between governments." We discussed earlier Pechota's distinction between a special and personal representative. Gordenker seems to reverse Pechota's definition.[63]

Hammarskjöld's initiative in the Temple of Preah Vihear incident provides an example of what has become known as the Secretary-General's "good offices." The concept of the Secretary-General's good offices has evolved out of his responsibilities under the Charter concerning the maintenance of international peace and security.[64]

Hammarskjöld's successor, Secretary-General Thant, continued to develop the political possibilities of this concept by quietly making available the Secretary-General's good offices whenever he thought it might be useful to promote a political settlement. It is important to note how this concept emerged from the independent initiatives of the Secretary-General acting, in large part, under his authority provided by Article 99 of the Charter.[65]

Given Hammarskjöld's highly innovative and practical interpretation on meaningful UN action, the question still remains concerning how the United Nations — and specifically the Secretary-General's office — can practice preventive diplomacy. Is it by emphasizing the possibilities for conflict prevention by the exercise of the Secretary-General's good offices, by gathering relevant information, and, if need be, by informing the Council of a possible threat to international peace? Or, does it require something more, something beyond the constitutional and procedural responsibilities of the Secretary-General to inform himself of a potential conflict, and — if need be — invoke Article 99? We explore this question by analyzing the legal and political consequences flowing from the first time in UN history that Article 99 was formally invoked, during the Congo crisis when Hammarskjöld explicitly used his authority under Article 99 of the UN Charter to convene the Security Council.

ARTICLE 99 AND EXECUTIVE ACTION

The Congo crisis, which erupted during the summer of 1960, was a decisive event within the history of the United Nations. It marked the first time that a Secretary-General specifically invoked Article 99. It may also represent the high point, so far, of great power trust in the United Nations' management of important international events. What began as a UN operation designed to facilitate the political transition of the Congo from a colony to an independent country turned into a political hornet's nest that caused many interested outside parties to question the effectiveness and even neutrality of the United Nations' involvement. As Brian Urquhart states:

> The crisis in the former Belgian Congo, which erupted with-
> in a week of that country's accession to independence on
> June 30, 1960, was to dominate the rest of Hammarskjöld's
> Secretary-Generalship. It was to bring him into a head-on
> collision with one of the major powers, the Soviet Union, and
> into serious disagreements with the three other great powers
> and with many smaller ones as well, and it was to pose prob-
> lems concerning the role and nature of the United Nations,
> and especially of the Secretary-Generalship, which haunt
> the Organization still. It was also to cost him his life.[66]

Hammarskjöld had anticipated trouble in the Congo, and he knew that events there would probably involve the United Nations. So, he arranged in May 1960 for Ralph Bunche to arrive in the Congo for Independence Day. Bunche was told to remain for a while as the UN representative on the scene.[67]

Because of the colonial legacy in the Congo, the Belgian population and military presence were bitterly resented by the Congolese citizens and army. Within a week after Independence Day, fighting erupted between Belgian forces still stationed in the country and Congolese civilians and army units. In early July, after the first Europeans were killed, Belgian airborne troops began to intervene actively in the internal situation of the country, supposedly to maintain "law and order."[68] Many Congolese saw the Belgian action as an attempt to reassert colonial domination. Ralph Bunche strongly objected to the Belgian intervention because he "clearly foresaw its consequences" — including the real risks of a wider war.[69]

Deteriorating events only confirmed the worst of Bunche's fears. Escalating Belgian military activity led the Congolese government to ask for military assistance from Ghana pending the arrival of a UN force.[70] As Urquhart states, these events led Hammarskjöld to invoke Article 99:

> These developments forced Hammarskjöld to conclude that
> an immediate and conspicuous military intervention by the
> UN was the only hope of getting the Belgian troops out and of
> avoiding both a complete breakdown of public order and
> administration and the risk of various forms of outside

intervention . . . so, on that morning, July 13, Hammar-skjöld decided to ask immediately for a Security Council meeting under Article 99, which had never formally been invoked for this purpose before.[71]

At the Security Council meeting, which convened at 8:30 p.m. on July 13, Hammarskjöld outlined his "proposals for meeting the Congolese government's request for assistance."[72] Among other things, he asked that a UN military force be created and sent to the Congo without delay in order to remove the Belgian forces from the area. Hammarskjöld felt a great sense of urgency about the deteriorating situation, so he argued for immediate Council action.[73]

The Council deliberated through the night and finally adopted, in the early hours of July 14, a resolution that called upon the Belgian troops to withdraw and authorized the Secretary-General to provide the Congolese government with "such military assistance as may be necessary until through the efforts of the Congolese government with the technical assistance of the United Nations, the National Security forces may be able, in the opinion of the government, to meet fully their tasks."[74] Armed with this resolution, Hammarskjöld worked tirelessly through the rest of the night to gather troops from donating countries for the UN operations, as well as arrange storage and supply areas.[75] In an amazing feat of administration (and political maneuvering), Hammarskjöld managed to have the first troops arriving in the Congo on July 15.[76]

Because the ensuing UN intervention in the Congo crisis has been extensively discussed and analyzed in the literature, we will only briefly review its history here.[77] The main focus of the following discussion will be on the constitutional issues raised by Hammar-skjöld's controversial handling of the Congo crisis, including his theory of "executive action" by the Secretary-General.

The disintegration of the Congolese government into competing centers of power — each with its favorite "great power sponsor" — is well documented.[78] There was a major threat to the centralized government posed by the secessionist movement, centered in Katanga Province and headed by Tshombe. There were deep tensions and feelings of distrust among members of the Central Congolese government centered in Leopoldville — tensions that eventually led to the splintering of the Congolese cabinet into separate factions; some favored the policies of Lumumba, the Prime Minister, and others favored Kasavubu, the titular president of a divided Congo. When the Soviet Union sided with Lumumba and the Western powers began to oppose him, the crisis in the Congo began to take on the ominous trappings of the Cold War. The shadowy intrigues of the neo-colonialists and Belgian mercenaries in Katanga and northern Rhodesia only added to the confusion.[79] Thus, the early Security

Council consensus, which was very fragile and incomplete to begin with (yet nevertheless allowed Hammarskjöld to deploy UN troops), began to disintegrate as the great powers began to choose sides.[80]

This understandably left the UN Congo operations in a precarious position. The increasing lack of a political consensus on the Security Council meant that Hammarskjöld and his advisors often had to make important decisions concerning the fate and future of UN operations in the Congo without political guidance. These decisions were often severely criticized by the great powers. In particular, the Soviet Union was extremely critical of Hammarskjöld's handling of the Congo crisis, especially after the murder of Lumumba by forces loyal to Kasavubu in February of 1961. In short, Hammarskjöld was trying to fill the political void both at UN headquarters and within the Congo. It was an impossible balancing act.

The problems that the United Nations encountered in the Congo led Hammarskjöld to speculate upon the proper response and function of the Secretary-General in situations where the political mandate for UN operations was unclear or fragile. As a result of these speculations, he enunciated a doctrine of executive action, intending to clarify the Secretary-General's role and responsibility when UN operations are conducted in uncertain political circumstances, for example, the Congo. He gave his most explicit description of these doctrines in his *Introduction to the Annual Report* of 1960–1961. In a key part of this report he states,

> The Secretary-General has been under the obligation to seek guidance, to all possible extent, from the main organs; but when such guidance has not been forthcoming, developments have sometimes led to situations in which he has had to shoulder responsibility for certain limited political functions, *which may be considered to be in line with the spirit of Article 99* but which legally have been based on decisions of the main organs themselves, under Article 98, and thus the exclusive responsibility of Member-States acting through these organs. Naturally, in carrying out such functions the Secretariat has remained fully subject to the decisions of the political bodies.[81]

Hammarskjöld's citation of Article 99 is curious; he states that "developments have sometimes led to situations in which he has had to shoulder responsibility for certain limited political functions, which may be considered to be in line with the spirit of Article 99." This interesting phrase is strategically placed within the context of his comments to justify the exercise of necessary executive steps by the Secretary-General.

Although the thrust of his remarks is clear, his phrase, "the spirit of Article 99," is confusing. Perhaps Hammarskjöld is referring to the inevitable "penumbra of uncertainty" that surrounds most rules of jurisprudence, especially in international law.[82] There is no definitive text of constitutional law that the Secretary-General can appeal to when making the types of political decisions to which Hammarskjöld refers. Thus, the shadow of uncertainty may well characterize the application of certain Charter Articles.

Yet, Hammarskjöld is referring to Article 99 in a very precise and carefully considered context. He is not referring to the vague uncertainty caused by the differing definitions of Charter Articles. Specifically, he is discussing the "spirit of Article 99" in situations where "police forces under the aegis of the United Nations have been organized for the assistance of governments concerned."[83]

As we have seen, Article 99 provides the Secretary-General with a preventive role and equips him with expertise and implied powers to help maintain international peace and security. The Article allows the Secretary-General to invoke the Security Council, if he believes it necessary to preserve the peace. Yet, the Article is silent on any duties of the Secretary-General once the Article is invoked. Presumably, once he has brought a matter to the attention of the Security Council, his political responsibilities under the Article cease. Once this Article is invoked, the legal basis for action by the Secretary-General — Executive or otherwise — inevitably shifts to incorporate the specific mandate of the Security Council; thus, Article 98 becomes the legal basis for further action by the Secretary-General, if the Security Council deems it necessary.

In short, no spirit of Article 99 lingers in the aftermath of the Article's invocation. The broad discretion of the Secretary-General to bring any matter before the Council should not be legally linked — even in spiritual, wraithlike form — to administrative and executive functions after the Article is invoked. To do so may lead to political difficulties — such as those that Hammarskjöld encountered in the Congo — that will have the inevitable result of diminishing the influence of the Secretary-General. If such linkage occurs, and then some action of the Secretary-General is seriously challenged or attacked — as in the Congo — then the preventive powers of the Secretary-General under Article 99 will be inevitably questioned or challenged. The outcome will be diminished discretionary power for the Secretary-General under this Article.

This discretionary power exists only before the Article's invocation. In particular, it cannot be invoked to justify executive action in peacekeeping operations. Reporting on such operations is inevitably requested by the Security Council; if a threat to the operation exists, it should be reported as part of the Secretary-General's mandate to administer the force. To link his discretionary powers under Article 99 to executive actions in UN peacekeeping might be construed as allowing the Secretary-General an independent role in the use of UN military forces. Yet, he has no such role unless specifically provided for by the UN Security Council. He most certainly has no such residual role emerging from the spirit of Article 99.

This is not to argue that the possibility of executive action by the Secretary-General does not exist. A specific mandate of the Security Council (or General Assembly) under Article 98 may ask the Secretary-General to exercise his own judgment or good offices in a certain issue or area. (See list of relevant Articles in Appendix II.) Yet, such executive action should never be linked to the Secretary-General's preventive role under Article 99. Once Hammarskjöld invoked Article 99 in the Congo crisis, the legal — and one might add, political — basis for his subsequent actions changed radically. By convening the Council, he had surrendered his discretionary powers as a watchman of the peace to become the Security Council's servant. At this point, any subsequent UN successes or failures, especially in the realm of UN peacekeeping, becomes the primary responsibility of the Council's members.

To act in an area as important as maintaining international peace and security, the Secretary-General must remain on solid legal ground. To push the legal definitions and limits of Charter Articles — especially Article 99 — into the realm of uncertainty is to risk the long-term irrelevance of Article 99 for the sake of providing a short-term justification for unanticipated activities by UN personnel in the field.

In fairness to Hammarskjöld, we note that his own choice of wording to describe Article 99 seems to reflect awareness of this danger. He is careful to condition his references to Article 99 by reasoning that the legal authority of such Articles comes from the main organs of the United Nations themselves. Even so, his invoking the "spirit of Article 99" is, for the reasons stated above, inappropriate.

It is understandable why Member-States of the United Nations, especially the great powers, are wary of giving the Secretary-General a broad mandate for executive action. As Hammarskjöld's experiences in the Congo illustrate, any action that is perceived to overstep his political role and responsibility under the Charter is severely challenged. The Soviet "Troika Proposal" was only one result of the political storm that resulted from Hammarskjöld's controversial handling of the Congo affair.[84]

A more lasting effect seems to be a general reluctance among the great powers to allow the United Nations — and specifically the Secretary-General — to occupy center stage in a political crisis. They are specifically wary of the Secretary-General undertaking executive steps in UN military operations. In view of the confusion between the broad discretion of the Secretary-General under Article 99 and the limitations and vagueness of specific UN mandates, this wariness seems to be, at least partially, justified.[85] However, it would be unfortunate if effective UN action for conflict prevention is frustrated by the continuing legacy of the Congo crisis. As we have seen, this legacy has produced serious confusion concerning the Secretary-General's responsibilities under Article 99 and his role under specific mandates by UN organs. This confusion can be minimized by maintaining a very clear distinction between the Secretary-General's discretionary powers under Article 99 before its invocation and his mandated powers under Article 98, especially after he has used Article 99 to convene the Security Council.

THE DEATH OF HAMMARSKJÖLD

Hammarskjöld's determined efforts in the Congo ended in tragedy. He was killed as he flew to Ndola to arrange a cease-fire with Tshombe between UN troops and secessionists in Katanga Province. The circumstances of his death are unclear and, to many, suspicious.[86] The only certainty in the aftermath of his death was that a gaping void had been created within the UN Secretariat, a void that his successor would have to try to fill. With his death, one of the most innovative periods in UN history — in terms of its institutional and legal development — came to an abrupt end.

NOTES

1. Joseph Lash, *Dag Hammarskjöld: Custodian of the Brushfire Peace* (Garden City, NY: Doubleday, 1961), p. 36.

2. Lash, *Dag Hammarskjöld,* p. 40.

3. Joseph Lash reports that Hammarskjöld believed that the independent initiatives of his office were "almost wholly built upon Article 99." See Joseph P. Lash, "Dag Hammarskjöld's Conception of His Office," *International Organization 16* (1962). Also see Oscar Schachter, "Dag Hammarskjöld and the Relation of Law to Politics," and Eric Stein, "Mr. Hammarskjöld, The Charter Law and the Future Role of the United Nations Secretary-General," both in *American Journal of International Law* (January 1962).

4. Dag Hammarskjöld, "Lecture at Oxford University," May 30, 1961, in Wilder Foote (ed.), *Servant of Peace: A Selection of the Speeches and Statements of Dag Hammarskjöld* (New York: Harper & Row, 1962), p. 335.

5. Hammarskjöld stated in his Oxford University speech that Article 99 carries "by necessary implication, a broad discretion to conduct inquiries and to engage in informal diplomatic activity in regard to matters which 'may threaten the maintenance of international peace and security.'" See Foote, *Servant of Peace,* pp. 334–35. Also see Stephen M. Schwebel, *The Secretary-General of the United Nations: His Political Powers and Practice.*

6. For instance, Hammarskjöld states in his Oxford University speech, "Article 98, as well as Article 99, would be unthinkable without the complement of

Article 100 strictly observed both in letter and spirit." See Foote, *Servant of Peace*, pp. 337–38.

7. Foote, *Servant of Peace*, p. 337.

8. See Hammarskjöld's "Introduction to the Annual Report 1960–1961," August 17, 1961, in ibid., p. 367. Hammarskjöld's statement, "The spirit of Article 99," is a most curious phrase, which we will extensively review below.

9. Hammarskjöld himself pointed out the novelty of his initiative, stressing to Chou En-lai in a confidential cable the "extraordinary nature of the initiative, this being the first time that the Secretary-General of the United Nations personally visits a capital for negotiations." Reported in Brian Urquhart, *Hammarskjöld* (New York: Alfred A. Knopf, 1973), p. 101. I am in debt to Urquhart's account of this incident throughout this section.

10. General Assembly Resolution 906 (IX), December 10, 1954.

11. Ibid. Also see Urquhart for an account of the origins of this resolution. Urquhart, *Hammarskjöld*, pp. 99–101.

12. See A/2888, December 17, 1954.

13. The Peking Formula is extensively discussed by Lash, *Dag Hammarskjöld*, as well as by Urquhart, *Hammarskjöld*. Both Lash and Urquhart point out that Hammarskjöld used this formula to meet later with the government of South Africa.

14. Urquhart, *Hammarskjöld*, p. 105.

15. This is Hammarskjöld's description of the Peking Formula, which he shared with Joseph Lash in an interview, April 10, 1960. See Lash, "Hammarskjöld's Conception," p. 349.

16. Mark W. Zacher, *Dag Hammarskjöld's United Nations* (New York: Columbia University Press, 1970), p. 129. Zacher is quoting Lash here; see Lash, "Hammarskjöld's Conception," p. 348.

17. Zacher, *Hammarskjöld's United Nations*, p. 128.

18. As Lash reports, this is a controversial interpretation: "Explicit in Hammarskjöld's development of the Peking Formula and his insistence upon his authority under the Charter as distinct from instructions given him by other organs of the United Nations was a doctrine of the autonomous character of the office of Secretary-General. It was not simply the agent of the other organs but coordinate with them." Lash, "Hammarskjöld's Conception," pp. 349–50.

19. Lash reports that Hammarskjöld asserted that his "authority was autonomous and coordinate with that of other organs and derived from the Charter as a whole." See Lash, "Hammarskjöld's Conception," p. 350. Also see Urquhart, *Hammarskjöld*, p. 105.

20. Urquhart, *Hammarskjöld*, p. 106.

21. Reported in ibid. Urquhart notes, "All quotes from the Hammarskjöld/Chou talks are from Hammarskjöld's own record of the talks," which are unpublished. In writing his biography of Hammarskjöld, however, Urquhart had access to these records.

22. For instance, Senator William F. Knowland, the Republican leader in the U.S. Senate, was calling for a naval blockade of mainland China unless the fliers were released. Emotions in the United States were high over their continued imprisonment, despite the fact that the Korean War had ended. See ibid., p. 97.

23. Under such circumstances, Hammarskjöld could hardly argue that the purpose of his trip was preventive and consistent with the "maintenance of international peace and security" (Article 99). Furthermore, it is extremely doubtful if the Chinese would have received him in such circumstances.

24. Lash, "Hammarskjöld's Conception," p. 347.

25. Urquhart, *Hammarskjöld*, p. 294.

26. Ibid. This is Urquhart's phrase. I am in general indebtedness to his account for this innovation.

27. A/3934/Rev.1, September 29, 1958. Also see Urquhart, *Hammarskjöld*.

28. Reported in Urquhart, *Hammarskjöld*, p. 294.

29. Dr. Ralph J. Bunche in a speech to the Ninth General Assembly of the International Press Institute, Tokyo, March 25, 1960. Also discussed in Urquhart, *Hammarskjöld*, pp. 294–95.

30. Urquhart, *Hammarskjöld*, pp. 295–96.

31. For a much fuller account of this first UN presence, see ibid., pp. 295–99.

32. Again, extensively reported in ibid., p. 352.

33. Ibid.

34. Vratislav Pechota, *The Quiet Approach: A Study of the Good Offices Exercised by the United Nations Secretary-General in the Cause of Peace* (New York: UNITAR, 1972), pp. 73–74.

35. In Chapter 9, I use the example of a personal representative to justify, in part, the sending of negotiating teams to the capitals of countries caught up in a crisis. The Peking Formula could also be cited in this context.

36. Urquhart, *Hammarskjöld*, p. 357.

37. Ibid., pp. 356–67. Urquhart provides a full account of events in Laos and the UN efforts there.

38. Ibid., p. 366.

39. SG/971, October 18, 1960, to the Fifth Committee of the General Assembly. Also reported in Urquhart, *Hammarskjöld*, pp. 353–54.

40. S/4213, September 6, 1959.

41. Ibid.

42. Urquhart, *Hammarskjöld*, pp. 342–43. The ensuing debate between Hammarskjöld and Sobolev is one of the great legal jousting matches of modern times.

43. Ibid., p. 343.

44. Leon Gordenker, *The UN Secretary-General and the Maintenance of Peace* (New York: Columbia University Press, 1967), pp. 149–50.

45. *SCOR*, 847 Meeting, September 7, 1959, paragraphs 11–12.

46. Ibid., paragraph 22.

47. Ibid., paragraph 17.

48. Ibid., paragraph 12.

49. Ibid., paragraph 26.

50. This was an extremely irregular and controversial vote; according to the Great Power Declaration of San Francisco, such votes are subject to the veto. Yet, Ambassador Ortona declared that the matter was a "procedural matter" based upon the vote — even though the Soviet Union voted against it. This was immediately objected to by the Soviets. See *SCOR*, 848 Meeting, September 7, 1959, paragraphs 80–89. For an explanation of the maneuvering that was going on, especially by the Western powers, during the Secretary-General debate on Laos, see Urquhart, *Hammarskjöld*, pp. 341–45.

51. Gordenker, *Maintenance of Peace*, p. 150.

52. Ibid. Also see Andrew W. Cordier, "The Role of the Secretary-General," in Richard N. Swift (ed.), *Annual Review of United Nations Affairs* (New York: Oceana Publications, 1960), pp. 4–5.

53. Urquhart, *Hammarskjöld*, pp. 343–45. Urquhart describes Hammarskjöld as profoundly upset by the subsequent course of events concerning the Council's debate over Laos but more or less powerless to stop the obviously manipulated direction of the Security Council debate. Thus, "Hammarskjöld was profoundly disturbed by the outcome of the Security Council proceedings."

54. Gordenker, *Maintenance of Peace,* p. 76. Also see Inis L. Claude, Jr., *Swords into Plowshares: The Problems and Progress of International Organization,* 4th ed. (New York: Random House, 1971), p. 313.

55. Claude, *Swords into Plowshares,* p. 313.

56. Gordenker, *Maintenance of Peace,* p. 76. Also see Hammarskjöld, "Introduction," *Annual Report,* 1960.

57. Gordenker, *Maintenance of Peace,* p. 152.

58. See, for example, Lincoln Bloomfield (ed.), *International Military Forces* (Boston: Little, Brown, 1964); Dag Hammarskjöld, "Report of the Secretary-General on the United Nations Emergency Force — Summary Study of the Experience Derived from the Establishment and Operation of the Force," UN Document A/3943, October 9, 1958; Stanley Hoffman, "In Search of a Thread: The UN in the Congo Labyrinth," *International Organization 16* (1962), 331–61; and Lester Pearson, "Force for the UN," *Foreign Affairs 35* (1957), 395–404. Pearson is commonly credited with originating the idea of peacekeeping forces.

59. Gordenker, *Maintenance of Peace,* pp. 76 and 152. Also see Claude, *Swords into Plowshares,* p. 314.

60. Gordenker, *Maintenance of Peace,* pp. 152–53. Also see Urquhart, *Hammarskjöld,* pp. 310–11.

61. Gordenker, *Maintenance of Peace,* p. 152.

62. Ibid., pp. 152–53.

63. Gordenker, *Maintenance of Peace,* p. 153. It is interesting to note that this appointment is described as a "special representative" of the Secretary-General. According to the distinction we developed earlier (note 34), such missions could be characterized as "personal representatives." Pechota makes note of the confusion that often exists between the two terms. Pechota, *The Quiet Approach,* pp. 72–75.

64. Pechota, *The Quiet Approach,* p. 2. This is regarded as the definitive study on the Secretary-General's "good offices."

65. See ibid., pp. 8–12. Also, Urquhart discusses the concept of good offices as well. See Urquhart, *Hammarskjöld,* pp. 310–11. Pechota stresses the interrelationship between preventive diplomacy and the concept of good offices.

66. Urquhart, *Hammarskjöld,* p. 398. I am in debt to Urquhart for much of the following discussion on the United Nations in the Congo. For an account that differs from his, see General Carl Von Horn, *Soldiering for Peace* (London, 1966).

67. Urquhart, *Hammarskjöld,* p. 389.

68. For a fuller account of the initial troubles of the Congo, see ibid., pp. 391–93.

69. Ibid., p. 393.

70. Ibid., p. 396.

71. Ibid.

72. Ibid., p. 397.

73. Ibid., p. 398.

74. Ibid.

75. Ibid., pp. 399–402.

76. Ibid., p. 401.

77. Besides Urquhart's excellent account in his biography of Hammarskjöld, there are a variety of books and articles written on the United Nations' operations in the Congo. See, for example, Arthur Lee Burns and Nina Heathcoate, *Peacekeeping by UN Forces: From Suez to the Congo* (New York: Fredrick A. Praeger, 1963); Per Frydenberg, *Peacekeeping Experience and Evaluation — The Oslo Papers* (Oslo: Norwegian Institute of International Affairs, 1964); Arthur L. Gavshon, *The Mysterious Death of Dag Hammarskjöld* (New York: Walker, 1962); Gordon King, *United Nations in the Congo: A Quest for Peace* (New York: Carnegie Endowment for International Peace, 1962); Connor Cruise O'Brien, *To*

Katanga and Back (New York: Simon and Schuster, 1962); and A. A. J. Van Bilsen, "Some Aspects of the Congo Problem," *International Affairs* (January 1962), pp. 41–51.

78. See sources listed in note 77.

79. See O'Brien, *Katanga and Back*.

80. Urquhart, *Hammarskjöld*, p. 443. The early Security Council "consensus" on the Congo was really incomplete because China, France, and Great Britain abstained. It is probable that it never really commanded the political support that it initially seemed to have.

81. Hammarskjöld's speech is reported in Foote, *Servant of Peace*.

82. Terry Nardin, *Law, Morality, and the Relations of States* (Princeton: Princeton University Press, 1983), p. 193. Nardin's book is, perhaps, one of the most significant statements on international law and politics since Hans Morgenthau's *Politics among Nations*. For an excellent review of Nardin's book, see Robert J. Myers, *WORLDVIEW*, March 1984.

83. Foote, *Servant of Peace*, pp. 366–67.

84. Urquhart reviews the Soviet proposed "Troika" extensively; see his *Hammarskjöld*, pp. 460–62, 466, 469–70, 525, and 527.

85. A good example of a vague mandate by the Security Council is the original mandate that it gave to the Secretary-General in the Congo operation, as well as subsequent mandates — as expressed in Council resolutions — that often left the Secretary-General without explicit guidelines. To offset this vagueness, which left him dangerously vulnerable politically, Hammarskjöld initiated the Congo Advisory Committee. See ibid., pp. 433, 436–38, 476–77, 486, 502, 509, and 513–14.

86. Ironically, Khrushchev — who opposed Hammarskjöld so bitterly in life — was deeply suspicious of the circumstances surrounding Hammarskjöld's death. In a view shared by many African leaders, Khrushchev believed that Tshombe, supported by the British and by Sir Roy Welensky, Prime Minister of Rhodesia and Nyasaland, was responsible for Hammarskjöld's death. See ibid., p. 472. Also Gavson, *Death of Dag Hammarskjöld*, passim. Finally, see Connor Cruise O'Brien, *Murderous Angels* (Boston: Little, Brown, 1968) for an imaginative and insightful account into the circumstances surrounding Hammarskjöld's death.

4
THANT AND WALDHEIM: THE STRUGGLE EBBS

U Thant of Burma became Acting Secretary-General after the death of Hammarskjöld in 1961. He came to the United Nations after serving as an assistant to U Nu during the time of Burma's emergence as a modern nation-state. For several years, he served as Burma's ambassador to the United Nations.

As a Buddhist, Thant was a very religious man who (like the Christian Hammarskjöld) sought to balance the stresses and strains of public life by sometimes retreating to profound inner reflection and contemplation.

U Thant was, in many ways, a model diplomat; he was unobtrusive yet able, compassionate yet realistic, effective yet often unappreciated. The press in the West, used to the self-promotion of politicians, especially when campaigning, almost always underestimated Thant. This was, apparently, no problem for Thant, who would sometimes greet friends and visitors by saying, "I empty myself to serve you."

A quiet and introspective man, Thant seemed in many ways to be a studied contrast to his dynamic predecessor.[1] Keenly aware of the brilliant although controversial legacy of Hammarskjöld, Thant was careful to avoid open clashes with the UN membership over policies and programs. He developed, through the Secretary-General's office, a "quiet approach" to the pressing problems of war and peace during his ten-year reign.[2] Some of his brilliant successes and innovations have gone almost unnoticed by legal and academic scholars. For instance, Thant's first major intervention came during the 1962 Cuban crisis.[3] During this dangerous nuclear confrontation, Thant displayed an extraordinary sense of timing and judgment as he launched his first preventive initiatives.[4] Yet, his contributions during this crisis have been overshadowed by scholars' fixations on the machinations and maneuverings of the superpowers.[5] He also strengthened and developed the concept of the Secretary-General's good offices and defended this development against continual attack.[6] Finally, he launched the first large-scale UN relief programs for civilians caught up in war and emphasized humanitarian assistance through the United Nations. To be sure, he also had his failures, especially in the area of peacekeeping.[7] Yet, his many successes outlived his few relative shortcomings, and history has yet to recognize fully his political contributions to the world at the time.

THANT AND THE CONGO

When Thant became Acting Secretary-General in the fall of 1961, he confronted the still raging conflict in the Congo. U Thant was able to salvage the United Nations from the quagmire of the Congo only with the greatest of difficulty. With Hammarskjöld's death, the great powers acquiesced to an increased UN role in the Congo; specifically, the new Kennedy administration strongly supported the Congolese central government. This was, apparently, a key factor in the eventual collapse of Katanga.[8]

After two more encounters with UN troops, the secession of Katanga came to an end in January, 1963 — thus ending the hopes of the neocolonialists and white supremacists for a last bastion in the Congo. The UN military force was withdrawn in June 1964, leaving a sizable UN civilian operation to help the central government.[9]

Even while the UN effort in the Congo was winding down, the controversy it created at UN headquarters in New York was heating up. Specifically, the problem remained concerning the United Nations' ability to pay for its Congo operations. The continuing failure of several members — in particular, France and the Soviet Union — to pay the assessed share of the United Nations' costs incurred from its Congo efforts led to the political paralysis of the General Assembly's nineteenth session and to the organization's near fiscal collapse in 1964.[10] Yet, Thant and the organization weathered this final Congo storm — in part due to some deft procedural maneuvering at the General Assembly's nineteenth session.[11]

Urquhart ends his lengthy analysis of the Congo operations on a labored, although hopeful, note:

> For some time after Hammarskjöld's death the Congo operation, which had caused so much controversy and dissension, was generally regarded with varying degrees of disapproval as an example of the type of involvement that the U.N. should avoid in the future. Later, however, the turmoil

in some other newly independent African countries, and the relative stability and prosperity of the Congo itself, caused a widespread reassessment of this judgment, and the Congo operation began to be regarded increasingly as an ultimately successful effort by the world operation in the face of almost insuperable difficulties.[12]

THANT AND THE 1962 CUBAN CRISIS

On the night of Monday, October 22, 1962, President John F. Kennedy announced to the world that a U.S. naval quarantine of Cuba would commence in response to the Soviet's efforts to build missile sites on the island.[13] Kennedy also demanded that the Soviets withdraw the missiles or face further U.S. action.

Imposing the U.S. naval blockade on Wednesday, October 24, presented the world with the terrifying prospect of a direct military clash between the superpowers that could escalate into nuclear war. In view of this very real — and growing — danger, Acting Secretary-General Thant decided to intervene actively in the crisis by opening direct communications with Washington and Moscow.[14] It should be noted that his intervention was uninvited by both superpowers although a great number of UN Member-States had encouraged his involvement.[15] U Thant began his independent initiative by sending a letter imploring restraint to both Kennedy and Khrushchev on Wednesday, October 24[16] — the same day that the U.S. naval quarantine began.[17] He also made additional comments during the Security Council debate on the crisis on Wednesday night.[18]

In his comments before the Council, Thant read his letters to Kennedy and Khrushchev.[19] In his letters, he pointed out that

> It is important that time should be given to enable the parties concerned to get together with a view to resolving the present crisis peacefully. . . . This involves on the one hand the voluntary suspension of all arms shipments to Cuba, and also the voluntary suspension of the quarantine measures involving the searching of ships bound for Cuba.[20]

The Soviets immediately accepted Thant's proposal.[21] Yet, the Americans categorically rejected Thant's call for suspension of the naval quarantine. As Arthur Schlesinger, a member of the Kennedy administration, states:

> U Thant made an unexpected intervention [on Wednesday, October 24] proposing that the Soviet Union suspend its arms shipments and the United States its quarantine to allow an

interlude for negotiations. Khrushchev accepted this thought at once and with evident pleasure; but, from our viewpoint, it equated aggression and response, said nothing about the missiles already in Cuba, permitted work to go forward on the sites and contained no provisions for verification.[22]

Despite the U.S. dismissal of Thant's proposal, President Kennedy indicated in his responding letter his support for the Acting Secretary-General's continuing search for a solution.[23]

U.S. commentators focus upon the failure of Thant's initial proposal as evidence of the United Nations' irrelevance during the Cuban missile crisis. For instance, in his book, *The Intermediaries: Third Parties in International Crises,* Oran Young states,

These are significant weaknesses in the resources of the Secretariat from the point of view of potential interventions in Soviet-American crises. The resultant problems were obviously illustrated by the attempts of the Secretary-General to intervene in the Cuban missile crisis of 1962. Although there were, in fact, some things that Thant could do constructively, it is quite clear that he suffered from a general lack of knowledge concerning strategic and technical matters. He was evidently unable to assess accurately what the effect of the steps he proposed would be on the military balance in the situation. He did not have available a very sound analysis of the crucial question concerning the military as opposed to the political and psychological importance of the installation of Soviet missiles in Cuba.[24]

Young's criticisms of Thant's proposal calling for mutual restraint are probably fair — as far as they go. However, it seems strange that Young emphasizes the military importance of Soviet missiles in Cuba when this is openly questioned, and even disputed, by the accounts of high Kennedy administration officials themselves.[25] Furthermore, Young seems to have an undue focus on a single aspect of Thant's intervention — namely, his Wednesday letter calling for mutual restraint. His focus prevents him from recognizing the importance of Thant's other efforts and proposals, including those made before the Security Council Wednesday night, October 24, 1962. Young is not alone in this regard; most U.S. and Western commentators on the crisis overlook Thant's other efforts — which were more successful in buying time for the superpowers.

THE SEARCH FOR COMMON GROUND: THANT'S KEY CONTRIBUTION

U Thant made his most significant proposal, not in his original letters to Kennedy and Khrushchev, but in his talk before the UN Security Council Wednesday night, October 24, 1962. He stated,

> I should also like to take this occasion to address an urgent appeal to the President and the Prime Minister of the Revolutionary Government of Cuba. Yesterday Ambassador Garcia-Inchaustegui of Cuba recalled the words of his President, words which were uttered from the rostrum of the General Assembly just over two weeks ago, and I quote: "Were the United States able to give us proof, by word and deed, that it would not carry out aggression against our country, then, we declare solemnly before you here and now, our weapons would be unnecessary and our army redundant." Here again I feel that on the basis of discussion, *some common ground may be found* through which a way may be traced out of the present impasse. (Emphasis added.)[26]

U Thant made this point in the context of requesting the Cuban government to suspend "construction and development of major military facilities and installations in Cuba" during the crisis. What is significant about his statement is that he introduced, near the beginning of this dangerous confrontation, the political terms of a salient solution that would eventually end the crisis; specifically, he pointed out that the Cubans (and presumably the Soviets) claimed that their weapons would be "unnecessary and redundant" if the United States pledged not to commit aggression against the country. Although these terms were made in the context of suspending construction, they became increasingly important as the crisis progressed. It is interesting to note that President Kennedy took note of Thant's comments before the Council in his written response (October 25) to the Secretary-General's original letter.[27] Presumably the Soviets also studied Thant's comments carefully.

Furthermore, Thant also interjected, in a very timely fashion, "salient escalation controls" that helped both the Americans and Soviets save face. A salient escalation control is a diplomatic "focal point" where a compromise or implicit agreement to halt further escalation may "converge" and arrest further deterioration of military or political stability during a crisis.[28] U Thant proposed his first successful salient escalation control in a letter to Khrushchev on October 25. In the letter, Thant expressed his "earnest hope that the Soviet ships already on their way to Cuba might be instructed to stay away from the interception area for a limited time only, in order to permit discussions of the modalities of a possible agreement which could settle the problem peacefully in line with the Charter of the United Nations." U Thant's request gave Khrushchev a plausible — and honorable — explanation for preventing an impending clash, and he accepted it. As Richard Walton states, "The Acting Secretary-General [was] responsible for the breathing space that avoided confrontation at sea — and possible escalation into nuclear war."[29]

Considering the danger of backing a superpower into a corner — whether it be the United States or the Soviet Union — Thant's proposal was a crucial face-saving device for Khrushchev and bought time — a most precious commodity during any crisis, especially a nuclear one. As Harland Cleveland states: "The UN, through the Secretary-General, served as a middleman in crucial parts of the dialogue between President Kennedy and Chairman Khrushchev which led to a peaceful solution."[30]

U Thant also proposed a salient escalation control to the Americans. Specifically, he suggested, in an October 25 letter to President Kennedy, that the Americans "do everything possible to avoid direct confrontations with *Soviet* ships in the next few days to minimize the risk of any untoward incident."[31] In his response to Thant on the same day, President Kennedy stated,

> If the Soviet government accepts and abides by your request "that Soviet ships already on their way to Cuba . . . stay away from the interception area" for the limited time required for preliminary discussion, you may be assured that this government will accept and abide by your request that our vessels in the Caribbean "do everything possible to avoid direct confrontation with Soviet ships in the next few days in order to minimize the risk of any untoward incident."[32]

The next morning, Friday, October 26, the U.S. Navy stopped the transport *Marucla,* a U.S. built liberty ship bound for Cuba under a Soviet charter from the Baltic port of Riga. Yet, it was a Panamanian-owned vessel. Hence, the Americans could accurately claim that they were observing Thant's request not to stop Soviet ships. As Robert Kennedy states about his brother's action: the *Marucla* had been carefully and personally selected by President Kennedy to be the first ship stopped and boarded. He was demonstrating to Khrushchev that we were going to enforce the quarantine, yet, because it was not a Soviet-owned vessel, it did not represent a direct affront to the Soviets, requiring a response from them. It gave them more time, but simultaneously demonstrated that the United States meant business.[33]

As news of the *Marucla* reached UN Headquarters in New York, the salient solution first proposed by Thant before the Security Council on October 24 was being cautiously and somewhat mysteriously explored by a Soviet diplomat in Washington. Alexander Fomin, a counselor with the Soviet Embassy — but also believed to be the head of intelligence operations in the United States — contacted ABC diplomatic correspondent John Scali. Fomin wanted "Scali to find out, through his contacts in the State Department, . . . whether the United States Government would be interested in a settlement which would include the dismantling of the Soviet missile sites under UN supervision in return for a U.S. pledge that there would be no invasion of Cuba."[34]

Fomin's proposal echoed the one Kennedy received in a personal letter from Khrushchev that Friday as well. Based on this personal letter, as well as Scali's conversation with Fomin, Robert Kennedy states, "I had a slight feeling of optimism as I drove home from the State Department that night."[35] Even so, he confesses to being "unclear" about why the Soviets had used such an unorthodox communication channel as Fomin to explore the proposal — a proposal that Thant had inserted earlier into negotiations during the crisis.[36]

As thoroughly discussed in the literature, the United States eventually did agree to the essence of this salient solution: to respect the territorial integrity and independence of Cuba in return for the withdrawal of Soviet missiles.[37] Yet, on Saturday, October 27, tensions flared again, in part, because of the downing of a U.S. U-2 surveillance plane. In a last-ditch effort to prevent war, President Kennedy sent a letter to Khrushchev on Saturday, October 27, accepting this proposal.[38] Khrushchev accepted it as well and announced the withdrawal of the missiles on Sunday, October 28.[39] As part of the arrangement to end the crisis, the Soviets agreed to UN supervision of the missiles' departure from Cuba. Stepping back from the brink of nuclear war, people throughout the world gave a grateful sigh of relief.

UN SUPERVISION AND VERIFICATION IN CUBA

Unfortunately, the United Nations' efforts to supervise and verify the withdrawal of Soviet missiles from Cuba were largely a disappointment — mostly because Castro refused to allow UN inspection teams onto the island.[40] Even so, the United States was able to verify to its own satisfaction that the missiles were being dismantled, and so the lack of UN supervision did not prevent reducing the crisis. However, the *mere possibility* of UN supervision was helpful during the crisis because it helped provide a way out of the deadlock.

Meanwhile, negotiations to end the crisis were continuing at the United Nations. Direct negotiations between the U.S. and Soviet governments continued at UN headquarters until January 1964 when both sides issued a joint communiqué stating that the conditions leading to the crisis in the Caribbean had ended.[41]

THANT'S INTERVENTION: AN IMPORTANT POLICY PRECEDENT

By actively intervening in the 1962 Cuban crisis, Thant established an important precedent for UN involvement in nuclear crises and thus broadened the scope of the Secretary-General's role in the prevention of conflicts. As we have seen, Hammarskjöld's theory of preventive diplomacy emphasized the necessity for UN involvement in potential or actual conflict situations outside the realm of superpower politics. In the Cuban crisis, Thant interjected his office directly into a dispute between the superpowers. In doing so, he legitimated the United Nations' interest and role in such crises, especially if others should occur in the future. It is significant that the superpowers not only allowed this to happen but made full use of the Secretary-General's intervention. As former Secretary of State Dean Rusk revealed only in 1987, President Kennedy was planning — if all else failed — a secret initiative through Thant's office.[42] In view of this, it would be implausible for the Soviets or Americans to argue in the future that the United Nations has no right to intervene in a threatening situation or dispute between them. The right has already been recognized and established. The political wisdom of doing so is another matter and depends upon the specific context of a crisis.

THANT AND THE SECRETARY-GENERAL'S GOOD OFFICES

U Thant cited his involvement in the Caribbean crisis as an example of exercising the Secretary-General's good offices.[43] It is important to note that he used his good offices without invoking Article 99. Indeed, this became a characteristic pattern of Thant's diplomacy — to search quietly and diligently for a solution without formally invoking Article 99 and thus inviting public debate of contentious issues.

After his intervention in the Cuban crisis, Thant had little time to rest. There were a variety of conflicts throughout the world in the early and mid-1960s: In Yemen (1962–1963), in West Irian (1962), between Cambodia and Thailand (1961–1968), between Rwanda and Burundi (1964), between India and Pakistan (1965 and 1971) and the ominous, growing involvement of the United States in Vietnam (1965–1975).[44] His attempts to help find a peaceful settlement in Vietnam earned him the enduring anger of the Johnson administration — although history may be kinder to his efforts. In all these situations, the Secretary-General tried, with various degrees of success, to employ his good offices. He often did so in a low-key and informal way, seeking informal contacts and consultations, and trying to determine — as he did in the Cuban crisis — whether any common ground existed between real or potential adversaries. He emphasized quiet diplomacy that was rarely visible to the public eye; Thant himself commented on this approach, stating that often while the Secretary-General is working privately with the parties in an attempt to resolve a delicate situation, he is criticized publicly for inaction or even lack of interest.[45]

U Thant's quiet approach to conflict prevention was, apparently, one of the main elements of his diplomacy. Unlike Hammarskjöld, who often worked in the public limelight and seemed to invite public scrutiny, Thant shunned the public's eye and preferred to operate in the background of events. Because of the behind-the-scenes nature of Thant's diplomacy, it is hard to analyze or evaluate his activities — or contributions — unless the objection of a Member-State brought an issue into the public domain. For instance, the Soviet Union publicly objected to Thant's exercise of his good offices upon, at least, three occasions — in the dispute between Cambodia and Thailand in 1966, in the situation that arose between Equatorial Guinea and Spain in 1969, and in the Bahrain case in 1970.[46]

Claiming that the UN Charter gave jurisdiction for such issues to the Security Council, the Soviets objected to Thant's involvement in these situations. For instance, in the Bahrain case (in 1970), the Soviet ambassador stated,

It is a matter of common knowledge that according to the Charter of the United Nations, questions of this kind and the decisions taken on them come within the jurisdiction of the Security Council. The statement in the [Secretary-General's] note that actions such . . . as this by the Secretary-General "have become customary in United Nations practice" cannot serve to justify these actions, for it is widely known that this illegal practice was forced upon the United Nations in the past . . . contrary to and in violation of the Charter . . . the USSR Mission to the United Nations considers it necessary to emphasize once again that under the United Nations Charter, decisions on matters connected with action by the

United Nations relating to the maintenance of international peace and security are taken by the Security Council.[47]

At the time, this was a familiar — although not traditional — Soviet viewpoint.[48] As pointed out earlier, the Soviets seemed to be overlooking or conveniently forgetting the responsibilities given to the Secretary-General under the Charter; specifically, Article 99 gives the Secretary-General a preventive role in the "maintenance of international peace and security" — an area the Soviets seem to be claiming is the exclusive jurisdiction of the Security Council. In contrast to the Soviet position, Thant believed that if two Member-States of the United Nations, locked in a real or potential conflict, wanted the Secretary-General to exercise his good offices in an ongoing effort to explore possible solutions, then the Secretary-General had an obligation to act. U Thant strongly defended the right of Member-States to call upon the services of the Secretary-General. In short, the initiative for employing his good offices often remained primarily with the Member-States themselves.[49]

The Soviets welcomed, and benefitted from, Thant's involvement in a dangerous dispute — the 1962 Cuban crisis — involving themselves yet denied this possibility in disputes involving others, for example, Bahrain. This fundamental inconsistency suggests that political, and not legal, considerations were the basis of the Soviet objections to the exercise of the Secretary-General's good offices during this period.

Although Thant defended the independent right of the Secretary-General to offer his good offices to those that might need his assistance, he did not — as a matter of practical policy — insulate his activities from the Security Council; instead, he continually consulted with Security Council members concerning his involvement in a situation or dispute. This practice of consulting with the Council sometimes led to procedural problems. One such problem developed over the Secretary-General's report to the President of the Security Council concerning the situation in Equatorial Guinea during March 1969. Pechota describes the episode:

In a written communication to the Secretary-General issued as a Security Council document, the President of the Council informed the Secretary-General that he had "brought to the attention of the members of the Security Council the content of our *consultation* [emphasis added]. The Secretary-General promptly replied that "[When] I saw you earlier today, I told you, as a *matter of information* [emphasis added], of my intention to send a representative to Equatorial Guinea. It was not a consultation in any sense. . . . It was not my purpose ... to establish any precedent of prior consultation."[50]

Thus, to his credit, Thant strongly defended the independence of his good offices and was very careful not to establish a precedent that may have limited the prerogatives of the Secretary-General.

THANT AND ARTICLE 99: LOST OPPORTUNITIES?

U Thant seemed reluctant to justify the use of his good offices in reference to Article 99 of the Charter. Furthermore, he seemed to have a very strong preference not to invoke the Article at all. For instance, he did not invoke Article 99 when he received the request from President Nassar to remove UN peacekeeping forces (UNEF) from the Sinai. He simply complied with the request, paving the way for the surprise Isareli attack that soon followed.[51]

Another time that he might have been eminently justified in invoking the Article — during the Indian-Pakistani crisis, which led to war in 1971 — he chose instead to send a note to the Security Council inviting the President and its members to consider with him ways to resolve the conflict. In justifying his course of action, Thant said, "The political aspects of this matter are of such far reaching importance that the Secretary-General is not in a position to suggest precise courses of action before members of the Security Council have taken note of the problem."[52]

So, instead of bringing the issue formally before the Security Council, Thant invited consultations in order to determinewhether the United Nations "with its varied resources for conciliation and persuasion" could play "a more forthright role" in the crisis.[53] Although Thant was unclear on this point, he seems to be arguing that he does not have enough information, both about the particular dispute and about the Council members' probable cause of action. Stating that he is not in a "position to suggest a precise course of action," he nevertheless reminds the Council of the "varied resources for consultation" that the United Nations can employ in the crisis. Thant did not argue — as Hammarskjöld did in the Laotian dispute — that because the Secretary-General's sources of information were inadequate, he had a duty to go directly to the area (or send a personal representative) in order to ascertain events. U Thant simply acknowledges that his judgment is incomplete; he does not acknowledge any obligation to gather more information so that he could suggest a "more precise course" of action. In view of the past statements emanating from the Secretary-General's office concerning his right to know, this seems to be a rather casual disclaimer of the Secretary-General's preventive role. Thus, he has been justly criticized for not acting in a situation when, because of the paradoxes of great powers politics, invocation of the Security Council via Article 99 might have been welcomed. As Sydney D. Bailey notes,

> The situation in the summer of 1971 was the kind of situation which the drafters of the Charter had had in mind when they decided to include Article 99 . . . when all members of the Council are inhibited from taking an initiative because of their relationship to one or other of the parties, it is in such situations that Article 99 attains its full importance.[54]

U Thant noted at the time that it could be politically counterproductive to convene the Council and then have the Council fail to take any concrete action or, even worse, exacerbate the dispute under review. Yet, at the least, he has an obligation to inform himself so that he can suggest a more precise course of action, if called upon to do so, especially when he is aware that there is a very serious potential conflict brewing. At the very most, he has the option to convene the Security Council so that the matter is brought to the attention of world leaders. Unfortunately in this situation, Thant seemed to have capitulated his preventive role after making a very modest and ineffective effort.

THANT AND HUMANITARIAN ASSISTANCE

In early 1971, East Pakistan was devastated by severe flooding. This natural disaster was soon followed by the outbreak of a bitter and bloody civil war between East and West Pakistan. As Gideon Gottlieb noted at the time, "The quick succession of tragic events in East Pakistan has left hundreds of thousands of persons dead or injured and has generated an exodus of over *nine million refugees to India* culminating in full-scale warfare between India and Pakistan."[55]

In response to this situation of massive suffering, Thant "initiated a UN East Pakistan Relief Operation (UNEPRO) without any supporting resolution from any United Nations Organ."[56] Thant justified this unprecedented action, stating, "I felt that my obligation under the Charter must include any humanitarian action which I could take to save the lives of large numbers of human beings."[57] The sole authorization for the operation came from President Khan's acceptance of Thant's offer to provide humanitarian assistance.

The United Nations' efforts had two operational aspects: the first was located in East Pakistan; the other, in India. In East Pakistan, UNEPRO quickly ran into major problems. Gottlieb succinctly describes the situation thus:

Substantial opposition to the operation developed from the Mukti Bahini, the armed forces of the Bangladesh government which had declared the independence of East Pakistan. The Bangladesh forces felt that UNEPRO had unwittingly been made to serve the ends of the West Pakistan "military occupational forces" and of the Razakara militia. Attacks on UNEPRO facilities and personnel led . . . to the recall of some of the operation in the wake of increasing hostilities in the province.[58]

UN humanitarian activities in India fared better. Under the leadership of Prince Sadruddin Aga Khan, international aid was quickly and effectively mobilized to aid refugees who had fled into India to escape the fighting.[59] Literally millions of people received some form of assistance from the United Nations — and from other relief agencies.

Aided by able assistants, Thant's decisive initiative in this situation undoubtedly helped to save thousands of lives. It also represented a significant new application of the Secretary-General's powers under the Charter. As Gottlieb noted,

Thant's explicit assertion that the Charter requires the Secretary-General to take humanitarian action, without any enabling resolution if need be, to save the lives of human beings in times of civil war, is an important development in the authority of the Office of Secretary-General under the Charter. It has now been unanimously endorsed by the General Assembly in Resolution 2790 (XXVI) of December 6, 1971.[60]

A plausible argument can be made that the Secretary-General's preventive role requires that he take active steps, as Thant did, during a conflict to minimize civilian casualties. A quick and lasting peace is often more difficult to achieve when systematic violence is aimed at civilian populations.[61] So, in order to prevent a wider war, and a sharp escalation in the fighting, the Secretary-General should have the authority and operational capacity to intercede in a particular conflict to prevent or minimize attacks against civilians.[62]

What makes Thant's intervention in East Pakistan so interesting is that the conflict was originally a civil war; therefore, Thant was entering into an area that some might say is within the domestic jurisdiction of the nation-state.[63] Yet, Thant was not deterred by this argument, and events vindicated his judgment. He was able to acquire the approval of the Pakistani president, as well as the assistance and support of a large number of Member-States. In doing so, he made it clear that the United Nations could effectively operate, even while a conflict was continuing, to mitigate the effects of violence through its humanitarian assistance and thus, presumably, prevent a further deterioration of events. That Member-States unanimously recognized his authority to do so confirmed Thant's belief that he had an obligation to act under the Charter.

THANT'S LEGACY

The record of Thant as UN Secretary-General is mixed even though his personal, behind-the-scenes diplomacy has been consistently ignored or underrated by history. Although he showed great skill in controlling escalation during the Cuban missile crisis and strongly defended the independence of the Secretary-General's good offices, he tended to minimize, or disregard, his preventive responsibilities under Article 99 in two key instances: UNEF in 1967 and the Indian-Pakistani problem in 1971. Yet, it is indisputable that he was a man of deep compassion and integrity, as his humanitarian initiatives in 1971 demonstrated. In taking such initiatives, he managed to give new meaning to the Secretary-General's preventive role.

In the fall of 1971, Thant's second term as Secretary-General ended. Already a sick man, with the cancer that would eventually kill him, he declined to serve a third term. This inevitable decision led to the most controversial election of a Secretary-General in UN history — the secret balloting by the UN Security Council that led to the election of Kurt Waldheim.

KURT WALDHEIM: "CARETAKER"
SECRETARY-GENERAL

The election of a UN Secretary-General is a critical time for the organization — as well as for the many Member-States. A strong UN Secretary-General could conceivably mobilize world public opinion behind a popular political initiative, such as confronting apartheid, criticizing the nuclear arms race, or ending nuclear testing. Yet, many of the Member-States either benefit from the political status quo or are reluctant to "rock the boat." Thus, they may favor the election of a weak Secretary-General whose record is mediocre or, as in the case of Waldheim, even dangerously suspect. For instance, the World Jewish Congress asserts that the United States, the United Kingdom, and the Soviet Union knew about Waldheim's war record by the late 1940s.[64] It is interesting to note that George Bush, the U.S. representative to the United Nations at the time, voted for the election of Waldheim. Yet, he has not answered the claim of the World Jewish Congress that the U.S. government — and the other great powers — certainly knew shortly after the war of Waldheim's real record with the German army during World War II.

Thus, there are some deeply disturbing questions about the election of Waldheim — questions that should encourage all members of the United Nations to play a much more active part in future elections of the Secretary-General. One question that remains unanswered concerns the way that Waldheim was elected by the Security Council. For instance, the Council used a secret ballot to elect the Secretary-General. Although this was done on the suggestion of the Soviet Union, it is unclear why the other permanent members of the Security Council agreed to this procedure. Secret balloting provides the permanent members an opportunity to use the veto power anonymously without being forced to reveal who they had voted for, or why. It also seems to be a way of absolving responsibility for the result of the voting.

Following this unusual secret voting procedure, Waldheim's name was recommended by the Security Council to the General Assembly, who made the final decision. The General Assembly, grateful that the permanent powers could agree on someone, duly appointed Waldheim as Secretary-General of the United Nations.

Perhaps the clear lesson from this incident is that the General Assembly should not be so eager to accept the first recommendation of the Security Council. The General Assembly must act as an effective check and balance to the maneuvering of the great powers who will seek, among other things, a candidate that will bow to their will. Above all, the General Assembly must ensure the appointment of an individual who will be a strong Secretary-General and who will take action, when possible, to promote the goals of the United Nations. At the very least, an assertive General Assembly could have helped prevent the fiasco caused by the election of Waldheim. Waldheim seems to have been a favorite selection of the superpowers because they wished to have a caretaker who would show no great initiative or energy. Waldheim did not surprise or disappoint them.

To his credit, Waldheim "actively sought a negotiating and intermediary role and was sometimes successful in his efforts."[65] He first invoked Article 99 in 1976 during the Cyprus crisis. Responding to his initiative, the Security Council continued to endorse UN peacekeeping efforts on the island and authorized the Secretary-General to attempt to mediate the dispute between Greek and Turkish Cypriots.[66]

He also proved himself to be a man of personal courage during his risky trip to Iran in a futile attempt to win release of the U.S. hostages. Yet, he was reluctant to assert his office or even run the risk of courting superpower disapproval. Thus, it is not surprising that his ten-year tenure in office was characterized by a lack of constitutional innovations, especially in the realm of international peace and security.

In fairness to Waldheim, it should be stressed that the early and mid-1970s were a time of detente with the opening of China to the West and a general relaxation in international tension. Of course, dangerous situations continued to emerge — in the Middle East (1973), in Southeast Asia with the ending of the Vietnam War, and in Cambodia (1975–1979). Yet, with the prominent exception of the 1973 war, these did not flare into high-risk East/ West confrontations. Although helpless to prevent the outbreak or escalation of hostilities, the United Nations played an important role in helping to end the 1973 war; however, most of the important negotiations during the period — SALT II Talks, the Sino-American rapprochement — occurred outside the United Nations.[67]

During his second term in office, Waldheim invoked his preventive powers under Article 99 during the Iranian hostage crisis, but it was not an effective initiative because the Iranians constantly delayed attending the Security Council debate, and he had no real plan or program to recommend. Of course, the Security Council voted for the immediate release of the hostages, but Waldheim provided no further strategy for resolving the conflict, and his initiative was simply lost in subsequent events.

During Waldheim's tenure as Secretary-General, the United Nations seemed to become completely peripheral to international politics. This development, which had its origins in trends that began in the 1960s, became very pronounced during the Waldheim period. The United Nations was attacked with seeming impunity; staff members were imprisoned around the world; and UN peacekeeping forces in southern Lebanon became popular targets for harassment by private armies.[68] Furthermore, under Waldheim, the United Nations reached a new low in world public opinion caused, in part, by the infamous 1975 "Zionism is racism" resolution passed by the General Assembly.

In normal times, the Secretary-General can do much to dampen the rhetorical excesses of the General Assembly by arguing that the United Nations should contribute to conflict resolution, not to intensifying a conflict. Admittedly, Waldheim recognized the danger of the "Zionism is racism" resolution and tried to prevent it. Yet, he was unable to mobilize the diplomatic strength needed to defeat it. Even so, a stronger and more respected Secretary might have prevented such a resolution from being adopted. For instance, in his book *Nation against Nation* Thomas M. Franck discusses how he (Franck) managed to deflect and, thus, defeat a similar resolution at an earlier date in Geneva during a conference of experts on racism and apartheid.[69]

Finally, revolutions were occurring in telecommunications and information management that could be very useful to UN operations, especially in the area of conflict prevention.[70] Yet the UN Secretariat seemed blissfully unaware of the new possibilities for peace. Of course, lip service was paid to the UN Charter and to the lofty aims of the Organization, yet the United Nations seemed to be characterized by institutional drift and benign neglect, especially in the late 1970s and early 1980s.

Waldheim ran for reelection in 1981 and was supported — through 16 votes — by Ambassador Jeane Kilpatrick of the United States. However, the Chinese vetoed every attempt to continue Kurt Waldheim in office. So, the Security Council finally agreed to recommend a relatively unknown diplomat from Peru, Javier Pérez de Cuéllar. Unlike his predecessor, Pérez de Cuéllar seemed determined to set out in new directions.

NOTES

1. For a perceptive and insightful account of Thant's personal style and of the influences that shaped his life and outlook, see June Bingham, *U Thant: The Search for Peace* (New York: Alfred A. Knopf, 1970).

2. This phrase, the "quiet approach" is Pechota's; see Vratislav Pechota, *The Quiet Approach: A Study of the Good Offices Exercised by the United Nations Secretary-General in the Cause of Peace* (New York: UNITAR, 1972).

3. Thant's intervention in the Cuban crisis of 1962 is discussed by Oran Young and Henry M. Pachter. See Oran R. Young, *The Intermediaries: Third Parties in International Crises* (Princeton: Princeton University Press, 1967), and Henry M. Pachter, *Collision Course: The Cuban Missile Crisis and Coexistence* (New York: Praeger, 1963). The Americans refer to the crisis as the Cuban missile crisis, and the Soviets refer to it as the Caribbean crisis. I take a compromise position and refer to it as the 1962 Cuban crisis throughout my discussion.

4. See, for example, Richard J. Walton, *Cold War and Counterrevolution: The Foreign Policy of John F. Kennedy* (New York: Viking Press, 1971), p. 230.

5. For a brilliant criticism of the scholarly "conventional wisdom" on the Cuban crisis, see Richard Ned Lebow, "The Cuban Missile Crisis: Reading the Lessons Correctly," *Political Science Quarterly 98* (Fall 1983).

6. Pechota, *The Quiet Approach,* pp. 4–9.

7. Thant's decision to withdraw UNEF from the Sinai is, perhaps, the most controversial decision of his career because it permitted the large-scale Israeli attack that soon followed. Even so, this decision has its articulate supporters. See Madeleine G. Kalb, "The UN's Embattled Peacekeeper," *New York Times Magazine,* December 19, 1982.

8. See Connor Cruise O'Brien, *To Katanga and Back* (New York: Simon and Schuster, 1962).

9. Brian Urquhart, *Hammarskjöld* (New York: Alfred A. Knopf, 1972), p. 593.

10. Inis L. Claude, Jr., *Swords into Plowshares* (New York: Random House, 1971), p. 328.

11. Ibid.

12. Urquhart, *Hammarskjöld,* p. 594.

13. For a definitive account of the crisis from a U.S. point of view, see Robert F. Kennedy, *Thirteen Days* (New York: W. W. Norton, 1969). For the Soviet perspective, see Ronald Pope, *Soviet Views on the Cuban Missile Crisis* (Washington, D.C.: University Press of America, 1982).

14. Thant's public communications with both Kennedy and Khrushchev are listed in the back of Robert Kennedy, *Thirteen Days,* "Documents."

15. Thant had been encouraged by numerous diplomatic delegations to intervene directly in the crisis, which he did. See Pachter, *Collision Course,* pp. 93–97; and Andrew Boyd, "The Unknown United Nations," *International Journal 19* 2 (1964), 207.

16. See Kennedy, *Thirteen Days,* pp. 181–82. Thant revealed the contents of the letters during the Security Council debate that night.

17. Ibid., pp. 65–72.

18. Ibid., pp. 180–82.

19. Ibid.

20. Ibid.

21. See "Chairman Khrushchev to Mr. U Thant," October 26, 1962, in Kennedy, *Thirteen Days,* p. 192.

22. Arthur M. Schlesinger, *A Thousand Days* (New York: Houghton Mifflin, 1965), p. 820. For the Soviet perspective on the U.S. response to Thant, see Pope, *Soviet Views,* pp. 204–5.

23. Kennedy, *Thirteen Days,* p. 185.

24. Young, *The Intermediaries,* p. 287.

25. The Kennedy administration was undecided, and seemingly confused, concerning the military significance of Soviet missiles in Cuba, especially in the early stages of the crisis. See Kennedy, *Thirteen Days,* p. 31. Robert Kennedy points out, "There were those, although they were a small minority, who felt the missiles did not alter the balance of power." Graham Allison also explores what he calls the "Politics of Issues" and cites Hilsman, one of the president's men in this crisis: "The United States might not be in mortal danger, but the Administration most certainly was." See Graham Allison, *Essence of Decision* (Boston: Little, Brown, 1971), pp. 193–95.

26. Thant's talk before the Council is recorded in Kennedy, *Thirteen Days,* p. 182.

27. Ibid., p. 185. In his reply, President Kennedy stated, "In your message and your statement to the Security Council last night, you have made certain suggestions and have invited preliminary talks to determine whether satisfactory arrangements can be assured."

28. I first used this term, defined in this way, in my presentation to UNITAR entitled "The UN Secretary-General and Nuclear Crisis Diplomacy: The Last Stop," March 21, 1984. Parts of this paper were reprinted in *WORLDVIEW,* November 1983.

29. Walton, *Cold War and Counterrevolution,* p. 230.

30. Harlan Cleveland, "Crisis Diplomacy," *Foreign Affairs 41* (1963). Cleveland was a senior official in the U.S. State Department during the Kennedy administration.

31. Kennedy, *Thirteen Days,* p. 187.

32. Ibid.

33. Ibid., p. 82.

34. Pope, *Soviet Views,* p. 133.

35. Kennedy, *Thirteen Days,* p. 90.

36. Ibid., p. 91. I believe that the unusual nature of this contact is probably related to internal Soviet power politics; by using Fomin, Khrushchev could hide his communications with the U.S. government from other Soviet leaders who,

fearing a rebuff, might have urged a stronger line, including no peace feelers.

37. See my article "Crisis Control and the United Nations," *WORLDVIEW*, November 1983, for an analysis of Thant's action.

38. Kennedy, *Thirteen Days*, pp. 102–4.

39. Ibid., p. 110.

40. Pope, *Soviet Views*, p. 223.

41. Ibid., p. 225. They publicly thanked him for his efforts, throughout the crisis, despite whatever private reservations they might have had. See, for example, Kennedy, *Thirteen Days*, pp. 192 and 213.

42. See J. Anthony Lukas, "Class Reunion: Kennedy's Men Relive the Cuban Missile Crisis," *New York Times Magazine*, August 30, 1987.

43. Pechota, *The Quiet Approach*, p. 12. I am in debt to Pechota's account in the following section on Thant's use of his good offices.

44. Ibid., p. 17.

45. Ibid., p. 1.

46. Ibid., p. 33.

47. Ibid., pp 33–34.

48. We saw in Chapter 1 how the Soviets were early supporters of Secretary-General Lie's efforts to enlarge the powers of his office.

49. Pechota, *The Quiet Approach*, p. 45.

50. Ibid., p. 50.

51. Sydney D. Bailey, *The Procedure of the UN Security Council* (Oxford, Clarendon Press, 1975), p. 75. For Urquhart's defense of this controversial decision, see Kalb, "Embattled Peacekeeper," p. 48.

52. Pechota, *The Quiet Approach*, p. 48.

53. Ibid.

54. Bailey, *The Procedure of the UN*, pp. 75–76.

55. Gideon Gottlieb, "The United Nations and Emergency Humanitarian Assistance in India-Pakistan," *The American Journal of International Law 66*, 362. I am in debt to Gottlieb's account in my following analysis.

56. Ibid., pp. 362–63.

57. Ibid., p. 363. Also see UN Press Release SG/1763/IHA 93, November 17, 1971.

58. Gottlieb, "India-Pakistan," p. 363.

59. Ibid., pp. 363–64.

60. Ibid., p. 364.

61. Thomas E. Boudreau, *Protecting the Innocent: Enhancing the Humanitarian Role of the United Nations in Natural Disasters and Other Disaster Situations* (New York: Council on Religion and International Affairs, 1983).

62. Ibid.

63. Article 2, paragraph 7, of the UN Charter prohibits the United Nations from intervening "in matters which are essentially within the domestic jurisdiction of any state."

64. Private conversations with the author, spring–summer 1988. The World Jewish Congress, with offices located in New York City, is quite open about sharing its extensive Waldheim file.

65. Leon Gordenker, "Development in the UN System," in Toby T. Gati (ed.), *The U.S., the UN, and the Management of Global Change* (New York: New York University Press, 1983), p. 30.

66. Thomas M. Franck, *Nation against Nation* (Oxford: Oxford University Press, 1985), pp. 125–26.

67. Hans Morgenthau noticed the trend to conduct important negotiations outside the United Nations and to minimize the role of the United Nations in international negotiations in the mid-1960s. See Hans Morgenthau, *Politics*

among Nations, 4th ed. (New York: Alfred A. Knopf, 1967), p. 474. Morgenthau believes that the decline began with the controversial nineteenth session of the General Assembly, discussed briefly above. UN staff believe that this trend was greatly accelerated during Waldheim's tenure.

68. Private conversation, former UN official from legal office.

69. Franck, *Nation against Nation,* p. 111.

70. The United Nations Association (UNA) issued, in 1971, an excellent study that recommended that the United Nations acquire a satellite mediated communications system. The report seems to have been simply ignored, and UN communications still do not have access to a global satellite system today. See *Space Communications and the United Nations: Increasing UN Responsibleness to the Problems of Mankind,* UNA National Policy Panel, May 1971.

5
THE STRUGGLE RENEWED: JAVIER PÉREZ DE CUÉLLAR

Before his appointment in 1982, the new Secretary-General, Javier Pérez de Cuéllar, was a distinguished international diplomat who served as Peru's permanent representative to the United Nations, as well as a United Nations Under-Secretary-General for Special Political Affairs. Before his service at the United Nations, he served as Peru's first ambassador to the Soviet Union. He had also headed Peru's embassy in Switzerland and served in missions to Britain, Bolivia, and Brazil. His appointment as Secretary-General surprised nearly everyone; yet, he proved, during his first term in office (January 1982–1987), to be a remarkably able and innovative Secretary-General. In stark contrast to his predecessor, Kurt Waldheim, he has a very active and energetic understanding of his preventive responsibilities under Article 99.

His first term in office was marked by dangerous political crises as well as severe challenges to the fiscal health and perhaps to the very future of the United Nations. By all accounts, he has met these crises energetically and skillfully. Although he is still in office, Pérez de Cuéllar may already be judged, during very difficult days at the United Nations, as one of the most successful Secretaries-General at the United Nations.

At the very beginning of his term, he took the unusual step of announcing that he intended to serve only one five-year term as Secretary-General. By doing this, he attempted to lessen the political leverage that the permanent powers have over a Secretary-General because of the reappointment process.[1] As it turned out, he ran for, and was appointed to, a second term. He did so because, by the end of 1986, the United Nations was facing a serious fiscal crisis, and he did not want to leave while the UN finances and future were so uncertain. So, even though he had a serious heart operation he continued to serve the United Nations. The following analysis of his preventive role includes only his first term — to the beginning of 1987.

THE FALKLAND/MALVINAS WAR:
THE BACKGROUND

Secretary-General de Cuéllar's first formidable test — the Falkland/Malvinas Island crisis — came after he had been in office for only a few months. As mentioned earlier, he became involved at a very late stage in the confrontation between Argentina and Britain. The U.S. mediation efforts, led by Secretary-of-State Haig, had ended in stalemate and raised serious issues about the role of a third party in international crises. Specifically, when the United States sided with Britain in the war, it left a gaping void in the interventionary efforts. Valuable time and contacts were lost as the Secretary-General and the Peruvians sought to fill the gap in mediation efforts.[2] One clear lesson of this is that third-party duties should be accepted only by those that can keep a commitment to impartiality and service throughout a crisis; otherwise, much momentum in mediatory efforts is lost, and lives are placed in jeopardy. Furthermore, considering the distances involved, Haig's use of shuttle diplomacy may have been an inappropriate technique.[3] Other interventionary tactics might have proved much more effective in the circumstances.

BAPTISM BY FIRE: THE SECRETARY-GENERAL
GETS INVOLVED

Because of Haig's "bailout" and the worsening military situation near the islands, the political circumstances of the Secretary-General's first intervention in the crisis could not have been more unfavorable. On May 2, a few days after the United States announced its support for England in the crisis, the British sank the Argentine cruiser, the *General Belgrano,* with a heavy loss of life. Two days later, the British frigate the *HMS Sheffield* was sunk. The war was intensifying even as the Secretary-General became involved.

On May 2, the Secretary-General gave to the two governments a "set of ideas" concerning a possible negotiated settlement.[4] These ideas

> Included the concepts of mutual withdrawal, the commencement of diplomatic negotiations for a definitive settlement of the dispute, the lifting of sanctions and exclusion zones, and the establishment of transitional

arrangements in the Falklands pending the outcome of diplomatic negotiations.[5]

By the end of the week (May 6), both the British and Argentine governments had indicated their willingness to explore further the Secretary-General's ideas. Then began what Anthony Parsons, the British ambassador to the UN at the time, describes as "the most intense and vigorous series of negotiations, attended by maximum public interest, until May 19th."[6] Ambassador Parsons elaborates upon the negotiations conducted during this time, stating,

> The Secretary-General saw myself and my Argentine colleague, Vice-Minister Eduardo Rocco, once or more often twice a day throughout the whole period, weekends included, working in an orderly and systematic way towards the elaboration of an agreement which would embrace the points in his original document, and which would put the Islands under temporary UN administration for a defined period during which negotiations for a final settlement would be carried out under his auspices.[7]

By all accounts, the Secretary-General's efforts during this period very nearly succeeded — even though first blood had already been drawn.[8] He began intense round-the-clock negotiations with both sides. By the weekend of May 15, a peaceful resolution of the crisis seemed within grasp.[9]

Yet, the possible peace seemed to slip through the fingers of the diplomats. Two factors seemed to contribute to the subsequent failure of negotiations. First, at perhaps the most crucial time of the negotiations, Ambassador Parsons was recalled to England for consultations, thus putting diplomatic efforts at the United Nations essentially on hold. After this weekend period, the British government stiffened its negotiating position and set a deadline for negotiations.[10] They were obviously preparing for war. The announcement of the British government's "final position" was regarded as a "stab in the back" by the Argentine government because they believed negotiations still had a chance.[11] From their perspective, the talks were sabotaged by the British government just at the point of agreement.

Although the Argentines bitterly criticized the British negotiating position during this crucial time, they were far from blameless themselves. After all, they had been the ones to initiate military action. Then, they apparently became trapped by their own aggression. In view of the massive popular swelling of support for the Argentine seizure of the islands, the ruling military junta began to believe that a negotiated settlement would be extremely unpopular with the thoroughly aroused public.[12] At the same time, the junta realized that the "British *were* coming" and that their own military position on the islands was precarious. Thus, they were caught on the horns of a dilemma. If they retreated, they feared revolution by their own people. If they stayed on the islands, they feared decisive defeat and humiliation. The junta apparently chose to face defeat on the islands in order to avoid revolution at home.

In this regard, the only fault of the British was that they did not build a golden bridge for their adversary's retreat.[13] Instead, they presented Argentina and the Secretary-General with a "final position." In view of the renewed British resolve to fight and Argentina's fear to retreat, the negotiations collapsed, and the war came.

THE BRITISH INVADE THE ISLANDS

On the evening of May 20, while the British invasion of the islands was proceeding, the Secretary-General announced the failure of his efforts before the Security Council.[14] At the request of the Security Council, he tried again, several days later, to arrange a cease-fire and negotiate a settlement even as the fighting was raging on the islands; however, the fiery winds of war swept away any realistic prospects for a stable peace. By mid-June, the British had reconquered the islands and reasserted their presence in the South Atlantic. The immediate issues were decided by violence and blood although the long-term issue remains unresolved to this day.

LEFT OUT IN LEBANON: THE SECRETARY-GENERAL ON THE SIDELINES

Even as the British were raising the flag of victory over the Falklands, the Israelis were pouring over their northern border and — after overrunning a UN peacekeeping force — plunging deep into Lebanon. The resulting fighting was severe as PLO and Israeli army units clawed at each other from Tyre to Beirut. Civilian casualties, caused by massive aerial and artillery bombardments, steadily mounted. The UN Security Council began to meet in marathon sessions while the Israeli army and navy encircled Beirut, trapping PLO leader Yasser Arafat. Thousands of civilians were also trapped in the city, and hundreds became casualties as the intense fighting continued.[15]

Throughout July and early August, there were repeated calls for a cease-fire from the Security Council; they were briefly honored and then inevitably ignored as both sides renewed fighting each other.[16] The fighting raged on until negotiations — arranged outside the context of the United Nations — led to cease-fire and the evacuation of the PLO from the city.

The evacuation of the PLO did not end the fighting; the Lebanese continued to fight among themselves, Palestinian refugees were massacred in Beirut, and the Soviets massively reinforced the Syrians, providing them with sophisticated SAM missiles and equipment replacements. Multinational peacekeeping forces, consisting of U.S., British, Italian, and French troops, were introduced into Beirut only to become targets themselves. Because the Soviets were bogged down in Afghanistan during this period, all the permanent powers of the Security Council except for the People's Republic of China had troops in combat situations.

The fighting had many anticipated and unanticipated results: the temporary dismemberment of the PLO, the outburst of massive peace protests in Israel, and the bloody attacks against the multinational forces in Beirut. As the invading Israelis withdrew, they also encountered heavy resistance from the formerly neutral Shiite Muslims of southern Lebanon who sought revenge for Israeli bombardments of their villages.

Although deeply concerned and disturbed by events in Lebanon, Secretary-General de Cuéllar had little direct role during the fighting. He was given important duties by the Security Council, especially dealing with the deployment of UN observers in and around Beirut during early August.[17] These UN observers had, besides their peacekeeping tasks, important humanitarian responsibilities as well. Furthermore, during the bloody Beirut fighting in the summer of 1982, some of the Secretary-General's subordinates were involved in the almost continuous efforts to arrange cease-fires. Yet, the principal parties involved — Israel, the PLO, Syria, and the United States — did not ask, or apparently even consider asking, him to accept primary and public responsibility for negotiating a peaceful settlement. In effect, the Secretary-General had to watch developments from the sidelines. A deeply thoughtful man, Pérez de Cuéllar pondered the problems of war and peace — which became very apparent in the spring and summer of 1982. He then shared his thoughts in his widely acclaimed first *Annual Report,* which he delivered in the early fall.

REFLECTIONS FROM THE SIDELINES: THE SECRETARY-GENERAL'S 1982 *ANNUAL REPORT*

In view of the war in Lebanon, it is not surprising that the Secretary-General dwelled at some length in his first *Annual Report* on the tendency of governments to avoid the United Nations during brewing conflicts or even while they wage war. He noted,

In order to avoid the Security Council becoming involved too late in critical situations, it may well be that the Secretary-General should play a more forthright role in bringing potentially dangerous situations to the attention of the Council within the general framework of Article 99 of the Charter. My predecessors have done this on a number of occasions, but I wonder *if the time has not come for a more systematic approach*. Most potential conflict areas are well known. The Secretary-General has traditionally, if informally, tried to keep watch for problems likely to result in conflict and to do what he can to preempt them by quiet diplomacy.[18] (Emphasis added).

One can see, in this short statement, the historical evolution of the Secretary-General's obligation under Article 99. Pérez de Cuéllar notes that the Secretary-General has "traditionally, if informally tried to keep watch" over international peace. Yet, in view of the obvious inadequacies and breakdowns of the current arrangements, he speculates whether "the time has not come for a more systematic approach."[19] In essence, Pérez de Cuéllar is proposing that the Secretary-General become a watchman of the peace and help alert the Security Council to impending conflicts before the outbreak of war. As he notes, this is a role that is clearly contemplated, if not required, by Article 99. Yet, as he frankly states, "The Secretary-General's diplomatic means are quite limited."[20] At this point, he suggests a solution to this problem that is also one of the clearest explanations of the Secretary-General's obligation under Article 99 on record: "In order to carry out effectively the preventive role foreseen for the Secretary General under Article 99, I intend to develop a wider and more systematic capacity for fact-finding in potential conflict areas."[21]

Because of the vagueness of the term "fact-finding," it may be more accurate — in the context of the Secretary-General's preventive role — to use the more general "information gathering," or simply "information management," as mentioned earlier. Such an admittedly bland term avoids the imprecision and confusion that surrounds "fact-finding." The problem then becomes one of developing a conceptual framework that specifies the exact relationship, if any, between information management by the Secretary-General and the prevention of conflict.[22] Currently, because of the different and often divided bureaucratic fiefdoms within the UN Secretariat, such a conceptual framework does not really exist, although reforms are currently being contemplated.

THE POLITICAL RESPONSE
TO DE CUÉLLAR'S SPEECH

Unfortunately, several significant political actors at the United Nations were not interested in the theoretical or practical questions raised by the Secretary-General's report, nor did they seem interested in having the Secretary-General assume the role of watchman of the peace — despite his obligation under the Charter. For instance, the Soviets immediately registered their disapproval of the Secretary-General's report, citing in particular the key sentence quoted above.[23] The Americans' response was a bit more delayed but initially as negative as the Soviets'. Ironically, the Americans objected because the Secretary-General was placing partial responsibility for developing a "wider and more systematic capacity" with a department within the Secretariat that was headed by a Soviet. Thus the Secretary-General's early efforts to improve and reform his information-gathering procedures immediately threatened to flounder upon the shoals of the Cold War.

Even so, in the aftermath of his 1982 *Annual Report,* the new Secretary-General proposed certain administrative changes within the UN Secretariat that were intended to provide him with a better and more systematic information-gathering capacity in potential conflict situations. The first actual reforms were then initiated. During this time, the United States withheld its contribution to the United Nations and prompted a severe financial crisis. Ironically, the reform efforts of the Secretary-General were actually encouraged by this crisis.

THE SECRETARY-GENERAL AND
HUMANITARIAN LAW

As we have already discussed, previous Secretaries-General have taken humanitarian steps to protect civilian populations during times of war or natural disasters. For instance, Secretary-General Thant developed a quiet tradition of systematic UN humanitarian assistance to the victims of armed conflicts and natural disasters. Furthermore, several new offices and administrative mechanisms were created during the 1970s to help facilitate delivery of international relief to victims worldwide.

However, many UN humanitarian aid programs have grown over the years in an ad hoc fashion, often in response to diverse political and bureaucratic pressures. Thus, there remains some confusion about the Organization's precise policy for providing humanitarian aid, especially in relation to armed conflict.

PROTECTING THE INNOCENT: BACKGROUND

By intervening for humanitarian reasons in an ongoing conflict, the Secretary-General can try to limit the scope of military violence. In doing so he can attempt to establish the grounds for a possible future settlement. By seeking to protect the civilian populations on both sides of a war, the Secretary-General promotes the self-interest of each side. In this way, the Secretary-General can, slowly and often with great diplomatic difficulty, become a trusted intermediary in the larger issues of the conflict. To a certain extent, this is exactly what happened in the Iran-Iraq War. This terrible war, initiated in 1980 by Iraq's invasion of Iran, was — in the winter and spring of 1983 — engulfing cities and the civilian populations of both countries. As neither side seemed willing to stop the fighting, the Secretary-General actively intervened to protect the innocent of both Iran and Iraq, as well as to seek some common ground between the combatants.

At this point, I must add a personal note. In the summer of 1983, I presented the first copy of my report "Protecting the Innocent: Enhancing the Humanitarian Role of the United Nations in Natural Disasters and Other Disaster Situations" to Secretary-General Pérez de Cuéllar.[24] Many of the recommendations in this report subsequently supported and reinforced the Secretary-General's humanitarian efforts in the Iran-Iraq War. The key recommendations — in terms of the United Nations' role in humanitarian law — are summarized in Appendix II.

THE WAR OF THE CITIES: IRAN AND IRAQ

In early May 1983, the government of Iran asked the Secretary-General to send a representative to view certain cities and civilian areas that had been subjected to military attack by Iraq.[25] The government of Iran also told the Secretary-General that, should the government of Iraq wish to invite UN representatives to inspect the civilian areas of that country as well, the government of Iran would welcome reciprocal visits. In mid-May, the government of Iraq said that it wished UN representatives to visit civilian areas in Iraq that had been subject to military attacks by Iran. After receiving these messages, the Secretary-General notified the Security Council that he planned to send a small mission to the two countries.

The mandate of the mission was to "survey and assess, as far as possible, the damage to civilian areas in the two countries" caused (or more precisely, claimed to have been caused) by military attacks.[26] The mission was also asked to ascertain, where possible, the types of munitions that could have caused the damage. The mission was not expected to ascertain the number of casualties or the value of property damage in specific areas; the primary task of the mission was to present an objective report on its inspections and observations to the Secretary-General.

The UN mission was headed by Brigadier-General Timothy K. Dibuama, military advisor to the Secretary-General. Besides UN personnel, there were also Swedish army specialists in munitions on the team, which was in the war zones from May 21 through May 30, 1983. The mission recorded, and reported upon, the extensive damage caused to civilian sectors in both Iran and Iraq.[27] Because it did not have a mandate to investigate independently reports of civilian deaths and injuries, the mission simply reported the figures given to it by the two governments concerning the civilian casualties in the areas it visited. The Secretary-General submitted the mission's report to the Security Council in late June 1983.[28]

One of the consequences of the visit was that the mission established a precedent for cooperation by the two governments with the United Nations in humanitarian concerns. The Secretary-General also twice achieved agreement from both sides not to bomb civilian cities. Although both initiatives eventually failed, many lives were saved. This built trust and acceptance for the direct involvement of the Secretary-General in humanitarian affairs, which was useful as efforts to end the war continued.

Yet, for the time being, the war persisted and inevitably escalated. In the winter and spring of 1984, the government of Iran made the serious allegation that the government of Iraq was using chemical weapons. The Iranians also requested the UN Secretary-General to investigate the areas of the alleged attacks.[29] Of course, Iraq opposed any unilateral UN initiatives or investigations. In view of this, the Secretary-General could have dodged the Iranian requests, simply stating that the necessary reciprocal agreement of both governments was missing. Such a timid response is always a temptation, especially because any UN action — without reciprocal agreement of the governments involved — is bound to draw the heated protests of the noncooperative government and its allies. However, as pointed out in *Protecting the Innocent,* the Secretary-General should not wait for an aggressor to approve of "humanitarian enquiry" concerning the civilian victims of aggression; the Secretary-General should decisively move to investigate and protect the civilians under attack, regardless of reciprocal approval.[30] At the same time, the Secretary-General could also seek the agreement of the reluctant government in order to protect, as much as possible, the civilians on both sides of the conflict.

To his credit, this is exactly what Secretary-General Pérez de Cuéllar did in the case of Iran's allegations. Acting upon his own authority and "[c]onscious of the humanitarian principles embodied in the Charter and of the moral responsibilities vested in his office," he requested four medical and military specialists to visit Iran and ascertain the truth of the allegations.[31] The team visited Iran in mid-March 1984. After completing its visit, the team unanimously concluded that chemical weapons had been used against Iranian civilians and soldiers. The report of the team was submitted to the UN Security Council, who strongly condemned Iraq's use of chemical weapons.[32]

THE WAR CONTINUES

During the spring of 1984, the Secretary-General received new reports of attacks against civilians in both Iran and Iraq. In particular, heavy civilian casualties caused by aerial attacks on the Iranian town of Baneh on June 5, 1984, had been confirmed by the International Committee of the Red Cross.[33] In response to these renewed attacks, the Secretary-General asked both governments for assurances that all deliberate military attacks by any means on purely civilian population centers in either country would cease. To reinforce this request, the Secretary-General proposed that observer teams, drawn from UN political and peacekeeping personnel, be created and stationed in each country. The mandate of each team basically followed the proposed tasks of "humanitarian fact-finding" missions outlined in *Protecting the Innocent* (see Appendix II). Although these teams were set up on his own initiative, the Secretary-General notified the President of the Security Council who, in turn, stated that the members of the Security Council agreed with the measures proposed.[34] The two governments also agreed to the stationing of quasi-permanent UN teams in their respective countries. On June 15, 1984, the Secretary-General set up the teams, placing one each in Iran and Iraq. At first, there were three members to each team. For a while, at least, attacks against civilians seemed to lessen.

For the next several months these teams continued to operate, and report, from Iran and Iraq. During the same time that these teams operated, the Secretary-General reported upon observance of the Geneva Convention concerning prisoners of war.[35] He also continually reported upon the use of chemical weapons against Iranian soldiers and civilians. Furthermore, he also expressed his alarm at the continuing escalation of the war, affecting not only the civilians of both sides, but also the neutral shipping in the Gulf as well. Through these initiatives, the Secretary-General created, in effect, a humanitarian regime in the midst of a savage and bloody war.

Yet, the existence of such a humanitarian regime is always a fragile and precarious accomplishment; in the absence of political settlement of the larger issues that perpetuate the war, any such regime is doomed to be a temporary arrangement. This is especially true in the Iran-Iraq War. Although attacks against civilians did seem to diminish for a while after the Secretary-General's direct interventions in both 1983 and 1984, this separate peace could not last long without diplomatic progress toward a final settlement of the war. Otherwise, the pressures to escalate the war, as well as accidental military incidents, would build and eventually topple any humanitarian regime intended to lessen the suffering of civilians.

This inevitably happened in the Iran-Iraq War. Attacks against civilians increased as the war continued, and the further use of chemical weapons was again documented by UN investigations in 1985 and 1986.

In view of this, the difficult lessons of invited intervention by the Secretary-General must be carefully evaluated. The key conclusion is that any humanitarian effort, to be lasting, must be coupled with successful political initiatives to end the fighting; otherwise, the success of the humanitarian efforts by the Secretary-General may be, at best, temporary.

Yet, such temporary victories have their value. The worst effects of the fighting were mitigated, if only for a while, and some civilian lives were undoubtedly saved by the Secretary-General's humanitarian initiatives. Furthermore, the mediating role of the Secretary-General to end the war was accepted, in large part, because of his humanitarian efforts. Currently, the Secretary-General is practically the only political figure in the world who commands the respect of both sides engaged in the fighting. Due in large part to the Secretary-General's efforts, a fragile cease-fire was tentatively accepted by both sides during the summer of 1988. One of his greatest achievements during this time was to get the five permanent members of the Security Council to work together to end the fighting. Because of his political and humanitarian initiatives concerning this conflict, he remains one of the world's best hopes for creating an enduring peace in the region.

THE RAINBOW WARRIOR: GOOD OFFICES OF THE SECRETARY-GENERAL

During his first term in office, Secretary-General Javier Pérez de Cuéllar provided his good offices to several other parties, besides Iran and Iraq, who were caught up in a dispute or fighting. He publicly intervened in Cyprus, western Sahara, and in the human rights issue in Poland. (These are studied in greater detail in *United Nations, Divided World*.)[36] There were also ongoing negotiations over Afghanistan, Namibia, and Cambodia. As mentioned earlier, these negotiations are in very sensitive stages, even though remarkable progress has been made. Thus, it remains for a future report to fully analyze the results achieved — and lessons learned — through these current diplomatic initiatives.

One of the most interesting recent uses of the Secretary-General's good offices was in the dispute between France and New Zealand over the sinking of the Greenpeace ship, *The Rainbow Warrior.* French agents had planted explosives on *The Rainbow Warrior* and sank the vessel, killing a Dutch photographer who was on board the ship. At least some of the French agents responsible for the attack were promptly captured by New Zealand authorities.

Although caught red-handed, France immediately insisted that New Zealand, in effect, release the bungling agents. In a move that seemed better suited for the bully in the school yard, France even made threats to retaliate against New Zealand's agricultural products in the European Common Market. Despite the hauteur of France, the French defense minister was forced to resign over the incident.

Because of the political tension and impasse between the two countries, the Secretary-General was asked to mediate a settlement. As a result the Secretary-General offered, in June 1986, his good offices to the governments of France and New Zealand, and both promptly accepted. Agreeing that his decision was binding, both governments gave the Secretary-General powers similar to an arbitrator's.

After extensive investigation, the Secretary-General proposed a solution: France would formally apologize to New Zealand and pay for compensation. The two French agents would be given over to French custody with the understanding that they would remain on an isolated French island in the Pacific for several years. In return, France agreed not to impede New Zealand's access to the EC. Both countries promptly accepted the solution.

Unfortunately, the French government promptly added more shame to its already dishonorable conduct during this incident — the two French agents involved in the murder of the Greenpeace photographer were promptly returned to France soon after release from their New Zealand prison. This act was in direct violation of the agreement carefully developed by the Secretary-General. Although the French government gave its word to abide by the settlement proposed by the Secretary-General, it disregarded the settlement and broke its own word as soon as its agents were released. This illustrates the weak political position of the Secretary-General. He has no power to impose political penalties or sanctions on those that flagrantly disregard international agreements. He can only hope that parties use his good offices to negotiate in good faith and honor the outcome. This is a frail, vulnerable hope in cases such as *The Rainbow Warrior,* where even a country's honor is readily sacrificed for political expedience.

THE WAR OF THE BUDGET: THE FINANCIAL CRISIS
AT THE UNITED NATIONS

Despite the victories and diplomatic setbacks during the mid-1980s, the Secretary-General had little time to rest. While disputes and wars continued to rage over the world, a different type of battle was looming closer to UN Headquarters that threatened to engulf the Secretary-General — the political battle over the United Nations' budget.

Declaring that the "United Nations is no longer a sacred cow," Senator Nancy Kassebaum introduced in 1985 an amendment to a State Department Funding Bill in Congress that limited U.S. contributions to international organizations to 20 percent of the total budget. This included the United Nations whose budget was funded 25 percent by the United States. The amendment passed both Houses and included the proviso that full U.S. funding would not resume unless and until the United Nations allowed its major contributors more control over the disposition of funds.[37]

The so-called Kassebaum amendment precipitated the most significant financial crisis at the United Nations in recent years. Along with other budget-cutting proposals, such as Gramm-Rudman, the Kassebaum amendment curtailed U.S. assessed contributions to the total UN system (including the specialized agencies) from roughly $442 million in 1985 to $385 million in 1986. The United Nations in New York stood to lose about 10 percent of its budgeted expenditures as a result.

IDEOLOGICAL IMPATIENCE OR
THE NEW ISOLATIONISM?

The U.S. motives behind the budget cuts were mixed and reflect the significant change in recent years in U.S. policy and perceptions toward the United Nations. The United Nations has undoubtedly earned its ideological enemies in the United States who view the world organization as bureaucratically bloated, financially mismanaged, and even an enclave, from the U.S. point of view, for Soviet spying. Doubtless, some of the United Nations' opponents represent the extreme right in U.S. politics and are threatened by the United Nations' strong public stance against apartheid, the arms race, and neocolonialism — as in Namibia.[38] Other opponents of the United Nations sincerely believe in the danger that the UN system presents to Western interests. For instance, there is a widespread, and understandable attitude, among U.S. decision makers that, although the United States might have to listen to anti-U.S. rhetoric and propaganda at the United Nations, it should not have to pay for it. For many decision makers in Washington, the Kassebaum amendment represents a warning "shot across the bow" to the United Nations: either attend to the important (and often private) business of diplomacy or find someone else to pay the bills.[39]

Yet, there is a more serious — and ominous — implication to the Kassebaum amendment that cannot be ignored: the growing threat of international isolationism in the United States. The United Nations Headquarters was deliberately located in the United States after World War II. This was done by the founding fathers of the United Nations to combat the post-World War I isolationist fervor of U.S. foreign policy — a fervor that fatally wounded the League of Nations because the United States refused to join. Since World War II, isolationism has been an ideologically dormant idea in U.S. foreign affairs; however, the increasingly shrill attacks against international organizations might indicate that a new ideological isolationism is emerging in the United States. Sober statesmen and commentators in the United States warn about the dangers of attacking international organizations too much and, thus, leaving the field to the United States' political opponents in the future.[40] It is too early to tell if the Kassebaum amendment is simply a "shot across the bow," or represents a growing isolationist trend in the United States.

Even so, there are some in Washington, D.C., who urge further financial cuts of the U.S. contribution to the United Nations.[41] Before considering such advice, the United States should first compare the daily costs of keeping the U.S. fleet in the Persian Gulf in 1987 with the yearly costs of the United Nations during the time of the Secretary-General's successful efforts to end the fighting between Iran and Iraq. Any such comparison will immediately reveal the vast financial discrepancy between the U.S. naval action and the United Nations diplomacy — not to mention the real risks and costs of a wider war involving the United States while its fleet policed the Gulf. This risk ended only after the Secretary-General managed, despite great odds, to gain a fragile cease-fire between Iran and Iraq.

THE UNITED NATIONS' RESPONSE
TO FINANCIAL CRISIS

In response to the Kassebaum amendment, the General Assembly formed, in late 1985, an 18-member panel officially called the Group of High-Level Intergovernmental Experts to Review the Efficiency of the Administrative and Financial Functioning of the United Nations.[42] The group contained representatives from 18 nations, including the 5 permanent members of the UN Security Council. The Group of Eighteen met 67 times between February and August 1986 and issued a final report to the General Assembly that year.[43]

THE GROUP OF EIGHTEEN REPORT

The report of the Group of Eighteen deliberations is a widely acclaimed document. Even the archconservative Charles M. Lichenstein, former U.S. deputy representative to the United Nations and now a Senior Fellow at the Heritage Foundation, describes the report of the Group of Eighteen as "an extraordinary document."[44] The final report of the Group of Eighteen contained a series of specific recommendations for streamlining UN bureaucratic and budgetary procedures.

The main recommendations contained in the Group of Eighteen report can be summarized as follows:[45]

There should be a substantial reduction in the number of staff members at all levels but particularly in the higher echelons. To this end, the overall number of regular posts should be reduced by 15 percent within a period of three years.

The number of posts at the level of Under-Secretary-General and Assistant Secretary-General should be reduced by 25 percent within a period of three years or less. There should also be a ban on rehiring retired Secretariat officials as consultants.

There should be a review of the nine political departments and offices that perform a wide variety of functions, with a view of consolidating and streamlining the organization's structure, especially in areas where overlap and duplication exist. As we shall see, this recommendation has led to an important — although little noticed reform — by the Secretary-General.

There should be no new Secretariat departments created without eliminating or consolidating existing ones.

With regard to the UN budget, the Group of Eighteen could not come to a consensus; instead, it made three separate recommendations, ranging from one that would, more or less, continue the current budget process to one that would give major donors almost complete control over the UN budget.[46] These budget recommendations have proved to be the most controversial proposals by the Group of Eighteen because they could give greater control of the UN budget to the United States and other significant donors.

The report by the Group of Eighteen has led to a flurry of activity within the UN diplomatic community and Secretariat. If anything, the report indicated that the era of "business as usual" at the United

Nations was rapidly coming to an end. In an institution as Byzantine and complicated as the United Nations, the idea of impending reform was suddenly in the air.

THE FOG OF REFORM

The notion of reform inevitably comes to any great institution like a fog; its very nature is elusive, threatening, and full of unseen obstacles.[47] This is especially true at the United Nations where the fog of reform has different meanings to different diplomatic delegations and Secretariat officials. For the superpowers, the fog of reform seems to represent the added opportunity to, and danger of, jousting with each other and jockeying for procedural, or even substantive, victories. For the nonpermanent members of the Security Council, the fog of reform represents the fugitive chance to improve their position and influence vis-à-vis the permanent members. For officials in the UN Secretariat, the descending fog represents either a threat to their well-entrenched bureaucratic fiefdoms or a convenient cover for pushing forward new ideas and programs that might advance the United Nations.

As we have seen, the thrust of the reform movement at the United Nations is two-fold; both the UN Secretary-General and the U.S. government have, for very different reasons, sought changes in the way the United Nations operates.

Since his 1982 *Annual Report,* UN Secretary-General Pérez de Cuéllar has expressed an interest in improving his preventive role. Specifically, he has continually sought to reform the political offices in the UN bureaucracy and make it more effective in preventing conflict. At the same time, there has been growing U.S. dissatisfaction with the United Nations in a variety of bureaucratic and budgetary areas. The subsequent withholding of substantial U.S. funds from the United Nations has provoked a crisis in the organization that is still continuing (1988). Yet, the U.S. actions have also led to a long-needed review of the way the UN Secretariat conducts business. The enforced streamlining caused by the United States coupled with the Secretary-General's own efforts at reform may, ironically, result in a stronger and more responsive United Nations.

An analysis and review of the entire reform movement at the United Nations go beyond the purpose of this study. Yet, the reform effort has already had an impact upon the nature of the Secretary-General's preventive role. Specifically, Secretary-General Pérez de Cuéllar has implemented a number of changes designed to enhance his capacity to predict and prevent international conflicts. His efforts to recast his office have been aided, unintentionally perhaps, by the Group of Eighteen's report. Other impending reforms concern strengthening his preventive role under Article 99 of the Charter. Although his efforts are little noticed by the press, Pérez de Cuéllar has demonstrated as imaginative and creative a flair for institutional innovation as Hammarskjöld.

In Part II of the book, "Reform and Renewal at the United Nations," we shall examine his current plans and programs in greater depth. Further recommendations concerning ways to strengthen the Secretary-General's preventive role will also be defined and developed. The ultimate goal of Part II is to present specific plans for strengthening the Secretary-General's capacity to preserve the peace in the future.

NOTES

1. If a Secretary-General has a serious clash with a permanent power on the Security Council, his chances of reappointment are diminished. For instance, after his support of the UN's Korean War effort, Secretary-General Lie was vigorously opposed by the Soviets until he stepped down in 1953.

2. The U.S. action apparently caught everyone by surprise. Many of my following comments and criticisms are based upon confidential interviews with negotiators actually involved in the effort to avert the war. Also see Ambassador Anthony Parsons' account of the Secretary-General's intervention: "The Falkland Crisis in the United Nations, 31 March–14 June 82," *International Affairs 59* (1983), 169–78.

3. In my CRIA publication *Protecting the Innocent* (New York: Carnegie Council, in *Ethics and International Affairs,* 1983), p. 23, I point out, "To rely upon a single source of communication and information during a crisis courts disaster. This is one reason why 'shuttle diplomacy' is sometimes desirable. It permits direct contact with political leaders and executive policy makers of a particular group or country. Yet, sometimes shuttle diplomacy is impractical, *especially when time is short and there are great distances to be traveled.*"

4. The Secretary-General recounted the sequence of his involvement to the Security Council on May 20, 1982 — the day that he announced that his efforts to end the crisis without war had failed. See also Anthony Parsons, "The Falkland Crisis."

5. Parsons, "The Falkland Crisis," p. 173.

6. Ibid.

7. Ibid.

8. Confidential interviews with UN mediators.

9. Parsons, "The Falkland Crisis," p. 173.

10. Parsons announced that a deadline had been placed on negotiations after he returned to New York from London May 17. See Parsons, "The Falkland Crisis," p. 174.

11. Confidential interviews in UN diplomatic community.

12. Confidential interviews in UN diplomatic community.

13. Coral Bell talks about the importance of building a "golden bridge" behind your adversary so that he can retreat without humiliation. See Coral Bell, "Decision Making by Governments in Crisis Situations," In Daniel Frei (ed.), *International Crises and Crisis Management* (Hampshire, England: Saxon House, 1978), p. 54.

14. His talk is reported and analyzed by Parsons, "The Falkland Crisis," pp. 169–78.

15. My CRIA publication, *Protecting the Innocent,* briefly reviews the impact of the fighting on civilians.

16. There were brief cease-fires repeatedly called that seemed to have only the effect of improving the military position of one side or the other. Even so, the Security Council never tired in repeating a call for a cease-fire. See, for example, S.C. Res. 516 (S/RES/516), August 1, 1982, and the "Report of the Secretary-General in Pursuance of Security Council Resolution 516," UN Doc. S/15334/Add.1.

17. Resolution 516, cited above, gave the Secretary-General the responsibility to deploy observers in and around Beirut. Resolution 521, passed by the Security Council after the refugee camp massacres, increased the number of deployed observers. See S.C. Resolution 521 (S/RES/521), September 19, 1982.

18. Javier Pérez de Cuéllar, *Report of the Secretary-General on the Work of the Organization* (New York: The United Nations, 1982), p. 8.

19. Ibid.

20. Ibid.

21. Ibid.

22. For an explanation of the role of theoretical frameworks in collecting data, see Neil Smelser, *Essay in Sociological Explanation* (Englewood Cliffs, NJ: Prentice-Hall, 1968), p. 57. His ideas are extensively discussed and supported in Richard Berstein, *The Restructuring of Social and Political Theory* (Philadelphia: The University of Pennsylvania Press, 1978). Also see Sydney D. Bailey, *The Procedure of the UN Security Council* (Oxford: Clarendon Press, 1975), p. 285.

23. Confidential interviews with a UN Secretariat official.

24. Thomas E. Boudreau, *Protecting the Innocent* (New York: Council on Religion and International Affairs, 1983). (Now called the Carnegie Council on Ethics and International Affairs.)

25. UN Doc. S/15834, June 20, 1983.

26. Ibid.

27. Ibid.

28. Ibid.

29. UN Doc. S/16454, March 30, 1984.

30. Boudreau, *Protecting the Innocent,* pp. 6–12.

31. UN Doc. S/16454, March 30, 1984.

32. Ibid.

33. UN Doc. S/16611, June 11, 1984.

34. UN Doc. S/16628, June 15, 1984.

35. UN Doc. S/16648, June 26, 1984.

36. Adam Roberts and Benedict Kingsbury, *United Nations, Divided World* (Oxford: Clarendon Press, 1988).

37. See Dante B. Fascell and Gus Yatron, "Congress and the United Nations," *Proteus* (spring 1988).

38. See, for example, the UN-related publications by the Heritage Foundation such as "The Charade of UN Reform," December 21, 1987. Published on the winter solstice, it is perhaps not coincidental that such an essay represents the absolute nadir of political commentary on the United Nations.

39. Official response from U.S. mission to the United Nations to written enquiry by author, spring 1988.

40. See, for example, the introductory comments of John Offner, review editor to *Proteus* (spring 1988). Also see the essay in the same journal by Peter Fromuth and Jeffrey Laurenti "Toward a Successor Vision," pp. 4–9.

41. See, for example, "The Charade of United Nations Reform," Heritage Foundation, December 21, 1987. It is not surprising that opponents of this group call it the "hysteria foundation."

42. United Nations General Assembly Resolution 41/231, adopted December 16, 1986.

43. See General Assembly Official Records: 41st Session, Supplement 49(A/41/49).

44. See Charles Lichenstein, "United Nations Reform: Where's the Beef?" March 10, 1987. "Backgrounder" (Washington, D.C.: Heritage Foundation, 1987).

45. So that there is little or no question concerning the results of this committee's work, I have used both official UN sources here, as well as the Heritage Foundation. See U.N.G.A. 41st Session, Supplement 49 (A/41/49), and/or Lichenstein, "Where's the Beef?"

46. See "The Charade of UN Reform," Heritage Foundation, December 21, 1987.

47. This section on reform is influenced by the wording in my report, *The Secretary-General and Satellite Diplomacy* (New York: Council on Ethics and International Affairs, 1984).

II

REFORM AND RENEWAL

> Something must be done, and done urgently, to
> strengthen our international institutions and to
> adopt new and imaginative approaches to the
> prevention and resolution of conflicts.
> — Secretary-General Pérez de Cuéllar
> 1982 *Annual Report*

In Part I, first we examined the legal basis of the Secretary-General's preventive role. We then discussed how all five Secretaries-General have interpreted, in a pragmatic day-to-day way, their preventive role and responsibilities under the UN Charter.

Building upon this, we now examine the Secretary-General's preventive role from a more analytical perspective. We first examine in Chapter 6 the three theoretical stages of this role: conflict identification, conflict analysis/intervention, and conflict settlement and legitimation (face saving). After each stage is defined and developed, we then discuss specific ways to reform and renew the Secretary-General's preventive role.

In Chapter 7, we examine the new Office of Research and the Collection of Information (ORCI) created by Pérez de Cuéllar in order to enhance conflict identification. We then analyze in Chapter 8 the suggested reforms designed to strengthen his ability to gather public information from around the world. In Chapter 9, we discuss ways to enhance the analysis/intervention stage of his preventive role. In Chapter 10 we review the present problems and future potential of UN telecommunications, and in Chapter 11 we examine prospective configurations for the proposed "Multilateral War Risk Reduction Center."

The purpose of the more theoretical treatment in the following chapters is to push the constitutional and operational possibilities, under the specific constraints of Article 99, as far as the Charter will permit. Ideally, the end result of this process will be the strengthening of the Secretary-General's preventive role.

6

WATCHMAN OF THE PEACE: THE THEORETICAL STAGES OF THE SECRETARY-GENERAL'S PREVENTIVE ROLE

> Arise, O Princes,
> Oil the shields!
> For the Lord said to me:
> "Go, set a Watchman.
> Let him announce what he sees."
>
> — Isaiah 21:5

In his 1982 *Annual Report,* Pérez de Cuéllar noted that the Secretary-General has "traditionally, if informally tried to keep watch" over international peace.[1] In essence, he is suggesting that the Secretary-General serves as an international watchman of impending threats to the peace and helps alert the Security Council to potential conflicts before the outbreak of war. As he notes in the same report, this is a role that is clearly contemplated, if not required, by Article 99.

In the aftermath of his 1982 *Annual Report,* the new Secretary-General proposed certain administrative reforms within the UN Secretariat that should provide him with a better capacity to identify potential conflict situations.[2] Yet, short-term reforms without a long-term vision of change can create as many problems as they solve. If done in an ad hoc way, each reform could cause, eventually, greater bureaucratic bottlenecks and Secretariat infighting rather than contribute to better conflict prevention.

Without a theoretical framework that both justifies and clarifies a specific reform, each effort to improve the Secretary-General's ability to prevent conflict threatens to become a piecemeal "band-aid" solution. In short, there is a need to develop a theoretical framework that can define and develop a clear and consistent link between the Secretary-General's obligation under Article 99 and his ability to gather, ascertain, and evaluate information concerning conflict prevention.[3]

In the following sections, the theoretical stages concerning the Secretary-General's preventive role are defined and developed. This will enable us to analyze and evaluate the proposed reforms of Secretary-General Pérez de Cuéllar in terms of their theoretical policy objectives as well as their practical day-to-day operations at the United Nations.

THE THEORETICAL STAGES OF THE SECRETARY-GENERAL'S ROLE

The sociologist Neil Smelser defines a theoretical framework as a level of logical ordering where models are embedded in definition, assumption, and postulates.[4] Professor David Singer believes that the "level of analysis" — which will be treated here as being synonymous with Smelser's phrase "level of logical ordering" — is a crucial choice in any scholarly enquiry.[5] This is because the level of analysis (or logical ordering) will influence, almost in a deductive way, all subsequent research. For this reason, the choices made at this point of theory building must be fully explicit. This is especially true when discussing the Secretary-General's preventive role because little theoretical work has been done in this precise area.

For the purposes of subsequent discussion, the preventive role of the Secretary-General will be divided into the following three stages or logical ordering: conflict identification, conflict analysis and intervention, and conflict resolution, which includes legitimation of a settlement or face-saving.[6]

CONFLICT IDENTIFICATION

Conflict identification requires that a potential or an actual international conflict is recognized at the earliest possible moment by the Secretary-General's office so that effective analysis and intervention can occur. This is, obviously, easier said than done. Thus, the precise problem of conflict identification is to create effective diplomatic and information management systems, employing multiple means of inputs, so that there is early alert and comprehensive coverage of any dangerous and destabilizing event that may threaten international peace and security. Secretary-General Pérez de Cuéllar had identified this area as needing significant improvement and implemented an innovative reform in the area: the creation of a new office, the Office of Research and Collection of Information (ORCI). He is also using the UN information centers to collect publicly available information from around the world.

THE INADEQUACY OF FACT-FINDING
FOR CONFLICT IDENTIFICATION

As discussed in Part I, all the UN Secretaries-General have struggled — with varying degrees of success — to assert their preventive role within the organizational and political context of the United Nations. For instance, Trygve Lie, the first Secretary-General, had to fight hard simply to assert his right to speak before the Security Council. Hammarskjöld struggled to assert the Secretary-General's right to gather information in a potential conflict area. Secretary-General Pérez de Cuéllar has expressed his determination to improve his office's ability to anticipate potential conflicts. In his first *Annual Report* (1982), he explicitly stated, "In order to carry out effectively the preventive role foreseen for the Secretary-General under Article 99, I intend to develop a wider and more systematic capacity for fact-finding in potential conflict areas."[7] Apparently, the Secretary-General presumes that the effectiveness of his preventive role will vary in relation to the ability of his office to gather facts, that is, fact-finding, in potential conflict situations.

Yet, without greater theoretical elaboration or empirical verification, a relationship between conflict prevention and fact-finding is certainly suspect. For instance, the United Nations Secretariat seemed to have ample information during spring 1982 that the British fleet was slowly sailing south toward the Falkland/Malvinas Islands. All the facts indicated that the British intended to retake the islands. Yet, the availability of these facts did not prevent the conflict from coming. On the contrary, the public accessibility to information seemed to simply heighten the stakes involved.

Part of the problem is the vagueness and inadequacy of the term "fact-finding." Informal interactions between diplomats and UN staff, private consultations between the Secretary-General and a head of state, or a concern expressed by a member of the Security Council can provide crucial information, but none of these activities can be characterized as fact-finding. (Indeed, sometimes the facts find the Secretary-General or his staff, even when they are not looking for them!) Critics point out the weakness of this phrase. In his book, *The Procedure of the UN Security Council,* Sydney D. Bailey states, "The trouble with facts is not that they are in short supply but that there is a superabundance of them. . . . Fact-finding in the UN context may consist of the painstaking collection of information using the most rigorous rules of evidence, or it may be the amassing of reports in order to bolster a predetermined political position."[8]

As we mentioned in Chapter 1, fact-finding has a limited role as an explicit action authorized by the Security Council; such action may include humanitarian fact-finding by the Secretary-General (see

Chapter 5). Yet, generally the method of fact-finding contributes more to the United Nations' political problems than to possible solutions. For instance, as we saw in Chapter 3, the UN fact-finding team sent to Laos in 1959 floundered upon the politics of the Cold War and seemed to create more troubles than clarity for the United Nations.

If fact-finding is so inadequate, the problem then becomes one of specifying the precise organization and structure of a "wider and more systematic capacity" for identifying conflicts. Is it defined and developed in organizational, political, or even technical terms? Or must the effort of the Secretary-General continue to be characterized as ad hoc groping and political improvisation — often after a crisis or war has already started? In short, is there a specific "level of analysis" that can provide a greater degree of logical order and convincing coherence to the Secretary-General's preventive role and responsibilities under Article 99 of the UN Charter?

A GLOBAL FRAMEWORK FOR
CONFLICT IDENTIFICATION

Specifically, the appropriate level of analysis for the conflict identification is, as already suggested in Part I, the entire Earth. The use of the globe as the basic unit of analysis is the preeminent characteristic of world order studies. Scholars from a variety of fields are beginning to examine the global implications of limited resources, environmental pollution, strategic studies, and economic development.[9] Despite their diversity, all world order studies share the common framework or level of analysis of looking at the "globe as a whole."[10] The meaning and significance of data collected, new information, or insights are ultimately determined by a demonstrable relationship to the entire Earth.

Using the globe as a whole to organize a wider and more systematic capacity has crucial implications for the size and scope of the Secretary-General's early warning and information management systems. For instance, in Chapter 7, I consider the need for the Secretary-General's early warning system to cover the Earth's commons, the oceans, the polar caps, and near outer space. This is especially important in view of the historical pattern of incidents on the high seas precipitating international crises.[11]

Even so, the United Nations is currently focusing upon country profiles to organize its early warning system. If the early warning system does not include coverage of the commons, 70 percent of the Earth's surface is exempt from the system. Thus, the simple change in perspective — from landlocked politics to the entire globe — is a good example of how the level of analysis employed can contribute to new insights and to new questions. We will return to this issue when we discuss the ideal system for conflict identification in the next chapter.

CONFLICT ANALYSIS/INTERVENTION

Once a potential conflict is identified, the incoming information must be analyzed by the UN Secretariat. The analysis stage involves evaluating all relevant information, extensive discussions among the diplomats at the United Nations, exploring alternative policy options, and outlining possible solutions to a potential conflict.

Of course, such analysis already occurs within the UN Secretariat. Yet, this stage of information flow through the Secretariat has never been adequately structured, particularly in reference to its crucial role in conflict prevention.[12] Although this has certain advantages, especially in terms of preserving a certain degree of flexibility and informality in working arrangements, it has also resulted in a great deal of bureaucratic inefficiency — the very sort of thing that has led the major powers, among others, to call for greater fiscal restraint during the mid-1980s.

Even if improvements in the analysis of information are made, the significant problem still remains: how can the Secretary-General intervene in a potential or actual conflict so that he can begin to exercise his preventive role? If he is invited by one or both of the parties, then the problem is solved. If he is not invited, then the question of whether or not he should intervene must be confronted. It should be emphasized that the Secretary-General's constitutional responsibilities do not disappear under Article 99 simply because he is not invited to exercise his preventive role. Yet, he cannot simply intrude into negotiations between potential, or actual, adversaries. Sometimes, when the danger is very great, as during the 1962 Cuban crisis, the Secretary-General can intervene without invitation and be welcomed. At other times, he must exercise greater diplomatic caution. In short, intervening in a crisis involves both a well-formulated diplomatic strategy and a delicate sense of timing.

At a certain point, the analysis and intervention stages become inseparable. The linkage of these two stages will occur when and if intervention by the Secretary-General is successful, that is, if he becomes an active participant in the ongoing negotiations. Thus, there is a dialectical relationship between the analysis and intervention stages. In a very real sense, these stages "heat up" and "fuse" together. This is physically, mentally, and emotionally the most tiring stage of conflict prevention for UN negotiators. For instance, during the Falkland/Malvinas crisis, some UN negotiators practically lived at UN Headquarters for over a month.[13]

SETTLEMENT/LEGITIMATION:
DIPLOMACY AS DRAMA

No nation can actively prepare for war and, at the same time, actively prepare for peace. War calls for the supreme sacrifice, and the people on the home front must be fully convinced that the expenditure of blood and treasure — the literal sacrifice of their sons, husbands, and brothers — is fully justified. Thus, it is no surprise that political leaders facing imminent conflict spend a great deal of time and energy arousing their own people, through pomp and propaganda, trying to prepare them for the coming war. This was especially true, for instance, in the Falkland/Malvinas crisis.

Specifically, the home fronts of both Britain and Argentina quickly became inflamed with deep popular emotions and began to exert a growing pressure upon the political context of diplomatic negotiations. The popular reactions of a nation's domestic population can narrow, with increasing severity, the diplomatic options that political leaders can exercise. Because the survival of one's own government is a key consideration of any political leader locked into a confrontation, the reactions and support of the home fronts are especially important during a crisis.

The danger is that the public pressures created by rising political tensions often trap governmental leaders into situations that can — from their perspective — be redeemed only through war. While diplomats may be busy trying to find common ground upon which to build a settlement, the public (and even the allies) of each government involved in a confrontation may be busy "burning bridges," thus making it almost impossible for political leaders to make concessions or even seek clarifications that may resolve the issue without bloodshed.

For instance, two days before the Argentinian invasion of the islands, workers led massive demonstrations against the junta in Buenos Aires. Two days after the invasion, there were massive demonstrations in Buenos Aires in favor of the junta's invasion.[14] Some may call the popular response simply the result of political manipulation; others may call it the frenzied outpouring of political madness — an orgy of defiance against a perceived injustice. There are, undoubtedly, elements of truth to both of these perspectives. Indeed, the junta itself seemed surprised by the popular support it had engendered. Despite the junta's protestations of peace, the dogs of war had been released.

To prevent this entrapment of leaders by their own people, the Secretary-General and his negotiating teams must help legitimate a peaceful solution to a crisis. In doing so, the Secretary-General helps to build golden bridges behind each potential adversary in a military showdown. The term "legitimating a settlement" refers to the political process by which a negotiated resolution of an international crisis becomes politically acceptable to the domestic audience, and allies, of the governments or regimes involved in the negotiations — as well as to the dissident centers of power within the negotiating governments themselves.

If the literature in political science and diplomacy is any indication, the need to legitimate a peace settlement is the most overlooked aspect of conflict prevention.[15] Despite this oversight, it is arguably one of the most important aspects of a negotiated settlement. In view of this, third-party negotiators — such as the Secretary-General — have a significant responsibility to help political leaders legitimate and justify a peace settlement, especially in the eyes of the domestic audiences or allies of the governments involved.

It is not enough for a third party to achieve the conceptual basis of a negotiated agreement. It must also provide some diplomatic assistance to political leaders so that they can convince their own people, and sometimes others within their own government, to accept a political settlement. In a diplomatic settlement it is often feasible, and always desirable, that all sides win. Thus, the settlement can be characterized and legitimated in the eyes of the home front as a victory.

The Secretary-General tried to do this during the Falkland/ Malvinas negotiations. For a variety of reasons, the Secretary-General's proposals in mid-May of 1982 represented a victory for both the British and Argentine governments. The British won in that the Argentine forces would withdraw from the islands to be replaced by UN forces. Argentina won because the British were willing to administer the islands and also conduct negotiations under the Secretary-General's auspices, which might very well have led to eventual Argentine control. Both sides could argue with conviction that they had achieved a victory. By characterizing the diplomatic settlement as a joint victory, the Secretary-General could help preserve the honor of each side.

The Secretary-General and the entire international community has a preeminent interest in helping a government legitimate a settlement in the eyes of the home front. If efforts are not made during the crisis to ensure governments that such international support will be forthcoming on a massive scale, then the popular pressure for a military solution may be overwhelming. This certainly occurred during the Falkland/Malvinas crisis when the Argentine government and, perhaps to a lesser extent, the British government felt trapped by the rising crescendo of bravado and jingoism on the home front. The results of the crisis are well known; the perishable opportunity to prevent bloodshed was lost, and the war came.

In the context of the United Nations, the most effective way to legitimate a settlement is through the personal involvement of the

Secretary-General. Before this stage of negotiations, the Secretary-General's public statements and travel should be restrained. Such diplomatic restraint is necessary to preserve trust, retain options, and prevent excessive expectations. He should stay in the center of the negotiating network, at UN Headquarters in New York City. But if negotiations reach the stage where both political parties privately agree to the Secretary-General's UN negotiated terms — but still fear public disclosure because of the demands of an inflamed citizenry — the need for the strong presence and participation of the Secretary-General may become necessary. At this stage of negotiations, he could begin his travels and public statements in earnest.

Another alternative is that the Secretary-General can invite the heads of state, or the government's foreign ministers, to UN Headquarters in New York to announce a settlement of the crisis. Such an announcement can occur simultaneously with announcements in the capitals of each government. The dramatic effect of such an act should not be criticized as histrionics. "When the alternative is death to hundreds or even thousands of people, the careful indulgence in a dramatic celebration of a diplomatic settlement at the UN seems to be a very small price to pay. It can also provide another highly visible 'stage' upon which the proposed settlement can be dramatically legitimated."[16]

The allies of each government should also be enlisted by the Secretary-General in order to legitimate a settlement. Once a settlement is announced, exclamations of support and congratulations should pour into the Foreign Ministry of each government. Heads of states of allied governments could be encouraged by the Secretary-General to travel to the capitals to congratulate personally the victorious and statesmanlike conduct of the governments' leaders. In the face of such support, domestic critics will find it difficult to condemn the negotiated outcome as weak or a disgrace.

This is not to say that the UN negotiators in the field should keep a low profile as well. It may be useful to prepare the domestic populations of all parties involved for a possible settlement by continually emphasizing the prospects for peace as symbolized by the presence of UN negotiators within the country. Also, UN negotiators in the field, in close cooperation with the host government, could devote some time and resources to the problem of preparing the public — the domestic population and the news media — for a negotiated settlement. The important factor is not simply that such support is achieved; rather, it is crucial that leaders locked together in a confrontation know that they can count on the Secretary-General and on their own allies to mobilize dramatic political and public support, thus creating irreversible political momentum, for a peaceful settlement.

In view of this, a potential crisis can be said to be peacefully resolved when the following three conditions are obtained.

It is based on the self-interests of the parties directly involved in the negotiations.

It is self-supporting in the sense that each party has a self-interest at stake in ensuring that the negotiated settlement is observed. Coercive constraints imposed by one party only ensure that the issue will explode again once the coercive constraints are removed or overthrown. The victors of World War I learned this difficult lesson with the subsequent resurgence of German nationalism under the Nazis in the wake of the humiliating settlement at Versailles. A bad peace agreement can help create a future war.

The agreement is self-regulating in the sense that all parties have an interest in policing the outcome and in correcting any deviations from the settlement within the context of their relationship.[17]

If the Secretary-General manages to obtain an agreement characterized by these three conditions, and the danger of war averted, then his preventive responsibilities are successfully completed.

NOTES

1. Javier Pérez de Cuéllar, *Report of the Secretary-General on the Work of the Organization* (1982) (New York: The United Nations, 1982), p. 8. (Hereafter 1982 *Annual Report.*)

2. Pérez de Cuéllar, 1982 *Annual Report.*

3. There seems to be a bankruptcy of ideas in the realm of information gathering by the United Nations; almost all commentators refer to "fact-finding" as a primary means of gathering information, even though it has — as we saw in Part I — a very difficult history and dubious value. For a comprehensive study on UN fact-finding, which reveals its faults as well as its possibilities, see Edwin Brown Firmage, "Fact-Finding in the Resolution of International Disputes — From the Hague Peace Conference to the United Nations," *Utah Law Review 421* (1971).

4. Neil J. Smelser, *Essays in Sociological Explanation* (Englewood Cliffs, NJ: Prentice-Hall, 1968), p. 55.

5. David Singer, "The Level of Analysis Problem in International Relations," in James Rosenau (ed.), *International Politics and Foreign Policy* (New York: The Free Press, 1969), p. 20.

6. This is my own characterization of the Secretary-General's preventive role. They were first used in my dissertation, *The Secretary-General: Watchman of the Peace,* completed at the Maxwell School, Syracuse University, 1985.

7. Pérez de Cuéllar, 1982 *Annual Report.*

8. Sydney D. Bailey, *The Procedure of the UN Security Council* (Oxford: Oxford University Press, 1975), pp. 279–85.

9. See, for example, Donella Meadows et al., *Groping in the Dark: The First Decade of Global Modeling* (Somerset, NJ: John Wiley, 1982); Donella Meadows, "Whole Earth Models and Systems," *CoEvolution Quarterly* (summer 1982), p. 100; or William Thompson (ed.), *Multiple Perspectives on the World Systems* (Beverly Hills, CA: Sage, 1982).

10. Meadows, "Whole Earth Models," p. 100.

11. This point is made in Dan Deudney, "Whole Earth Security: A Geopolitics of Peace," Worldwatch Paper No. 55 (Washington, D.C.: Worldwatch Institute, 1983).

12. See my report, *The Secretary-General and Satellite Diplomacy* (New York: Carnegie Council, 1984). This assertion is based upon my own analysis of the impoverished state of the literature — and of diplomatic practice — in this crucial area.

13. Private discussions by author with members of Secretary-General's negotiating team, spring 1983.

14. R. Reginald and Dr. Jeffery M. Elliot, *Tempest in a Teapot: The Falkland Islands War* (San Bernardino, CA: Borgo Press, 1983), p. 98. Also see Lawrence Freedman, "The War of the Falkland Islands, 1982," *Foreign Affairs 61* (1), 196–210.

15. The literature is largely silent on this question. The idea of "legitimating" a settlement to the home front seems to strike diplomats as "showmanship," that is, "selling" an agreement to domestic audiences. This is often viewed as somehow beneath the role and responsibility of a successful negotiator; yet, a very good agreement or settlement can fail if it is not legitimated in the eyes of domestic audiences. It is the final touch of responsible, and successful, diplomacy. At least one former diplomat realizes this; see Connor Cruise O'Brien, *The United Nations: A Sacred Drama* (New York: Simon and Schuster, 1968).

16. See O'Brien, *The United Nations: A Sacred Drama*. This is an insightful description of the United Nations as political theater.

17. This is my own definition of conflict resolution based upon a paper I presented in Ireland; see Thomas E. Boudreau, "Peace Studies: The Irish Initiatives at the First International Conference on Peace Building," Shannon, Ireland, April 1986. This paper is also in *Gandhi Marq,* Spring 1990.

7

GLOBAL WATCH:
TOWARD A
COMPREHENSIVE SYSTEM
OF CONFLICT IDENTIFICATION

As discussed in Chapter 1, Article 99 of the Charter gives the Secretary-General broad powers and prerogatives in determining whether a "matter . . . may threaten the maintenance of international peace and security." In view of this responsibility, it would be unwise to argue that the Secretary-General must limit his purview of political problems to known "hot spots" in the world, such as the Middle East or southern Africa. As the Falkland/Malvinas War indicates, threats to international peace and security may quickly develop in some of the most unexpected and isolated parts of the world.

In other words, the Secretary-General cannot choose the time and place of potential threats to the peace; instead, the potential conflicts will govern the scope and timing of the Secretary-General's preventive efforts. Yet, his efforts may well fail unless there is — consistent with his responsibilities under Article 99 — effective coverage of all potential conflict areas.

ENHANCING EARLY WARNING: ORCI

Until recently, the gathering and analysis of information by the UN Secretariat was done on an ad hoc basis. There was little systematic integration of the Secretariat's information management responsibilities, especially in the crucial area of early warning for potential conflicts. In order to improve conflict identification within the UN Secretariat, Secretary-General Pérez de Cuéllar approved, shortly after the end of his first term, the creation of the Office for Research and the Collection of Information (ORCI).[1] This new office represents one of the main reforms concerning his preventive role under Article 99.

ORCI consolidates a variety of functions that were formerly performed by a number of offices within the Secretariat. The responsibility of the new office is to collect and disseminate political news and information within the Secretariat, as well as to carry out research and drafting of reports for the Secretary-General. ORCI also has a mandate to mobilize the expertise of the nongovernmental organizations (NGOs) such as universities, think tanks, and foundations. The ultimate purpose of the new office is to provide the Secretary-General with an effective early warning system. The specific mandate of the office is as follows:

(a) To assess global trends;
(b) To prepare country, regional, subregional, and issue-related profiles in close consultation with officers dealing with negotiation and conflict resolution functions in the Secretariat;
(c) To provide early warning of developing situations requiring the Secretary-General's attention;
(d) To maintain current information in data systems, consulting with inside and outside data banks, as appropriate;
(e) To monitor factors related to possible refugee flows and comparable emergencies;
(f) To carry out ad hoc research and assessments for the immediate needs of the Secretary-General;
(g) To receive, consolidate, and distribute political information from the media and from the United Nations information center on developments related to peace and security, for use by the Secretary-General and his senior staff;
(h) To prepare and edit drafts of the Secretary-General's public statements, messages and reports.[2]

For the purpose of analysis, we shall focus upon "a" through "c," as well as "g." These four functions are the key building blocks of an effective early warning system. (A fifth function, concerning the creation of data banks, is discussed in Chapter 10, which deals with the UN telecommunications.)

However, before analyzing each function in greater detail, it is useful to develop a model for conflict identification. Such a model, presented below, helps pinpoint the strong and weak links of the Secretary-General's early warning system.

IDENTIFYING THE WEAK LINKS:
A THEORETICAL MODEL

The Secretary-General's early warning system can be conceptualized as a "simplified information systems model," a term borrowed from system analysis. The basic information system model consists of three components: inputs, analysis (or processing), and outputs.[3] This simplified model provides a useful conceptual basis evaluating global conflict identification by the Secretary-General.

UN Headquarters already possesses strong processing or analysis skills in the form of a highly experienced and professional senior staff, and multiple outputs distribute information about the United Nations. For instance, the Department of Public Information (DPI), which works with the world media, is one of the largest offices in the United Nations and is currently being upgraded and streamlined.

A key factor in ensuring the accuracy of early warning assessments is a globe-spanning system of multiple inputs that receive and send important information to the office of the Secretary-General in a timely fashion. Such diverse inputs are clearly the weak link of UN conflict identification.[4]

The Secretary-General and his staff are keenly aware of the need for multiple inputs, and have taken a number of steps to improve the diversity of information received from the field. This is one of the key reasons why he established ORCI; the Secretary-General hoped to enhance the inputs to his early warning system. In view of this, we will review these efforts within the context of ORCI's new mandate from the Secretary-General.

FUNCTIONS OF THE OFFICE

Assessing Global Trends

As mentioned earlier, the geographical shape of the globe as a whole determines the organization and structure of the wider and more systematic capacity sought by Secretary-General Pérez de Cuéllar. Thus, the first function of ORCI — "To assess global trends" — is fully consistent with his preventive role and responsibilities under Article 99.

As discussed in Chapter 1, the Secretary-General has expansive powers to consider and analyze any matter that may, in his opinion, threaten international peace and security. This obviously includes traditional categories of threat perception, such as increased diplomatic and political tensions or actual military movements. Many practicing diplomats and scholars are also increasingly aware of the importance of social, economic, environmental, humanitarian, and even health trends that may contribute to international tensions. For instance, as the current head of ORCI, Dr. James C. Jonah states,

> Another reason for the creation of ORCI was the . . . need to make the Secretary-General and his representatives fully aware of new results of multidisciplinary research, as it pertains to global trends having direct bearing on expected political developments (e.g., what would be the political implications of a sudden deviation in the world debt crisis, global warming, increased terrorism, drug trafficking or AIDS?).[5]

As an experienced diplomat, Dr. Jonah is aware of the possible impact on political tensions of very diverse, and apparently unrelated, forces in international affairs. Thus, if the Secretary-General's early warning system is to be truly effective, it must receive, analyze, and integrate information concerning trends from a wide variety of sources throughout the world.

Furthermore, there is no reason for the Secretary-General to limit his concern to identified threats to the peace. Because the purpose of Article 99 is prevention, the Secretary-General should feel free to monitor, and comment upon, any matter that promotes the maintenance of international peace and security. Thus, positive economic, social, or environmental developments that enhance international cooperation and stability come under his global purview.

The information from the Secretary-General's enhanced early warning system should then be periodically shared with the Security Council. The Secretary-General currently provides a review of UN and global events in his *Annual Report*; however, more can be done to keep key constituencies, such as the Council, fully informed of emerging global trends. For instance, the Secretary-General could formally report to the Security Council every month, after the change through rotation of the Security Council President, upon important developments that he is monitoring throughout the world. These regular monthly presentations could be entitled "Global Watch" reports and would identify key potential issues that should be continually and carefully monitored by the Council and his office.[6]

Finally, the enhanced early warning system provides the Secretary-General with an unparalleled opportunity to present a global vision to Member-States and to the world. He can help focus world attention on the pressing problems of peace in the years ahead. As one UN official points out, ORCI provides him with the capacity to articulate strategic visions and, thus, take a leading role in tackling the root causes of instability in the twenty-first century.[7] He could do this most effectively by enhancing the electronic media outputs through the UN Department of Public Information. Packaged video clips or even a UN cable TV station could be used to present the UN perspective to the world.

Country versus Regional or Subregional Profiles

Another key responsibility of ORCI is to prepare profiles of various regions in the world, including so-called country profiles. Unfortunately, the gathering of country profiles — which requires the gathering of information on every UN member — could become, especially during a crisis, highly controversial and politically unwise. Few countries might be willing to allow the United Nations to gather profiles dealing with sensitive matters, especially within their own borders.

The potential political sensitivity of this issue was demonstrated soon after the office was established. Several U.S. senators objected to ORCI's functions because they suspected that the collection of information could be a cover for gathering secret intelligence. The Secretary-General sought to reassure the senators that only publicly available information would be gathered and analyzed by ORCI. Furthermore, the U.S. mission to the United Nations, headed by the professional diplomat Vernon Walters, quickly reassured the senators that the United States supported the creation of ORCI and was closely monitoring the situation.[8] Although the senators quickly dropped their objections, the incident illustrates the potential political sensitivity of ORCI's conflict identification function.

Because of this, a UN profile system should be planned and organized by using international borders within a specific region as the basic unit of analysis. Such regional or subregional profiles — also mentioned in the ORCI mandate — might include several Member-States of the United Nations.[9] In short, a group or even a pair — such as Iran-Iraq or Israel-Syria — of nation-states are put together using their joint and outermost political boundaries as the basis for the profile. Organizing profiles based upon regional or subregional political boundaries ensures that analysis of incoming information can proceed without violating Article 2, Paragraph 7, of the UN Charter, which states, "Nothing contained in the present Charter shall authorize the United Nations to intervene in matters which are essentially within the domestic jurisdiction of any state."

Furthermore, a growing threat in international affairs is the danger of military incidents in the Earth's commons — the oceans, the polar caps, and outer space.[10] These commons are potential skirmishing grounds during a crisis. As Daniel Deudney of Princeton University points out:

Looking at transparency technologies as the center of superpower strategic competition, it is no surprise that some of the most explosive crisis situations of the cold war have resulted from attacks on sensory platforms — particularly aircraft and ships — in legally ambiguous or overly provocative situations. . . . The archduke Francis Ferdinand of World War III may well be a vital serial or low-orbit sensory platform shot down in some ambiguous situation during a superpower crisis.[11]

Thus, any planning of an early alert system should include an operational ability to monitor the Earth's commons. The UN Secretariat is decidedly weak in this area. The plan to develop an early warning system based on country profiles does little or nothing to improve the situation. (The concept of "electronic offices" in the Security Council could conceivably monitor such situations; we review this idea in Chapter 10.) The regional and subregional profiles could include periodic satellite shots of the commons in the area. (Such satellite information is becoming increasingly available commercially, and this trend will continue.) The subregional profiles should also include analysis of international borders, especially those threatened by political tension or violence. Although lacks and gaps will inevitably occur, such a profile system is a necessary prerequisite for the Secretary-General to fulfill his preventive role.

Early Warning of Developing Situations

A key to effective early warning is to have multiple sources of information. For instance, the information gathered by ORCI according to regional or subregional profiles should not be at the expense of other, already existing, inputs to the Secretary-General's reporting system. If properly integrated into the Secretary-General's early warning system, redundant inputs ensure that, if one profile or input misses important information, another input will note it and report it to the Secretary-General.

Furthermore, although coordination of the various inputs of the Secretary-General's reporting system is desirable, centralization of information management should be avoided. Below the level of the Executive Office of the Secretary-General, no single department should have complete control over all aspects of the early warning system. In short, other inputs can — and should — supplement ORCI's specific functions. For instance, in the U.S. State Department, lower-level officials can issue an alert, which senior officials, their immediate superiors, are obligated to pass on even though they may object or think that the alert is premature.[12] The UN early warning system could operate in a similar way. Such a decentralized system of multiple means ensures that the right information gets to the right person at the right time.

Yet, ORCI need not view itself simply as a center within the United Nations that identifies potential conflicts. The same skills — in-depth familiarity with the local situation and the key actors — that are required in conflict identification can also be very helpful in conflict analysis and intervention. Thus, once a conflict is identified, the ORCI staff should shift its focus and provide an interventionary infrastructure consisting of an expertise in a specific area so that it can aid the Secretary-General in finding a solution to a growing conflict. One way to do this is to make ORCI responsible for intensive consultations with the highly trained and knowledgeable diplomats in the UN community around UN Headquarters in New York. Any promising ideas or new information can then be directly integrated into the Secretary-General's analysis of events.

Monitoring the Global Media

Another key function of ORCI is the responsibility to monitor the world's media. To do this, ORCI has acquired access to several of the world's leading newswire services. They are monitored during the working week, eight hours a day, by staff in the office. This function, formerly located in a department controlled by a Soviet, proved to be quite controversial because the Western powers strongly objected at the time. Not surprisingly, after the location of this media-monitoring function was placed in ORCI, it received strong support from these same countries, including the United States.[13]

At first sight, the monitoring of the media seems rather innocuous if not meaningless; after all, the wire services are a public source of information available to all. Yet, the media is still a valuable source of information. The news services, spread throughout the globe, are often the first to detect long-term trends or impending trouble. Furthermore, a composite analysis that results from a variety of Western, Soviet, and third-world media sources can be a valuable source of data often lacking if one simply uses one country's media. Such composite analyses are currently completed for the Secretary-General; three times during each working day he receives a new bulletin that summarizes significant events around the world. Once a day, he receives a press review, a summary of major editorials dealing with UN affairs from around the globe.

However, major political developments are no respecter of working hours. Obviously, the current eight-hour day, five-day week coverage is simply inadequate if the Secretary-General is to play an important part in anticipating international conflict. For instance, because current coverage is incomplete, the Secretary-General sometimes finds out about important developments as he reads the newspapers on his way to work.[14] In view of his important responsibilities, he must have better and earlier warning of impending events.

To do this effectively, the monitoring of the world's media needs to be expanded within ORCI to 24-hour coverage. This is a major task, involving several different languages and numerous wire services. The first step is to increase coverage to 12 hours a day, then to 24 hours a day, and finally to provide weekend coverage as well. Because of the severe budgetary crisis at the United Nations, this expanded coverage must be done within existing resources. This can be accomplished only gradually because it may require moving staff positions or promotions from other departments.

Given the inadequacy of current coverage, the expanded news service is a modest first step toward upgrading the inputs necessary for effective conflict prevention. The information obtained and made available by the expanded news service will be in the nature of publicly available news reports and unauthenticated wire service reports. No intelligence gathering or analysis will be involved. These reports will simply be related in the form "UPI states . . ." or "Tass reports. . . ." Well-established operating procedures already govern the selection and distribution of this information.

Once comprehensive coverage is established, incoming information can be managed and distributed in a variety of ways. For instance, one suggestion is to use a combined news service/computer relay system. According to the authors of this idea

> Such a project does not require sophisticated data systems, only a facility for the transmission/relay of . . . news service stories through the computer. The computer's data bank would have various "hot words" such as "coup d'etat," "military buildup," "earthquake," etc. If such a word were to arrive in the terminal via the . . . ticker service, the entire news story would be automatically shifted into a "hot file." It could then be forwarded directly to the Secretary-General.[15]

Ideally, a watch officer, who could be permanently on duty, would monitor all incoming information, including contacts from UN diplomatic delegations, and alert, if necessary, the Secretary-General. Currently, there is always someone on duty at the United Nations who can reach the Secretary-General. Perhaps the duties of this person could be expanded to include monitoring the media, when and if the expansion of the news service occurs.

Obviously the incoming information can be utilized in a variety of other ways once it is within the Secretary-General's reporting system. The most important step is to increase coverage of the news services to a comprehensive 24-hour day, every day of the week. Given the importance of accurate and relevant information in conflict prevention, this step is a modest, indeed minimal, goal. Thus, the Secretary-General's current efforts to improve the informational inputs through the expanded news service are admirable and long overdue.

THE IDEAL EARLY WARNING SYSTEM

Because of the United Nations' current (and probably continuing) fiscal crisis, any ideal early warning system must obviously be developed within the constraints of existing financial resources. In order to envision the system of conflict identification that would result if the suggestions made above were implemented, we need to return to the organizing paradigm of the system, the globe. In order to ensure comprehensive coverage, a series of globe-spanning inputs and profiles should be fully integrated into the Secretary-General's early warning system. First, there are the regional, subregional, and issue profiles being developed at UN Headquarters. These profiles include known hot spots as well as ambiguous legal and political situations. They also include, when necessary, coverage of developments upon the Earth's commons — the oceans, the polar caps, and the trust territories.

Second, there are the UN information centres reporting weekly to the ORCI and to the Executive Office of the Secretary-General. Third, there are the permanent diplomatic missions of the UN Member-States in New York City; they provide constant background information and often provide the first hints of impending trouble. Fourth, there are the ad hoc sources of information — the NGO's, the individual scholarly reports, and the unofficial expressions of concern. Then, there are the substantive inputs consisting of the often controversial UN fact-finding teams dispatched by the Security Council or by the General Assembly. There are also the computerized information management systems and data banks — another responsibility of ORCI — that can gather all the information from these various inputs and provide an analysis according to prearranged formulas based upon proven experience and correlations.

Also, as already mentioned, a key input would be the alert system within the UN Secretariat that allows junior officers from any political department, especially those in the field, to "kick upstairs" an early warning alert to the Executive Offices of the Secretary-General without senior officials interfering with or stopping the initiative. A safeguard to this system is to make any such alert part of the junior officer's professional portfolio; thus, a series of false alarms might suggest a pattern of poor judgment that should disqualify the individual from greater responsibilities.

The commons of outer space could be periodically examined and profiled in its entirety by the Outer Space Division in the PSCA. In this way, a global early warning system can be tentatively constructed using existing resources at the United Nations.

Finally, and perhaps more important, there is the Secretary-General himself. He has the key role in conflict prevention through the United Nations. He is at the epicenter of a globe-spanning system of conflict identification. He can focus the entire UN system upon a single potential conflict. He can also mobilize the resources of the UN community and bring them to bear upon a specific problem. His judgment, experience, and intuition are the crucial final ingredients to an effective conflict identification system.

ENHANCING THE ROLE OF THE SECRETARY-GENERAL

Throughout the preceding discussion the preventive role of the UN Secretary-General has been either emphasized or implied. In many ways he is the most important participant and presence in an ongoing and effective early warning system.

Yet, the job of the Secretary-General has steadily grown over the years in terms of its complexity and administrative responsibilities. Currently, the Secretary-General must constantly balance the daily demands of administering the global UN bureaucracy with his crucial diplomatic responsibilities to help prevent war — an almost impossible balancing act. He cannot do either task well indefinitely if his time is constantly divided between major diplomatic and administrative tasks. How, then, can he establish clear priorities?

It must be remembered that a primary purpose in creating the United Nations was, as the Charter Preamble states, to "save succeeding generations from the scourge of war." Consistent with this, a variety of commentators have emphasized that the United Nations is ultimately judged by its ability to prevent international conflict.[16] In view of this, the Secretary-General must view his preventive role as his primary responsibility. To focus on this role the Secretary-General should increasingly delegate some of his day-to-day administrative responsibilities.

Even though he already does this to a great extent, more can be done. The best way to do this is to enhance the political and administrative roles, respectively, of the Chef de Cabinet to the Secretary-General and the Under-Secretary-General for Administration and Management. The UN Charter rightly requires the Secretary-General to be the "chief administrative officer of the Organization" (Article 97 — see Appendix I), but he has, in effect, already delegated much of his daily bureaucratic responsibilities to the Under-Secretary-General for Administration and Management.

This role should be formalized. This Under-Secretary-General, selected for his or her strong administrative and management skills, should have the primary, delegated authority to run the internal administrative affairs of the UN Secretariat. In short, this Under-Secretary-General should be responsible for all routine administrative matters, including complaints, under the direct supervision of the Secretary-General, who retains final authority.

Similarly, the Chef de Cabinet already reviews many of the political and diplomatic matters that come to the Secretary-General's office. This role should also be formalized in the sense that any policy recommendations should be first reviewed by the Chef de Cabinet and then forwarded to the Secretary-General with a specific recommendation. Such policy reviews do not include early warning analyses from ORCI or any other input in the UN system. As mentioned earlier, these go directly to the Secretary-General.

Finally, many of the symbolic duties and meetings of the Secretary-General could be assumed by the Protocol and Liaison Service within the office of the Secretary-General. One way to do this would be to ask a retiring senior diplomat, who has served his or her delegation with distinction, to serve as ambassador or even chancellor of the United Nations. This person would serve under the Chief of Protocol and represent the United Nations at ceremonial functions and receive nongovernmental, or even governmental, delegations that do not address the primary administrative, political, or diplomatic responsibilities of the Secretary-General. Funding for this honorary and temporary position (one or two years) should come from existing pension and office budgets. As is already done, to some extent, at the UN, the presidents of the Security Council and/or the General Assembly could also accept, when appropriate, representative or ceremonial functions. These steps could collectively relieve some of the crushing scheduling problems of the Secretary-General so that he can concentrate on the crucial task of preventing war.

NOTES

1. Although planning for this new office took place in 1986, the mandate for the Office for Research and the Collection of Information (ORCI) was issued shortly after the end of the Secretary-General's first term. See *Office for Research and the Collection of Information,* Secretariat document ST/SGB/225, United Nations, March 1, 1987, New York. Also see UN Press Release, "Secretary-General Announces Structural Modifications Relating to Secretariat Political Functions," March 2, 1987, SG/SM/3970 or G/1051.

2. See UN Press Release, March 2, 1987.

3. For an introduction to the basic "input-analysis-output" model of information management, see John G. Burch, Jr., and Felix R. Strater, Jr., *Information Systems: Theory and Practice* (New York: John Wiley, 1974), Chapter 1. Also see Chapter 3, "Analysis of Systems." See Chris Mader and Robert Hagin,

Information Systems: Technology Economics, Applications (Chicago: Science Research Associates, 1974), p. 3. I am also in debt to their brief discussion of a "simplified information systems model." Also see Henry S. Brinkers (ed.), *Decision-Making: Creativity, Judgement, and Systems* (Columbus: Ohio State University Press, 1972).

4. This area has been identified by Secretary-General Pérez de Cuéllar himself. See his 1982 and 1983 *Annual Reports.* Also see his mandate for ORCI (in note 1).

5. James O. C. Jonah, "Office for Research and the Collection of Information (ORCI): The UN Secretary-General's New Arm of Analytical Information and Early Warning," Unpublished paper presented at UN/Yale Conference, Warsaw, Poland, spring 1989.

6. I use the term "Global Watch" to describe the specific preventive powers of the Secretary-General under Article 99. However, a recent book by The United Nations Association of the United States creatively uses this term to describe an expanded UN watch on a variety of factors that influence international well-being. See Peter J. Fromuth (ed.), *A Successor Vision: The United Nations of Tomorrow* (Boston: University Press of America, 1988).

7. See Tapio Kanninen, "Towards Effective War Risk Reduction within the United Nations Framework," Paper prepared for the Conference on the Reduction of the Risk of War through Multilateral Means, Kingston, Ontario, October 7–8, 1988.

8. Letters from his office to this author in response to an enquiry on this matter, April 29, 1988.

9. I first suggested the use of such "regional or subregional" profiles in my dissertation. My discussion of such a system of profiles became a key resource in the design and development of ORCI. See Thomas E. Boudreau, *Watchman of the Peace: The United Nations Secretary-General and the Prevention of International Armed Conflict,* Ph.D. dissertation, Syracuse University, 1985.

10. See Daniel Deudney, "Whole Earth Security: A Geopolitics of Peace" (Washington, D.C.: Worldwatch Institute, 1983), p. 32.

11. Ibid., p. 32.

12. For a description of how such a junior officer "early alert" system works in U.S. diplomacy, see Thomas G. Belden, "Indicators, Warnings, and Crisis Operations," *International Studies Quarterly 21,* 1 (March 1977). This system is discussed within the context of the United Nations in Thomas E. Boudreau, *Secretary-General and Satellite Diplomacy* (New York: Carnegie Council, 1984), pp. 22–23.

13. Letter from U.S. Mission to United Nations to author, April 29, 1988.

14. Private discussions with senior UN officials.

15. This idea was developed by two Secretariat members of the UN/Yale project on multinuclear diplomacy — David Biggs and Tapio Kanninen. See Tapio Kanninen, "Introducing Systematic Capacity for UN Fact-Finding in Potential Conflict Areas: A Study on the Feasibility to Establish a System of Country Profiles and Early Warning Indicators," Unpublished paper submitted to the Graduate School, City University of New York, June 1983.

16. A number of commentators (including the Secretary-General himself) have made this observation. See, for instance, Adam Roberts and Benedict Kingsbury, *United Nations, Divided World* (Oxford: Clarendon Press, 1988). Also see Mark W. Zacher, *International Conflicts and Collective Security 1946–77* (New York: Praeger, 1979).

8
A MODEST PROPOSAL: IMPROVING THE INPUTS

INTRODUCTION

A variety of proposals have been made during the past several years suggesting ways to enhance the United Nations' ability to gather information about potential crises. I discuss three such "modest" proposals in this chapter: Ambassador Anthony Parsons' call for the United Nations to create temporary UN ambassadors (1983); my own suggestion that the UN membership create both UN Embassies and UN ambassadors (1978, 1980); and Secretary-General Javier Pérez de Cuéllar's decision to use the UN Information Centres as inputs, that is, as means to gather information about potential crisis situations (1983).[1] All three proposals are explored and evaluated in terms of the ideal model of the Secretary-General's early warning system developed in the last chapter. By doing so, we can define their potential contribution in conflict identification more precisely.

THE WEAK LINKS

Portraying the Secretary-General's early warning system as an information systems model allows us to identify the system's "lacks and gaps" that inhibit the gathering, analysis, and distribution of information relevant to conflict identification on a global scale. The Secretary-General has already pinpointed the greatest weakness within the Secretariat; in a section of his 1983 *Annual Report* (that echoes his 1982 report) he states, "I have also, within the Secretariat, initiated steps in order to be alerted in advance to incipient problems. I look forward to working with the Council in order to develop a wider and more systematic capacity for fact-finding in potential conflict areas."[2] Although he does not use the language of systems analysis, the Secretary-General is, in effect, saying that the inputs to his reporting system are the weak links. His efforts over the past few years have been unquestionably focused upon improving the United Nations' ability to gather information throughout the world. During the past several years, there have been a variety of suggestions concerning ways to enhance the gathering of the information needed by the Secretary-General in order to fulfill his responsibilities under Article 99.

ANTHONY PARSONS' CHATHAM HOUSE SPEECH

One of the more interesting proposals that advocated improvements in the inputs was made by Ambassador Anthony Parsons at the Stevenson Memorial Lecture at the London School of Economics/Chatham House on February 15, 1983.[3] Ambassador Parsons represented Great Britain at the United Nations during the period of the Falkland/Malvinas War.

Ambassador Parsons first states that, in order to take preemptive action in coordination with the Security Council, the Secretary-General needs his own sources of information. Ambassador Parsons points out that, at present, the Secretary-General "has to rely for the most part on the public media which can, with great respect, be both inaccurate and lacking."[4]

For the most part, the Secretary-General is "dependent on other people to provide him with the information on which to make his assessment." Parsons sees this as a major problem.

To remedy this situation, Parsons recommends that "UN political presences" be established on a temporary basis in "the major trouble spots of the world." These UN political presences would be headed by individuals called UN ambassadors whose duty it would be to report directly to the Secretary-General: "Their reporting would be confined to assessments of the degree of tension in regional disputes and the danger of the tension rising to the point of conflict."[5]

Although he does not define his proposals in such terms, Ambassador Parsons clearly develops his suggestion concerning UN ambassadors within the context of the Secretary-General's reporting system.[6] The main purpose of the UN ambassador is to report back to the Secretary-General in UN Headquarters about a potential conflict. Armed with relevant information, the Secretary-General could then alert the Security Council about an incipient dispute.

By focusing upon the inputs to the Secretary-General's reporting system, Parsons helps to identify the weaknesses of the present arrangements whereby the Secretary-General is dependent on other people. He is clearly concerned about improving the Secretary-General's access to information concerning potential conflicts. In this sense, his proposal is useful in pointing out the glaring deficiencies of a system that requires the Secretary-General to rely upon the public media for information about a brewing conflict.[7]

Yet, there are formidable legal and political problems with his proposal. First, as Ambassador Parsons is well aware, sending a fact-finding mission or personal representative of the Secretary-General to a potential conflict area is often a sharply controversial political issue, especially within the context of the Security Council.[8] In view of some of the legal problems with this approach, it is hard to see how this might improve information gathering by the Secretary-General. His proposal might simply be an unwanted invitation for the Secretary-General to engage in new and unnecessary political and bureaucratic battles for marginal gains of dubious value.

Furthermore, the responsibilities of the UN ambassador may be too narrowly defined. By limiting his reporting functions solely to "assessments of the degree of tension in regional disputes and the danger of the tension rising to the point of conflict," Parsons prevents the ambassador from reporting upon problems of an economic, environmental, social, cultural, or humanitarian character that may have very important long-term implications for the peaceful prospects in a region.[9] Also, a very limited reporting mandate — confined to tension assessment — would mean that the UN ambassadors operate solely under the jurisdiction of the Security Council. Thus, the potential contribution of UN ambassadors could be heightened by giving them a broader mandate that included peacebuilding as well as peacekeeping or tension assessment functions.[10]

Finally, the temporary nature of the tension assessment will probably be inadequate in terms of ascertaining the long-term trends and causes of potential conflict within a region.[11] There is a need for long-term, continuous reporting and assessments concerning the roots of conflict, including economic, social, and humanitarian aspects; therefore, the inputs to the system — whether they be UN ambassadors or observers — should be placed on a permanent and procedural basis.

In short, the weaknesses of Parsons' proposal are that the mere request by the Secretary-General to place a UN ambassador may cause a hotly contentious political and legal debate, especially if the sole purpose of the UN ambassador is to report to the Secretary-General upon political problems in a major trouble spot in the world; the Security Council may debate the problem to death, as it has done in the past. The reporting of a temporary UN ambassador would be just that — temporary. Such reports provide no institutional opportunity to develop long-term assessments concerning potential disputes, nor does it allow establishing an in-depth analysis and empirical data base concerning the specific problems and personalities involved in a conflict in a certain area. The limited mandate of the temporary UN ambassadors does not permit the consideration of other issues that may play an important role in an incipient conflict.

In view of the difficulties with the temporary nature of Parsons' UN ambassadors, one must wonder if the cure is worse than the disease, especially in terms of raising false expectations that cannot possibly be fulfilled.

MODEST PROPOSAL II: A NEW DIPLOMATIC ORDER

In contrast to Parsons' proposal calling for the dispatch of temporary UN ambassadors, there is the proposal I made several years ago (first published in the fall of 1978 and then revised and republished by the Stanley Foundation in 1980 and circulated throughout the UN community), which called for establishing permanent UN diplomatic posts headed by a UN ambassador.[12] Specifically, I pointed out that a new

Diplomatic Order can grow out of the current field operations of the UN system. Many of the specific preconditions of a new international diplomatic system already exist. The idea of a New International Diplomatic Order offers an integrative approach that will:

(1) promote the consolidation and effectiveness of the growing UN system,

(2) provide the United Nations and its Member-States with greater educational, administrative, and diplomatic capabilities,

(3) help preserve international peace and security.[13]

Recognizing the difficulties of administering and supporting UN diplomatic posts in every state, I suggested, "It might be advisable to implement a UN diplomatic presence by first establishing regional embassies." I went on to elaborate upon the functions of UN Embassies, stating,

In the beginning of a new program such as a UN diplomatic presence, it might be difficult to administer and support diplomatic posts in every Member-State. Therefore, it might be advisable to implement a UN diplomatic presence by first establishing regional embassies. Ideally, regional UN Ambassadors would be available to any Member-State in an area that might have a development problem or request international intervention to settle a dispute. By first establishing regional embassies, the United Nations could test the concept of a UN Embassy and gain valuable experience in the administration of a diplomatic presence. If the regional embassies succeed, then the concept of a universal diplomatic presence would gain credibility.[14]

Admittedly, my proposal has a variety of weaknesses concerning its relevance and feasibility. First, I did not suggest — as Ambassador Parsons did — the use of UN ambassadors (although I used that term) as part of the Secretary-General's reporting system. Even so, I did point out the value that UN ambassadors might have in preventing conflict and aggression. For instance, in discussing the advantages of a UN diplomatic presence, I specifically stated,

A primary incentive for allowing the establishment of a UN presence in a host country would be that the continuous stationing of impartial UN diplomats could, in an unexpected situation of crisis, enhance the security of the host country. The ability of impartial UN observers to preserve a troubled peace has already been proven effective in such crisis situations as Indonesia, Cyprus, Kashmir, and Egypt. . . . However, a peacekeeping presence during a crisis could be replaced or augmented by a continuing UN diplomatic presence to minimize the temptation of aggression against a host country. Such a UN presence could not hope to prevent determined aggression, but the known presence of impartial, international observers might serve to *restrain* any excesses which might accompany aggression. Recognized UN diplomats, armed with film cameras, travel privileges, and diplomatic immunities could act as an added restraint against aggression by virtue of their potential to present the world with a vivid account of the aggressor's activities.[15]

Clearly implied within this passage is the UN diplomat's ability to report to UN Headquarters and even to provide the United Nations with filmed reports, that is, "armed with film cameras."

However, problems with my proposal have become apparent over time. The first is that creating diplomatic posts in potentially every Member-State would be prohibitively expensive. In view of the United Nations' current budgetary difficulties and restraints, it is inconceivable that Member-States would consider, let alone consent, to a universal diplomatic presence. Thus, if such UN posts are ever established, it will probably be on a regional basis.

Second, I am now convinced that labeling these regional UN posts as UN Embassies might be misleading. To argue by analogy that the United Nations should establish an "embassy" might confuse the innovative purposes of such an institution.[16] In view of this, it might be useful to use some other term to describe the permanent posts that are an integral part of the inputs to the Secretary-General's reporting system.

But, before dismissing the analogy entirely, we should take note of some of the interesting — and perhaps useful — characteristics of an international embassy. These characteristics should be carefully examined and considered, especially within the context of the conflict identification by the United Nations.

The first and foremost characteristic that should be carefully considered in this context is the permanence of an embassy. Creating permanent diplomatic posts has had several long-term institutional, legal, and political ramifications. For instance, in his book, *Renaissance Diplomacy,* Garrett Mattingly explains that the development of modern diplomacy began with the exchange of the first permanent posts between the city-states of the Italian peninsula in the late Middle Ages.[17] This meant that temporary (and sometimes "last ditch") diplomatic missions between city-states were increasingly replaced by permanent, procedural institutions. This in turn greatly enhanced the ease and certainty of communications between the ruling elites of different cities and provided an important safety valve in the volatile politics of the era.[18]

Second, and perhaps more important, the creation of permanent posts led to regular reporting from the field back to the sending city or state. The advent of regular reporting had a tremendous impact on the development of diplomacy. As Mattingly points out, regular reporting by the early permanent diplomats of the Italian city-states led to the creation of the first foreign offices and ministries in the home government.[19] The need to analyze reports sent home by diplomats and the opportunity to keep an up-to-date record of one's potential allies or enemies encouraged the development of professional foreign offices with a recognized expertise in foreign affairs.

Third, the inputs — the gathering of information — by these first permanent diplomatic posts became largely a procedural, that is, noncontroversial, matter. First regarded as little better than spying, the regular reporting of permanent diplomats eventually became a routine matter. Of course, spying through diplomatic channels did — and does — occur. Even today, one occasionally hears of the dismissal of a diplomat because of spying activities into sensitive matters of state. However, these abuses should not negate the fact that a vast amount of helpful information is now procedurally processed through diplomatic channels throughout the world. In fact, providing information to the home government is one of the primary duties of the permanent ambassador of a nation-state. Speaking of the U.S. diplomatic service, Thomas Bailey states, "A primary duty of the ambassador is to send home to Washington detailed descriptions and analyses of what is going on in the host country in reports (dispatches) that are prompt, clear, candid, succinct, interesting, comprehensive and accurate."[20]

Bailey's comment is useful in pointing out that diplomatic reports have become a procedural matter, often far removed from the fiery political debates concerning ideology or policy. Such reports are often limited to providing facts. Similarly, if information gathering by the Secretary-General is to be useful or even possible, it must be placed on a procedural basis as well and must be as free as possible from debilitating political debate. Gathering information in a potential conflict situation must become part of the rules of the game in international affairs.[21]

Although the term "UN Embassy" might be misleading, there are decided advantages in incorporating some of an embassy's characteristics and procedures into the Secretary-General's reporting system. The greatest advantage may well be the development of regular, procedural reporting that requires constant interpretation and analysis in UN Headquarters. This information can be shared, in turn, with the relevant UN organs. The question then becomes, "How could permanent and procedural 'inputs' to the Secretary-General's reporting system be created and administered, and what would they be called?"

MODESTY OR ELEGANCE?: SECRETARY-GENERAL PÉREZ DE CUÉLLAR'S PROPOSAL

As has been mentioned in Chapter 5, Secretary-General Pérez de Cuéllar recently instituted a major reform in order to enhance his early warning system. He requested that the directors of the UN Information Centres, who are stationed around the world, submit a "weekly regional report on peace and security" to the Executive Office of the Secretary-General.[22]

This reform represents a bold institutional innovation because an entirely new information flow into the UN Secretariat has been created.[23] The Information Centres have suddenly become supplementary sources of information within the Secretary-General's reporting system. Before the Secretary-General's reform, the Information Centres had primarily served as distributors — outputs — of news from the United Nations.

In view of the preceding discussion on Ambassador Parsons' and my "modest" proposals, the advantages of the centres as procedural inputs becomes immediately apparent. A key advantage is that such inputs avoid the often lengthy political debates that precede sending UN fact-finding teams to a specific region. The political costs of these efforts are such that they are rarely used; they simply engender too much controversy. In contrast, procedural inputs are already beyond the purview of substantive debate within the Security Council or General Assembly.[24] They thus avoid the political bloodletting that is often associated with other methods of information gathering by the UN Secretariat.

Also, the Information Centres provide continuous information to the Secretary-General; they do not disband or disappear once a report is issued — as do ad hoc field missions.[25] In fact, some of the more recent UN agreements with host countries specifically provide for the permanency of the centres. Even without this permanency being mentioned, both the United Nations and the host governments seem to assume that such centres shall exist indefinitely within the borders of the host country. The permanency of the centres is not explicitly provided for, but it is presumed.[26] In short, the Information Centres can be construed as both procedural and permanent inputs to the Secretary-General's reporting system.

Furthermore, the potentially contentious debate concerning the creation of UN Embassies or a temporary UN presence is completely avoided by this reform — even though the UN Information Centres now fulfill many of the proposed functions of a UN diplomatic presence.[27] Specifically, the director of the UN Information Centre can serve as an international observer who bears witness to the international interest in preventing or peacefully solving potential crises peacefully.[28]

As we have seen, Parsons' proposal — that the Secretary-General use temporary UN ambassadors on special assignments — does not fulfill the need for a permanent, procedural reporting system; in fact, it does the opposite. It precludes the development of such a system by offering an alternative that promises to get embroiled in the daily political battles at the United Nations. The simple appointment of such an ambassador, or the Secretary-General's announcement that he intends to send an ambassador to a major trouble spot, will almost inevitably cause a sharp debate within the contentious Security Council. A major power watching over its client's interests in a conflict may interpret establishing a special mission and sending out ambassadors to a troubled area as interference or as providing recognition to a party on the other side. Because of this reaction, it is eminently desirable to establish a permanent and procedural process for continuous conflict identification by UN Secretarial personnel.

Another key advantage of the Information Centres is that they already constitute a worldwide network of inputs. There are over 60 centres, including ones in South America, Africa, the Middle East, and throughout Asia.[29] By using the centres to assess public information, the Secretary-General simply restructures an institutional resource in such a way as to maximize UN coverage of potential crisis situations while minimizing new organizational expenses. In effect, the Secretary-General has created a truly global early warning system out of existing resources — a truly innovative administrative feat.

Finally, the Information Centres promise to provide what up to now the Secretary-General has sorely lacked — a system of regular regional reporting from the field. The importance of regular reporting to the emergence of modern diplomacy has already been discussed. The need for such reporting was also emphasized by Ambassador Parsons. My proposal calling for UN Embassies develops an elaborate scheme that could be used to gather such regular reports, although at much greater cost. In contrast, the Secretary-General's decision to use the Information Centres as inputs provides what is, in essence, an elegantly simple and inexpensive way of ensuring regular reports from around the world — without (so far) the enormous political costs and controversy that might be associated with the use of ad hoc UN ambassadors or embassies. The use of UN Information Centres as inputs ensures that expenses are kept to a minimum while providing worldwide regional coverage of potential crisis situations. Thus the superiority of the Secretary-General's reform becomes immediately apparent. I cannot speak for Ambassador Parsons, but I am gladly willing to concede that the Secretary-General's use of Information Centres is a much better, and less controversial, arrangement than other proposals. In effect, he is creating a worldwide system of inputs that provides a truly comprehensive early warning system within the UN Secretariat — something that has been lacking and sorely needed.

If this reform is adopted and institutionally develops, then an entirely new dimension of international diplomacy can be anticipated. The UN Secretary-General will possess a truly worldwide system of early warning inputs that can help keep his office fully informed about incipient conflicts. Such a permanent and procedural system of inputs will enable him to fulfill his obligation under the Charter to stay fully informed about matters that might threaten the maintenance of international peace and security. If this occurs — and there are signs that the reform is succeeding — then the adequacy of the inputs into the Secretary-General's reporting system will be no longer the subject of sharp debates or of modest proposals.

NOTES

1. I first developed the idea of UN ambassadors, and of UN Embassies in Thomas E. Boudreau, "United Nations Diplomacy: An Immediate and Ultimate Need," *Unified World 12* (September 1978). I was entering my first year of graduate

school and was unaware that Waldheim had privately made a similar proposal at about the same time. My revised essay was also republished as "A New International Diplomatic Order," Occasional Paper #24, The Stanley Foundation (1980) (hereafter referred to as "NIDO"). Ambassador Parsons also discussed the idea of UN ambassadors in his Stevenson Memorial Lecture at the London School of Economics/Chatham House on February 15, 1983. See G. R. Berridge and A. Jennings (eds.), *Diplomacy at the UN* (New York: St. Martin's Press, 1985), pp. 48–58.

2. Javier Pérez de Cuéllar, *Report of The Secretary-General on the Work of the Organization 1983*. Available through Public Inquiries at the United Nations.

3. Reported in *Diplomacy at the UN,* pp. 48–58.

4. Ibid.

5. Ibid.

6. Parsons does not use the term "reporting system," nor does he analyze information gathering by the UN Secretary-General in terms of inputs, analysis, and outputs. Even so, he does explicitly link the responsibilities of the UN ambassador to information gathering for the Secretary-General. Thus, I evaluate his proposal in this section in terms of the model I developed in Chapter 6. See Parsons in *Diplomacy at the UN,* pp. 48–58.

7. Ibid. Parsons' speech helped to draw public attention to the glaring inadequacies of the United Nations' information-gathering capabilities.

8. A classic example of the divisive arguments that often occur when a Member-State suggests that the United Nations send out a fact-finding team, or information-gathering mission, is the Laos debate in 1959. For the Laos debate see UN *SCOR* 847 Meeting, September 7, 1959, p. 8; UN *SCOR* 848 Meeting, September 7, 1959, pp. 1–30.

9. In Thomas E. Boudreau, *Protecting the Innocent: Enhancing the Humanitarian Role of the United Nations in Natural Disasters and Other Disaster Situations* (New York: The Council on Religion and International Affairs, 1983), I talk about the role that the General Assembly can play in promoting international peace and security precisely because its mandate is larger than that of the Security Council. I specifically mentioned the need to enquire into successful economic, social, cultural, educational, and health programs in order to promote greater international awareness. By limiting mandates to issues dealing solely with conflict, the United Nations can impose restraints upon itself that make it impossible for the staff or the organization as a whole to take a more effective role in conflict prevention.

10. Boudreau, *Protecting the Innocent,* p. 15. I discuss the idea of roving regional representatives with a broad mandate that would report to UN Headquarters.

11. A senior UN official within the Executive Office of the Secretary-General has stressed to me the importance of "ascertaining the long-term trends" within a particular region. These trends become apparent only through regular reporting that is systematically evaluated in terms of their implications for international peace and security.

12. Boudreau, "NIDO," passim.

13. Ibid., p. 5.

14. Ibid., pp. 12–13. I also recommend such regional arrangements in Boudreau, *Protecting the Innocent,* pp. 14–15.

15. Boudreau, "NIDO," pp. 17–18.

16. The most comprehensive treatment of modern diplomacy is to be found in the Vienna Convention on Diplomatic Relations, which was signed on April 18, 1961, at a conference of 81 states. It entered into force on April 24, 1964. Also see E. Denza, *Diplomatic Law: Commentary on the Vienna Convention on Diplomatic*

Relations (New York: Oceana, 1976); A. Watson, *Diplomacy: The Dialogue between States* (London: Eyre Methuen, 1982); Hans Morgenthau, *Politics among Nations* (New York: Alfred A. Knopf, 1967). The legal meaning and scope of diplomatic functions, including that of an embassy, are extensively discussed in the convention and the commentaries cited above.

17. Garrett Mattingly, *Renaissance Diplomacy* (Cambridge: Riverside Press, 1955), p. 71. Mattingly's discussion of diplomacy during these times is the classic in the field.

18. Ibid.

19. Ibid., pp. 109–11. This evolution is an interesting example of institutional development. Mattingly discusses how the placement of the first permanent diplomats in the field created the need to have home offices that could receive and analyze the diplomats' returning reports. This led to establishing the first foreign ministries.

20. Thomas Bailey, *The Art of Diplomacy: The American Experience* (New York: Appleton-Century-Crofts, 1968), Chapter 3.

21. Admittedly, this is unlikely, even though such a development would be consistent with the UN Charter, especially with Article 99.

22. This innovation by the Secretary-General is fully discussed in Chapter 5 above. Also see Thomas E. Boudreau, *The Secretary-General and Satellite Diplomacy* (New York: Carnegie Council on Ethics and International Affairs, 1984).

23. Ibid.

24. By definition, a procedural input provides information that is obtained by an official UN agency or operation or by UN personnel permanently stationed in the field. The regular, routine reports sent back to UN Headquarters by such personnel are not subject to substantive debate within the Security Council. In short, regular reporting from the field is not a substantive question subject to a veto. See Chapter 6 above.

25. For example, the Secretary-General's mission to Lesotho — sent in the wake of the December 1982 South African attack on that country — was simply a temporary task force that was disbanded once its final report was issued. See "Assistance to Lesotho: Report of the Secretary-General," S/15600, February 9, 1983.

26. The United Nations does legally have permanent posts in host nations; the UNDP renegotiated its Standard Basic Agreements (SBA), which govern the field operations of the resident representatives with the governments of Member-States. The new SBA specifically states that the "UNDP may maintain a *permanent* mission, headed by a resident representative, in the country." See UNDP/ADM/LEG/39 rev. 13, January 22, 1980.

27. Boudreau, "NIDO," pp. 17–18.

28. Ibid.

29. See Peter I. Hajnal, *Guide to United Nations Organization, Documentation & Publishing* (Dobbs Ferry, NY: Oceana Publications, 1978), Chapter 12, "United Nations Information Centres."

9

AN OUNCE OF PREVENTION: ENHANCING THIRD-PARTY INTERVENTION

THE ANALYSIS INTERVENTION STAGE

After a potential conflict is identified by the early warning system, the incoming information must be analyzed by the UN Secretariat. This is where the preventive role of the Secretary-General takes on its greatest significance and where conflict prevention takes place — if it occurs at all. If an impending conflict is judged to be a threat to international peace and security, the Secretary-General must decide upon an intervention strategy based upon the information he has received. In many ways this is the most sensitive stage of the Secretary-General's preventive role.

Of course, such analysis and intervention already occur within the UN Secretariat. Yet, this stage of the information flow through the Secretariat has not been theoretically or operationally organized in an adequate fashion, particularly in reference to its crucial role in conflict prevention.[1] In this chapter, we examine several sequential steps the Secretary-General can take to prevent conflicts. These steps occur in the analysis/intervention stage of the Secretary-General's preventive role. The words "analysis" and "intervention" will be used interchangeably because the two processes become identical in a successful preventive effort by the Secretary-General.

From a theoretical perspective, four possible procedural steps are involved in the progressive efforts by the Secretary-General to prevent a conflict. The word "procedural" is emphasized because the implementation of the various intermediary stages should become automatic once a potential conflict situation is identified. If the conflict cannot be prevented at the first level of analysis, the second level should be automatically activated. This automatic escalation of the various levels is the basis for procedural prevention through the Executive Office of the Secretary-General.

UN INFORMATION TEAMS (UNITS): THE FIRST LEVEL OF ANALYSIS

As already mentioned, conflict identification occurs through the early warning system; however, this statement is only partially accurate. Within the context of the United Nations, conflict identification has not really occurred until the Secretary-General — having been alerted to a specific situation by incoming information by senior staff, by diplomats in private consultation, or by his own critical evaluation of events — assigns a department or specific office within the UN Secretariat the responsibility to act upon all incoming information relevant to the incipient dispute. Or, the Secretary-General can create an ad hoc unit — such as a UN interdepartmental or interagency team — to analyze information and events. By assigning a potential conflict to an existing department or to an ad hoc unit, the Secretary-General ensures that he has informed himself should more extensive preventive procedures become necessary.

Ongoing analyses of this nature are already done on a routine basis within the Secretariat. For example, all information dealing with UN peacekeeping operations is directed toward the Office of the Under-Secretary-General for Special Political Affairs. Because most peacekeeping operations are on a fixed-term mandate from the Security Council, this office has to analyze all relevant information and prepare periodic reports for review by the Secretary-General. If the Secretary-General approves the report, it is submitted to the Security Council for its review and approval as well. Thus, this office has "major reporting functions, including the drafting of reports of the Secretary-General and to the General Assembly. This office is also responsible for the drafting of other documents, including a variety of policy statements, press statements and speeches."[2]

Informal discussions with the diplomats of Member-States assigned to the United Nations are often important sources of information concerning potential crises. Diplomats can alert the Secretary-General to a growing problem, as well as explore with him the terms of a possible solution. Without the approval of their host government, UN diplomats may not be able to negotiate a settlement to an incipient dispute; but they can and do serve as an early warning system that provides important clues to an emerging conflict.

This initial stage of intervention and analysis is often the most appropriate level for planning long-term efforts to promote social and economic development. As mentioned in Chapter 1, the Secretary-General's preventive responsibilities must encompass areas of the world where threats to the peace exist because of hunger, poverty, or the abuse of humanitarian law. Located in the center of the UN system, his office can be a powerful catalyst in mobilizing positive sanctions, developmental aid, and humanitarian relief. This is peacebuilding through international cooperation — one of the most promising ways to prevent conflicts in the future. As such, organizing interdepartmental or interagency teams for these purposes is fully consistent with his preventive role.

This first level of analysis in the UN Secretariat is important in determining whether a potential threat to international peace exists and, if so, its size and scope. More information may be required in order to obtain a more complete picture of the situation. If this is the case, then the information search must be intensified by initiating the second level of analysis — direct consultations with the relevant governments, regimes, or ethnic groups (such as in Cyprus) involved in a potential dispute.

CONSULTATIONS: THE SECOND LEVEL OF ANALYSIS AND INTERVENTION

United Nations Consultations involve direct talks between the Secretary-General and his senior staff with senior officials of the governments or regimes involved in a potential conflict situation. These consultations can occur either in the capitals of the governments concerned or at UN Headquarters in New York.

The purpose of these consultations is to solicit the views of senior governmental policy makers, experts, and significant regional ethnic leaders concerning an incipient conflict. The consultations also enable the Secretary-General and his staff to keep fully informed about a developing situation. They are often informal or confidential and provide the UN Secretariat with a realistic understanding of the problems and possibilities of peace in a specific area. It should be emphasized that such consultations already occur; however, their potential role in conflict prevention is rarely emphasized.[3] It may well be desirable that these consultations become a routine and procedural matter whenever a potential conflict is identified.

One possible effect of these consultations is to increase the integrative complexity of information that is being processed through the UN Secretariat. Integrative complexity is "a dimension of information processing characterized at one pole by simple responses, gross distinctions, rigidity and restricted information usage, and at the other by complexity, fine distinctions, flexibility and extensive information search and usage."[4] This theory was developed by Peter Suedfeld and Philip Tetlock in order to analyze communications within and between governments before two intense international crises: the summer of 1914 and the fall of 1962. They found that "complexity of the messages produced by government leaders was significantly lower in crises that ended in war. As the crisis approached its climax, complexity declined in 1914 and increased in 1962."[5] Suedfeld and Tetlock believe that the results of their study demonstrate the "usefulness of information processing complexity, which can be measured objectively in a wide variety of materials, for analyzing political and diplomatic events."[6]

Suedfeld and Tetlock's research concerning the integrative complexity of information provides a useful means of measuring and evaluating the information gathered by UN inputs. Ideally, the various levels of analysis would result in the increased complexity of information processing that will allow the Secretary-General — as well as the relevant diplomatic delegations — to find possible policy alternatives, salient escalation controls, and even solutions to an incipient confrontation. In short, one purpose of the consultation level of analysis is to enhance the integrative complexity of information processing between potential adversaries. If this effort is successful, then the likelihood that an incipient conflict can be prevented, not just identified, is increased.

The primary purpose of the consultations is to keep Secretariat officials, especially the Secretary-General, better informed about potential conflict situations. These consultations are exploratory and enable the Secretary-General to fulfill his obligation under Article 99 to keep himself fully informed about possible threats to the peace. If the Secretary-General suspects that such a threat may exist, he can intensify his search for a potential solution by formally offering his good offices.

THE SECRETARY-GENERAL'S GOOD OFFICES: THE THIRD LEVEL OF ANALYSIS AND INTERVENTION

The third level of analysis and intervention involves the use of the Secretary-General's good offices in order to defuse a potential conflict situation. This level has been very adequately described by Vratislav Pechota in his UNITAR study entitled *The Quiet Approach: A Study of the Good Offices Exercised by the United Nations Secretary-General in the Cause of Peace.*[7]

Pechota points out that the "Secretary-General's good offices are essentially of two types: those he undertakes in pursuance of a request from a competent organ of the United Nations, and those he himself decides to undertake within the competence of his office."[8]

The primary purpose of the Secretary-General's good offices is to serve the parties directly involved in a brewing dispute. Yet, it should not be overlooked that the Secretary-General can gather a great deal of relevant information through the exercise of his good offices. Often, the information he receives cannot be disclosed. Even so, it enables him to keep himself fully informed about a potential conflict situation and to try to do something to avert war. This is why his good offices have evolved into "an effective and in some respects unrivalled instrument for settling international disputes peacefully."[9]

When effective, the exercise of the Secretary-General's good offices almost inevitably increases the integrative complexity of information. This is because policy decisions become better informed as nuances are understood and explored, as rigid images are challenged, and as judgments become conceptually more complex. In short, the exercise of the Secretary-General's good offices can help overcome — in a polite and procedural way — the rigid world views of political leaders that sometimes contribute to increasing tension and conflict.

Unfortunately, the limitations of the Secretary-General's good offices are often quite pronounced. First, the exercise of these offices often requires the direct participation of the Secretary-General in all important negotiations. Obviously, this limits the number of issues in which the Secretary-General can intervene — there is simply so much that one person can do. Second, there are only a limited number of people involved in the negotiations. Whereas this has distinct advantages in terms of ensuring privacy and confidentiality, it also limits the amount of information, experience, and creative problem solving that can be brought to bear on a pressing problem. Finally, the exercise of the Secretary-General's good offices does not provide any support for the implementation of an agreement; the parties themselves are required to implement this solution. Unfortunately, parties locked together in a conflict often need the help of a third party to legitimate and even orchestrate a peaceful settlement. As already briefly discussed, this was one of the key missing factors in the Falkland/Malvinas War.

The limitations of the Secretary-General's good offices are not unique and reflect many of the problems found in traditional diplomatic approaches to conflict prevention. For instance, Suedfeld and Tetlock analyze information that results from only three major types of diplomatic interactions during a crisis: the interactions between the leaders within a government and interactions between leaders of opposing governments. In the case of the 1914 crisis, they also examine a third type: interactions between leaders of allied nations. They then scored the written communications that resulted from these three types of interactions according to their integrative complexity.[10]

Their analysis does not account for, or measure, the integrative complexity of information that is communicated between or among a group or team of third-party negotiators. This is a significant omission, because for the purposes of our current discussion, that is, the good offices of the Secretary-General, such interactions are crucial. In short, several other types of interactions that were not a factor and were not mentioned by Suedfeld and Tetlock can be promoted through the use of the Secretary-General's intervention. These are: interactions between executive decision makers and third-party negotiators; interactions between diplomatic representatives of executive decision makers and third-party negotiators; interactions between third-party negotiators and allies of the governments locked together in confrontation; and interactions among the third-party negotiators themselves, that is, the Secretary-General and his staff, including those at UN Headquarters and those in the field.

It is important to identify these seven types of interactions in order to emphasize the possible locus points where the analysis and integrative complexity of information relevant to conflict prevention can be enhanced. An ideal negotiating framework is obviously one that encourages all seven types of diplomatic interactions during an incipient conflict or crisis. To rely primarily, or even solely, upon simply a few modes of interaction can impoverish the search for a diplomatic solution by failing to bring to bear all the potential diplomatic resources available. The specific problem then becomes one of mobilizing all possible diplomatic interactions within the context of the Secretary-General's preventive role in order to enhance the integrative complexity of information concerning a crisis and, thus, try to prevent war.

The Secretary-General's good offices, however, do not always manage to mobilize all seven types of diplomatic interactions.[11] What is specifically needed is a systematic way to ensure that all these major types of diplomatic interactions, which are also crucial information exchanges, occur during an incipient crisis. This is the purpose of the UN framework for international negotiations, which we will discuss in the following section.

A UN FRAMEWORK FOR INTERNATIONAL NEGOTIATIONS (UNFIN)

Sometimes the Secretary-General's good offices fail to bridge the widening gulf between governments and/or political parties, and the threat of military hostilities becomes more imminent. If the preceding steps of procedural prevention fail, the Secretary-General could, in close consultation with the Security Council, implement a framework for international negotiations that deliberately intensifies the search for all relevant information and possible solutions, especially when the danger of war seems to be growing.[12] In such situations, the Secretary-General has an obligation to keep himself fully informed about unfolding events and to try to enhance the integrative complexity of information so that the potential conflict can be avoided.

A UN framework for international negotiations (UNFIN) consists of the following procedures, which can be implemented on the outset of a crisis, that is, a situation in which time is short, basic interests are at stake, and the danger of war grows. It consists of the following steps:

The dispatch of UN negotiators, headed by an Under-Secretary-General or diplomat of comparable rank to the capitals of the potential adversaries during the first hours of the crisis.

The creation of alternative channels of communications between the ruling elites of the potential adversaries via these negotiating teams and the Executive Office of the Secretary-General's Office.

The mobilization of the diplomatic communities in the conflicting capitals of the potential adversaries and in New York City to aid in the UN effort to defuse the crisis and to help develop proposals for ending it.

The introduction of these proposals by the Secretary-General into the ongoing bilateral negotiations.

A commitment by the United Nations to help implement any agreement between potential adversaries designed to reduce tensions, including verifications procedures.[13]

The use of UN negotiation teams is based, in part, upon three past practices involving missions by the Secretary-General or his staff overseas. The first precedent is Dag Hammarskjöld's trip to Peking, which resulted, eventually, in the release of 11 captured U.S. airmen. Hammarskjöld argued that his trip to the People's Republic of China, which did not belong to the United Nations at the time, was based upon his authority under the Charter and was not based upon the instructions given to him by the General Assembly on the matter.[14] This interpretation of the Secretary-General's preventive role resulted in the famous Peking Formula. As Mark Zacher explains, "The essence of this formula [is] that when a state does not recognize the authority of the Security Council or the General Assembly which the Secretary-General has been asked to try to implement, *he can request and undertake negotiations under his independent diplomatic powers flowing from the Charter.*"[15] (Emphasis added.)

A second historical precedent that supports the use of UN negotiating teams is the concept of a UN presence. Dr. Ralph Bunche, the former Under-Secretary-General for Special Political Affairs and a Nobel Peace Prize winner, explained, "The important aim of the UN 'presence' is the establishment of some sort of UN arrangement on the spot with the purpose of watching local developments, holding a finger on the pulse *and keeping UN*

Headquarters fully informed about developments in the area."[16] (Emphasis added.) This definition of a UN presence would apply to UN negotiating teams as well. One purpose of such teams would be to gather information and to keep UN Headquarters fully informed about important developments.

A third historical precedent that applies to UNFIN is the use of a personal representative by the Secretary-General. Such representatives have been used in the past to carry out the Secretary-General's good offices. As Pechota explains, "The appointment of personal representatives . . . who will assist the parties to a dispute to resolve their problems, seems to be subject to only two requirements: consent by the parties concerned and notification to the Security Council of the decision."[17] Such personal representatives have been appointed by the Secretary-General in a number of potential conflict situations.

The purpose of UNFIN is to intensify the search for relevant information and possible solutions by mobilizing the diplomatic community, as well as all possible political and technical support in order to avoid war.

It should be emphasized that the very presence and participation of UN negotiators in ongoing discussions between potential adversaries can serve as a moderating influence.[18] They can also strengthen the hand of governmental leaders who urge conciliation because during the incipient stages of a crisis there are often competing centers of policy and power within each government involved in a confrontation. Some high-ranking government officials may favor conciliation while others may favor force. Diplomatic communications through regular channels do not always identify these competing centers of power, and diplomats cannot always support those officials who favor conciliation. However, when located in the capitals of countries in conflict, high-ranking international diplomats are in a unique position to identify and strengthen the voice of conciliatory government leaders. It is thus important that UN officials representing the Secretary-General go directly to the leaders of the nations locked into a confrontation and communicate, via diplomatic pouch, personal visits, or on secure communications channels, back to UN Headquarters in New York.

A UN framework for international negotiations can also enhance the integrative complexity of information flowing between political leaders and international negotiators. The research of Graham Allison, Peter Suedfeld, and Philip Tetlock suggests that effective crisis diplomacy requires multiple points of contact and communications between governments during a crisis.[19] To rely upon a single type, or source, of communication and information is to court disaster because important nuances of meaning tend to be transmitted ineffectively amid the inevitable "noise" of the crisis. Of course, negotiations directly between two potential adversaries will always have the greatest weight and significance, especially during a crisis; however, third-party intervention by the Secretary-General can create supplementary channels of communication that ensure that all options are fully explored and adequately considered by national policy makers.[20] Thus, as part of the framework, the Secretary-General should strive to create, in effect, additional channels of communication and information. However, this will require, among other things, a significant upgrading of the United Nations' current communication capacity, now limited to a spotty satellite, radio, and telex network.

The underlying assumptions for increasing diplomatic interactions are that such interactions between experienced diplomats and a primary mediator, such as the Secretary-General, can help broaden the base of negotiations by increasing the number of alternatives considered, increase the information search and information processing of the UN Secretariat, ensure that all political and diplomatic perspectives are considered during crises when time is very short, and ensure that all possible solutions are explored.

If this is done, the problem then becomes one of mobilizing the diverse diplomatic interactions (and decision maker interactions) at an early enough stage in a crisis so that the integrative complexity of information can be maximized. A UN framework for negotiations is one way to do this and thus ensure that all peaceful options are fully explored before a gauntlet is finally flung.

NOTES

1. The need for such systematic organization is discussed within the context of the United Nations in Thomas E. Boudreau, *Secretary-General and Satellite Diplomacy* (New York: Carnegie Council on Ethics and International Affairs, 1984).

2. UN Doc. A/C.5/32/15.

3. See Ronald Fisher, "Third-Party Consultation as a Method of Intergroup Conflict Resolution," *Journal of Conflict Resolution 27,* 2 (June 1983). For a related study, also see F. Y. Chai, *Consultations and Consensus in the Security Council* (New York: UNITAR, 1971).

4. Peter Suedfeld and Philip Tetlock, "Integrative Complexity of Communications in International Crises," *Journal of Conflict Resolution, 21,* 1 (March 1977). See also H. M. Schroder, M. J. Driver, and S. Streufert, *Human Information Processing* (New York: Holt, Rinehart & Winston, 1967).

5. Suedfeld and Tetlock, "Integrative Complexity," p. 169.

6. Ibid.

7. Vratislav Pechota, *The Quiet Approach: A Study of the Good Offices Exercised by the United Nations Secretary-General in the Cause of Peace* (New York: UNITAR, 1972).

8. Ibid., p. 2.

9. Ibid.

10. Suedfeld and Tetlock, "Integrative Complexity," p. 169.

11. Pechota, *The Quiet Approach,* passim. For instance, Pechota does not discuss the possibility of third-party negotiating teams talking among themselves, nor does he discuss the possibility of such teams talking with allies of the parties involved. Of course, because the use of such teams is a relatively new idea within the context of the United Nations, these possibilities go beyond the traditional application of the Secretary-General's good offices.

12. The idea of a UN framework for international negotiations (UNFIN) was first discussed in an international context in Thomas E. Boudreau, "Buying Time in a Crisis," *WORLDVIEW,* November 1983. The idea comes from an Iroquois technique of conflict resolution. The Iroquois Indians, who live throughout upstate New York, are governed by the oldest constitution in the Western world, "The Great Law of Peace." Hence, they have extensive experience in conflict resolution and frequently travel abroad on their own passports. Their confederacy is an example of one of the most successful political unions on earth, and it has much to teach those who still struggle for peace in a politically fragmented world. (Based on personal interviews 1982–1984.)

13. Boudreau, "Buying Time in a Crisis," passim.

14. See Chapter 3; also see Mark Zacher, *Dag Hammarskjöld's United Nations* (New York: Columbia University Press, 1970).

15. Zacher, *Dag Hammarskjöld,* p. 128.

16. Brian Urquhart, *Hammarskjöld* (New York: Alfred A. Knopf, 1973), p. 294.

17. Pechota, *The Quiet Approach,* p. 74.

18. J. A. Rubin and B. R. Brown, *The Social Psychology of Bargaining and Negotiation* (New York: Academic Press, 1975).

19. Suedfeld and Tetlock, "Integrative Complexity," p. 169. See also Graham T. Allison, *Essence of Decision: Explaining the Cuban Missile Crisis* (Boston: Little, Brown, 1971).

20. This is assuming that the Secretary-General is invited to intervene and that the Secretary-General and his staff are not overwhelmed by the "noise" and rumors that inevitably surround and suffuse any serious diplomatic negotiations. I call this the "wheat/chaff" problem of diplomacy.

10

SATELLITE DIPLOMACY:
AN ANALYSIS OF
UN COMMUNICATIONS

And thefts from satellites and rings
And broken star I drew,
And out of spent and aged things
I formed the world anew.

— Ralph Waldo Emerson
Songs of Nature

BACKGROUND: CURRENT COMMUNICATIONS

The Secretary-General cannot exercise his preventive role effectively without adequate global communications. Yet, opponents of the United Nations can derive great satisfaction from the knowledge that many modern corporations in midtown Manhattan have greater international communication systems than does the entire UN organization. The current UN communication system is barely adequate for a global organization. It is clearly inadequate for communicating with potential conflict areas.[1]

Although the UN Secretariat is now far more aware of this problem than previously, and important changes are being contemplated, most UN Member-States do not consider improvements in this area a top priority.[2] Until they do, the technical state of UN communications will continue to be an embarrassment to the organization.

For instance, the Secretary-General currently lacks the ability to communicate from UN Headquarters on secure channels with his representatives in the field, especially when these representatives stray beyond the spotty UN radio and satellite network. The United Nations has only recently acquired a modest satellite communication channel linking, via Geneva, the Secretariat in New York with peacekeeping operations in the Middle East. Thus, given the current technical capacity of UN communications, the Secretary-General would be unable to communicate on a real-time basis with most of his senior officials engaged in sensitive consultations overseas or with UN negotiating teams during a crisis.

The primitive nature of UN communications presents profound problems for any effort by the Secretary-General during an incipient conflict. For instance, if the Secretary-General had to confirm or deny information about a suddenly developing crisis in Asia or Africa, his ability to intervene effectively could be outstripped by fast-paced events — unless he had adequate means of gathering information and communicating with the leaders of the countries involved.

Such a state of affairs in UN communications is simply unacceptable, especially if Member-States are serious about entrusting the Secretary-General with important preventive tasks. In order to correct this situation, Member-States must lend their support to a program to upgrade immediately the telecommunications capacity of the United Nations.

The need for access to a global network of telecommunications is especially acute. Although it has been several decades since the launching of Sputnik, the United Nations still has no access to a comprehensive global satellite system — even though many departlments within the Secretariat are eager to obtain this capacity. It would be neither difficult nor unduly expensive to lease the services of an existing international satellite consortium and, thus, quickly acquire a truly global telecommunications system. Such a simple step can take UN telecommunications from pay phone diplomacy to the space age.

"WHERE ARE THE MAPS": THE NEED FOR DATA BANKS

As the Falkland/Malvinas crisis erupted in the spring of 1982, the UN Secretariat made a startling discovery — there were no maps of the islands at UN Headquarters. Indeed, there is not a set of detailed maps available at the United Nations for many potential hot spots in the world.

To correct this, a centralized computer data set — or data bank — should be developed at UN Headquarters to deal specifically with conflict prevention.[3] This data bank, located within the new Office of Research and the Collection of Information, could be organized into three general subsets. First, there could be a data index containing the citations of all UN documentation concerning specific disputes or potential conflicts that have been or are under active consideration by the UN Security Council. Furthermore, there should be a data index of relevant research on conflict prevention by the various departments of the Secretariat, such as UNITAR, and by private universities or scholars around the world. Much of this data already exists in bits and pieces in various UN departments, such as the Dag Hammarskjöld Library. The collection of this data in an indexed computer bank is simply a more efficient way to make the information available. The Information Systems Division already has the computer facilities needed to organize and operate such a data bank — as well as a limited data set already on file that is used by the Department for Disarmament Affairs for research purposes. A third key data bank must be a comprehensive collection of detailed maps for the entire Earth. Such information is readily available, relatively inexpensive, and — as the Falkland/Malvinas crisis illustrates — urgently needed if the United Nations is to intervene effectively.

A knowledgeable UN official has suggested that this computer bank could well pay for itself if the United Nations were simply to charge the Member-States for UN-related research or for the specific UN computer services.[4] Not only would this keep UN operating costs at an absolute minimum, but it would benefit most Member-States as well. These computerized services would be far cheaper than the services of a research officer or team paid to locate the relevant data in different UN departments. Many of the smaller delegations to the United Nations simply do not have the resources necessary to conduct continuous research. Charging individual diplomatic delegations for the services rendered would also impose a certain degree of financial restraint and discipline on the UN computerized operations and, thus, recommend this program to the major powers, who are concerned about increasing costs at UN Headquarters.

Once this data bank is created, a variety of steps can be taken to integrate communications and link the information flow concerning conflict prevention with the office of the Secretary-General, the UN Security Council, and individual diplomatic delegations. As one top UN official said, this will ensure that, during a crisis, the "right information gets to the right person at the right time."

For instance, the Security Council chambers could be linked electronically with the data bank, UN TV studios, and the expanded news service in ORCI. There are several ways of doing this. Each diplomatic delegation could have a small table-top audiovisual monitor, or video monitors could be placed in strategic and highly visible locations around the room, or there could be a combination of table-top audiovisual monitors and large video screens. Whatever system of electronic linkage the Security Council chooses, it should complement the electronic offices of each diplomatic delegation that could be located near the Council chambers.

ELECTRONIC OFFICES AND
THE SECURITY COUNCIL

The permanent members of the Security Council have global intelligence and diplomatic services that can gather information and relay it rapidly to their representatives sitting on the Security Council. Many of the nonpermanent members of the Council do not have such support services. Thus, equal access to information is a special concern to the nonpermanent members who sometimes complain that they do not have relevant information concerning events under discussion. They also complain that their diplomatic representatives are often isolated from important information during long Council sessions. There are, of course, ways to relay information or new instructions to diplomats sitting around the Security Council. Diplomats can leave the Council chambers and call their home missions. Until the mid-1980s, they went to a room within UN Headquarters where news from the wire services was posted.[5] In an electronic age, however, such informal arrangements are simply too clumsy and inadequate.

To help correct this situation, it should become a matter of UN principle and policy that every member of the UN Security Council have a small electronic office near the Council's chambers. Each electronic office would possess modern information management facilities, such as a word processor, a computer terminal, and an audiovisual monitor. Each office can be linked up with the home mission as well and have phone lines to the outside. Because of security considerations, none of these offices would be linked to any UN department. Telecommunication lines running to and from UN Headquarters could consist of optic cabling, which is difficult to tap. The expenses for operating these rooms would be borne by the members of the Security Council; the United Nations cannot, and should not, be expected to pay for the offices' upkeep and equipment. Space is a problem, so these offices should be small and used solely to facilitate the information flow and official business of the Security Council.

The presence of electronic offices near the Council chambers linked with home missions will ensure that each diplomatic delegation has, literally at its finger tips, all the relevant and up-to-the-minute information on an issue being discussed or debated. A better information flow during Council sessions will help ensure the timeliness and relevance of Security Council resolutions. This information flow can be facilitated by modern techniques of information management.

All these steps — the creation of a data bank, the electronic linkage of the Secretary-General's office and the Security Council's chambers, and the small electronic offices for diplomatic delegations on the Security Council — are designed to improve the ongoing analysis of information and events within UN Headquarters. These improvements can facilitate the work that is already being done by diplomats and UN officials. Yet, as the United Nations acquires a global network of satellite-mediated telecommunications through a commercial consortium, an entirely new set of possibilities for conflict prevention and dispute settlement is created. A new form of diplomacy — satellite diplomacy — becomes possible, if not inevitable.[6]

SATELLITE DIPLOMACY

Satellite diplomacy can be defined within the context of the United Nations as the use of satellite-mediated telecommunications to promote the peaceful uses of outer space through international cooperation and to enhance international security in a manner consistent with the principles and purposes of the UN Charter.

A primary prerequisite of satellite diplomacy is the demilitarization of outer space. In order to develop its peaceful possibilities, outer space must be free from destabilizing weapon systems, as well as threats originating on Earth to early warning satellites. Thus, it is crucial that the superpowers negotiate a treaty that prevents the arms race from spreading into outer space. As Secretary-General Javier Pérez de Cuéllar stated, "Military competition in this limitless area is bound to have devastating consequences in terms of mutual confidence and mutual security."[7]

If weapons can be kept out of outer space, an entirely new conception of international peace and security becomes possible. Because of the ongoing advances in telecommunications technology, it is becoming eminently feasible and cost effective to develop new international satellite security systems. The UN study on the proposed International Satellite Monitoring Agency (ISMA) reflects the growing interest in using outer space to ensure peace on Earth.[8] If data from the ISMA were made available to every defense ministry, every university, every wire service, as well as to the United Nations, it would be very difficult for any aggressor to hide the mobilization of military forces for a large sustained attack. This would give new meaning to the traditional concept of collective security.

Of course an emphasis on the peaceful uses of outer space is not new to the United Nations. The General Assembly has an ongoing committee in this area that has done outstanding work for many years. There is an Outer Space Division and an Expert on Space applications in the Department of Political and Security Council Affairs. Yet it is fair to say that almost all the work done by these various committees and offices has focused upon how UN Member-States can take advantage of the peaceful possibilities of outer space.

Very little work has been done on improving the access of the UN Secretariat — specifically the office of the Secretary-General — to a global system of satellite-mediated telecommunications.

This is surprising because satellite-mediated telecommunications can enormously enhance the effectiveness of the UN Secretariat and, in particular, of the Secretary-General's preventive role. Three examples will be discussed briefly in order to illustrate the potential, and even inevitable, applications of space-age technology to the Secretary-General's ongoing efforts to gather, analyze, and distribute information relevant to conflict prevention. These are audiovisual reports by the Secretary-General to the Security Council, which might include live reports from UN teams in the field (these would be especially useful in protecting UN members — such as the "frontline states" in southern Africa — from attack); live electronic meetings via videoconferencing between the Secretary-General and the national leaders located anywhere in the world; and collective security consultations between the senior policy makers of the five permanent powers of the Security Council and the Executive Office of the Secretary-General.

AUDIOVISUAL REPORTS BY
THE SECRETARY-GENERAL

Using currently available telecommunications, it is possible to link the Security Council electronically to the UN TV studios nearby, which are run by the UN Communications Service, so that live, or taped, audiovisual reports can be received from the Secretary-General. Such reports can greatly enhance the Secretary-General's ability to share official reports with both diplomats and the watching world. He can provide audiovisual supplements to his regular reports on peacekeeping, humanitarian missions, and potential conflict situations.

In fact, the Security Council already receives written or photographic materials, which is circulated around the table and, after perusal and examination by the diplomats of the Council, is often incorporated into the official records or supplements of the meetings. Audiotapes provide a basic record of the Security Council's meetings and are kept on file by the Secretariat. Thus, the use of audiovisual reports by the Secretary-General would build upon the already established practices of the Council.[9]

Obviously there will be conflicting ideas among UN staff about just what constitutes the proper perceptions to include in the Secretary-General's report; therefore, UN staff might be encouraged to provide the Secretary-General with audiovisual reports that express both a majority and minority point of view. Such a process would inevitably lead to disagreements among the staff; but it is far better to carry on disputes behind the closed doors of a UN film-editing room than on the battlefields of warring states. Furthermore, the subject matter of certain audiovisual reports, especially those dealing with civilians or refugees caught up in war, will probably command a tragic consensus; pictures of bombed-out hospitals, dead civilians, and homeless refugees require no political or philosophical debate for their impact.

Once approved by the Secretary-General, the audiovisual reports will be shown to the Security Council on a procedural basis. Afterward, the reports will be distributed, via the UN outputs, to news agencies, governments, and NGOs around the world. Because audiovisual technology is now spreading to many underdeveloped regions of the world, the Secretary-General's audiovisual reports provide a way to reach out effectively to untold millions who otherwise might have very little interest in, or involvement with, the United Nations.[10]

LIVE TV REPORTS TO THE SECURITY COUNCIL

The telecommunication technology already exists that would allow the Security Council to receive live TV reports from UN negotiating teams or other staff in the field. These reports would require, among other things, a mobile satellite station, or uplink, as well as ongoing access to a satellite transponder. The Communications Service is currently recommending that such a mobile uplink be obtained.[11] Of course, live reports from the field present command and control problems for the Secretary-General; yet these problems are not insurmountable and are outweighed by the deterrent power of live UN TV reports shown before the UN Security Council and, consequently, broadcast throughout the world.

The possibility of presenting live audiovisual reports to the Security Council could be part of an international satellite security system that could be operated by an international satellite cooperative.[12] (The idea of such a cooperative originated with Howard Kurtz and his late wife, Harriet; the Kurtzes' idea was passed on to the French government, which, in turn, called for a feasibility study on an International Satellite Monitoring Agency (ISMA). The study was completed in the early 1980s.) All UN Member-States could be linked, via satellite, to UN Headquarters as part of this cooperative or as part of the ISMA. In cases of sudden attack, any Member-State could send live audiovisual reports to the Secretary-General, who, in turn, would relay the report to the Council. The footage for such live or taped audiovisual reports could be gathered by small mobile UN teams in the field. Video equipment for taped reports is increasingly inexpensive. Mobile, live reports would obviously require a much more sophisticated, and expensive, operational capacity.

DETERRENT DIPLOMACY AND SOUTHERN AFRICA: A CASE STUDY

If equipped with state-of-the-art telecommunications, the Security Council and the Secretary-General could work together more effectively in order to preserve international peace. One situation that still cries out for more determined international action is the regional crisis in southern Africa caused by the existence of apartheid and the South African regime's history of attacks upon, or attempts to destabilize, its neighbors, the frontline states.[13] This is still important and necessary — even though there have been limited, recent reforms — because apartheid is not dead and buried. Hence, the possibility of civil war — white versus black or even white versus white (the conservatives) — continues.

In view of this, the Security Council could, in close coordination with the Secretary-General, promote deterrent diplomacy by strengthening the United Nations' presence in the area. Deterrent diplomacy can be defined as the preventive possibilities of anticipatory action by significant international actors.[14] One way deterrent diplomacy can be strengthened within the context of the UN efforts in southern Africa is through enhancing the electronic outreach of negotiators who are trying to prevent international aggression. For instance, mobile UN telecommunication teams could be stationed in the capitals of the frontline states — coupled, officially or unofficially, with military missions of the embassies from the permanent members of the UN Security Council, which already are stationed in several of the countries concerned. If the apartheid regime attacks any of these countries — as it periodically does — mobile UN teams could send a filmed or even live audiovisual report to the Security Council.

Ideally, the combination of mobile, telecommunication teams coupled to the UN Headquarters' new ability to engage in real-time collective security consultations could act as a deterrent to the apartheid regime's aggression, thus helping to contain the Afrikaner and bringing a modest, yet invaluable, degree of added security and stability to the frontline states. At the very least, Afrikaner aggression would have to take into account the new diplomatic capability of the international community. As a Rand study on multilateral crisis centers points out:

> Plans to mask a staged sequence of events would somehow have to accommodate the uncertainties brought on by the existence of a fast and versatile system of intergovernmental communications. . . . Establishing mechanisms that force more rapid and elaborate deception planning will tend to deter, especially when the price of failure is high.[15]

Because the South African regime will be keenly aware of the added uncertainties created by enhanced UN communications, especially when electronically coupled with a UN presence in the frontline states, its aggression might be modified and reduced in scale. Admittedly, a more likely possibility is that the apartheid regime will consider the UN teams themselves as potential targets for military or covert action. Hence, there is an obvious need to couple these teams, officially or unofficially, with the military missions of the permanent members in the area.

Furthermore, the office of the Secretary-General, in close cooperation with the Security Council, or even the General Assembly, could also receive and review satellite surveillance of southern Africa from the ISMA or from individual Member-States.[16] Once shared with the appropriate UN organ, this information could be distributed to the news media throughout the world. Such information could be especially useful in enforcing possible future strategic sanctions against South Africa in the areas of oil, mining, and shipping.[17] For instance, oil tankers in South African ports could be easily identified from space — thus helping to trace the Afrikaners' international sources of supply. Such information could give real power to the often empty international calls for an economic embargo of the South African regime.

OTHER POSSIBILITIES OF SATELLITE DIPLOMACY

Electronic Meetings

If UN negotiating teams are sent out to different parts of the world, or if the Secretary-General sends a personal representative to the capital of a nation on the other side of the globe, they can all meet together despite the distance via satellite-mediated teleconferencing. Such electronic meetings between executives on different continents are already commonplace in commercial and diplomatic enterprises.

According to public sources, the various US intelligence services also use voice conferencing as a link in times of crisis.[18] The National Operation and Intelligence Watch Officers Net (NOIWON) allows the operations centers of the CIA, DIA, NSA, State INR, J-3, and the White House watch to call a secure voice conference at any time. There is also the National Operations and Intelligence Analyst Net (NOIAN), involving all these offices except the White House. Another system, CONTEXT, has also reportedly been developed for NOIAN's use. This system allows experts and officials to prepare joint reports, propose alternative drafts, and share documents when severe time constraints do not permit them to leave their offices.

The United Nations, and specifically the Office of the Secretary-General, could develop similar capabilities as part of the electronic linkage of UN Headquarters. A variety of offices within the Secretariat could thus be linked internally as well as tied into the satellite systems for overseas transmissions. It has recently been recommended that the United Nations create a "situation room" for better crisis control.[19] Yet in a bureaucracy as labyrinthine as the United Nations, such a room might create as many problems as it solves.[20] Furthermore, as the U.S. NOIWON and NOIAN systems illustrate, new technology is rendering obsolete the idea of collecting key information in a single location. Modern information systems make it possible, even desirable, to link a variety of offices and experts into the decision-making process. It is important to avoid creating a single source of information, or a single source of analysis, and to begin developing instead multiple means of inputs, analysis, and outputs. Thus, such electronic linkage of key policy makers permits decentralized decision making, which itself might promote the integrative complexity of information processing. For this reason it is desirable to establish a variety of situation rooms providing specific expertise or dealing with specific issues — such as peacekeeping and nuclear verification — and to link and integrate them electronically into the Secretary-General's reporting system.

Videoconferencing: Meeting Face-to-Face via Satellite

Videoconferencing — live, televised, simultaneous, and interactive meetings conducted via satellite among several different offices around the world — can be extremely useful in a variety of UN activities. It can be useful to offset the growing costs of UN-sponsored conferences and travel by UN officials. Many of these possibilities are also discussed in the UNISPACE Report and in the report on Communications by the Joint Inspection Unit.[21]

Videoconferencing can also provide the means by which the Secretary-General may meet directly and discreetly with the heads of government without travel. The UN TV studios could easily be used for this once a satellite channel is obtained from a commercial consortium. Such meetings could serve as a forum for informal consultations as well as for exploring areas of mutual concern — particularly during times of international tension or crisis. In this way, videoconferencing offers an informal means of information gathering and enquiry by the Secretary-General.

In a related development, the U.S. government instituted in the early 1980s a videoconferencing link, EURONET, between Washington, its UN mission in New York, and five of its embassies in Europe.[22] U.S. officials point out that "EURONET ushers in a new communications era for the U.S. government. It will replace the slow and sometimes ineffective transmission of vital diplomatic material by airplane or letter that we have traditionally relied on."[23]

Videoconferencing can also serve as an electronic equivalent to shuttle diplomacy during periods of international crisis, helping to bring together the Secretary-General and his negotiating teams located in different countries. The whole idea of shuttle diplomacy is to meet face-to-face with key decision makers. Videoconferencing permits such face-to-face discussions without extensive and tiring jet travel.

Videoconferencing can also add an entirely new dimension to third-party mediation during a crisis because the very architecture of third-party intervention — its organization and structure — is a crucial factor in preventing or resolving conflicts.[24] This is, in part, the reason for using UN negotiating teams that can meet directly with the parties involved in a potential dispute. Because the parties involved in a potential or actual conflict often feel beseiged or isolated, the UN negotiating team can help remove the barriers of mistrust and fear that creep over government officials during a crisis and, thus, help to defuse a tense situation. But, it is important that the UN negotiating teams meet among themselves to compare notes, consider options, and hammer out possible solutions. They can do this electronically — that is, via electronic meetings — even though they may be thousands of miles apart. Each negotiating team, stationed within the grounds of a neutral embassy, could be equipped with a mobile satellite station and, thus, be directly linked with UN Headquarters in New York. Because every nuance, including voice and facial expression, may be an important source of information in delicate negotiations, and especially during a crisis, videoconferencing might improve communications between all involved parties.

There are problems with this form of communication. It may not be possible to fully protect satellite transmissions, even when electronically scrambled, from the eyes and ears of national intelligence services. Yet, if communications are varied, and use a variety of sources, such as using videoconferencing that is electronically scrambled plus information received through traditional diplomatic pouch services, a solution to part of this problem may be possible.

Of course, technical fixes have a very limited role in diplomacy. Despite access to elaborate telecommunications, UN negotiators may be unable to prevent war. Certainly elaborate electronics and sophisticated satellites are no substitute for conceptual analysis or creative imagination. Thus, enhanced telecommunications might make only a marginal difference. Even so, such seemingly minor improvements in the ability to communicate and transmit information during a crisis can be important when decisions are being made that may mean the difference between war and peace, especially in an increasingly multinuclear world.

NOTES

1. I first mentioned this in a report personally presented to the Secretary-General in 1983. Thomas E. Boudreau, *Protecting the Innocent: Enhancing the Humanitarian Role of the United Nations in Natural Disasters and Other Disaster Situations* (New York: Council on Religion and International Affairs, 1983), p. 16. Many of the ideas in this chapter were first developed in this report.

2. There is not only greater awareness of this problem within the Secretariat; the Secretary-General requested that the Secretariat prepare a comprehensive proposal to upgrade its communications systems. See his report, "Communication System of the United Nations Report of the Secretary-General," November 20, 1984, A/C.5/39/39. This report was issued the same day that my second report, *The Secretary-General and Satellite Diplomacy* (New York: Carnegie Council, 1984) was presented to him.

3. The first time I heard this idea mentioned was in a discussion with a diplomat who serves as a nonpermanent representative on the Security Council. Since then, I have heard it discussed by senior officials within the UN Secretariat as well. Nor is the idea a new one; Lincoln P. Bloomfield of MIT reminded the Secretary-General of his ten-year-old CASCON proposal while at a dinner in New York at the home of the U.K. permanent representative in the spring of 1985.

4. This was suggested by a senior UN official who is knowledgeable about UN data and communications facilities.

5. There are, of course, the support services provided to diplomats sitting on the Security Council by UN Secretariat officials, such as documentation and the transfer of messages, if necessary. Yet, several diplomats have mentioned the lack of modern communication facilities near, or within, the Council chambers.

6. I first used this term "satellite diplomacy" in Boudreau, *Protecting the Innocent,* p. 28.

7. "Secretary-General's Message Opening 1984 Session of Conference on Disarmament," UN Doc. SG/SM/3521, February 8, 1984.

8. UN Doc. A/AC.206/14.

9. For a discussion of this, see Boudreau, *Protecting the Innocent,* p. 21.

10. Ibid.

11. Internal memo prepared by the UN Communication Service, spring 1984.

12. The idea of an international or global satellite cooperative was first developed by Howard and Harriet Kurtz. I first became aware of their work this past year, and I believe it has great promise as a way to help preserve international peace in the future.

13. For a recent study of South African assaults, see Arif Shahid Khan (India), "Apartheid on the Attack: Recent Developments (September 1987–March 1988)," UN Centre against Apartheid, April 1988, Information Note No. SCA/GE/88/2.

14. This is my definition; the term "deterrent diplomacy" describes the preventive possibilities of anticipatory action by significant international actors. For instance, in Boudreau, *Protecting the Innocent,* I pointed out that listing the individual names of innocent victims in UN reports may marginally deter attacks on civilians in the future.

15. See Dale M. Lande et al., "Improving the Means for Intergovernmental Communications in Crisis" (Santa Monica: Rand, 1984).

16. See the *Study on the Implications of Establishing an International Satellite Monitoring Agency,* Report of the Secretary-General, Preparatory Committee for the Second Special Session of the UN General Assembly Devoted to Disarmament, August 1981.

17. The UN General Assembly has periodically called for such sanctions. See, for example, *Sanctions against South Africa: The Peaceful Alternative to Violent Change* (New York: UN Publications, 1988).

18. Thomas G. Belden, "Indicators, Warnings, and Crisis Operations," *International Studies Quarterly 21,* 1 (March 1977).

19. William Langer Ury and Richard Smoke, *Beyond the Hotline: Controlling a Nuclear Crisis* (Cambridge: Nuclear Negotiation Project, 1984).

20. When the Carnegie Council Crisis Management project reviewed this idea with UN officials, their response indicated that such a situation room would create problems of access for the UN Secretariat. Because implementing this idea would apparently cause more problems than it would solve, the proposal was dropped in favor of one for a multilevel information management system as outlined in this chapter.

21. "Report of the Second United Nations Conference on the Exploration and Peaceful Uses of Outer Space," A/CONF.101/10 Vienna, August 9–21, 1982. Also, the idea of the United Nations using videoconferencing for diplomatic purposes was discussed in Boudreau, *Protecting the Innocent,* pp. 22–24.

22. "EURONET Satellite System Shrinks the World," *USIA World* (published by the United States Information Agency) *2,* 11 (December 1983).

23. Ibid.

24. This point is also made in Boudreau, *Protecting the Innocent,* p. 23.

11
A UN MULTILATERAL WAR RISK REDUCTION CENTER

MULTILATERAL THREATS AND
WAR PREVENTION DIPLOMACY

There are currently at least six nuclear-armed states in the world — Britain, China, France, Israel, the United States, and the Soviet Union. India has exploded a nuclear bomb and is suspected by Pakistan to be building an arsenal and requisite delivery systems. There are also several other near-nuclear nations, including Pakistan, Argentina, Brazil, South Africa and, lately, Iraq.[1] There is also the growing danger of regional conventional weapon rivalries, including the increasing dangers of ballistic missile proliferation and chemical warfare. Current superpower arms-control negotiations, including the 1987 INF agreement, do not address the plans of England and France to expand their nuclear arsenals. In view of these developments, a former UN diplomat warns, the world is "almost infinitely more complicated" than the basic Cold War of U.S.-Soviet confrontation; hence, "the main dangers to peace come, not directly from either of the superpowers, but from the ambitions and fears of a number of minor powers, unpredictably interacting with superpower rivalry."[2]

In other words, with many actual or potential nuclear powers, there are increasingly significant multilateral threats to international peace. This is even more apparent when the possibility of terrorist groups obtaining missile materials, or even a nuclear bomb, is seriously considered. This is a danger that the Secretary-General specifically mentioned in his 1986 *Annual Report*.

Yet, surprisingly, there is not an adequate framework in the scholarly literature on strategic issues that established the complex parameters and interrelationships of war prevention diplomacy in a multinuclear world. Scholars and policy makers have focused in the past upon the U.S.-Soviet rivalry without analyzing in depth the increasing dangers confronting multilateral diplomacy. Three growing dangers in a multinuclear world immediately come to mind.

The first is nuclear terrorism. If a substate group seizes or acquires nuclear materials and makes a bomb, the great powers will obviously want to know if they had any assistance from another state. The dangers of mutual recrimination, blame, and — especially if a bomb detonates in a city — retaliation are very real. With the world moving toward a plutonium economy in the 1990s, the possibility of terrorists acquiring a bomb grows.[3] In such a situation, there is a demonstrable need for a third party, such as the Secretary-General, to urge restraint, help unite the nations of the world on a common plan, urge restrictions and, most of all, help prevent retaliatory alerts or military action based on incomplete information.

A second danger stemming from the "ambitions and fears of a number of minor powers, unpredictably interacting with superpower rivalry" is a regional conflict — like that in the Middle East — escalating into a superpower confrontation. If this seems unlikely — despite the several bloody regional conflicts raging in the world today — it is important to remember that World War I began with a single shot in the quiet, remote city of Sarajevo.[4] The point is that the path of escalating violence, like a growing fire, is often unpredictable, fast, and furious. This possibility grows as strong yet volatile regional actors such as Iraq or South Africa develop new missiles and chemical or even nuclear-weapon arsenals.

Finally, a nuclear bomb never exists in ominous isolation; it is the epicenter of vast political, bureaucratic, and military command and control structures that span across the world. The organizational structures of the nuclear powers increasingly overlap and electronically interact; hence, there is the danger of interactive multinuclear alerts occurring simultaneously.[5] The result could be confusion, especially among the nuclear powers who might interpret an alert mobilization as evidence of aggressive intent. This is especially true in Europe where four independent nuclear powers maintain strategic, intermediate (France), or tactical nuclear delivery systems. Hence, as Paul Bracken warns, the danger of escalation is very real as the "number of interrelated choices involving the *many organizations* that control nuclear weapons further complicates the difficulty of management."[6] (Emphasis added.) In such a multinuclear alert situation, a third party such as the UN Secretary-General — if equipped with a direct communication link to world leaders — could play a useful, even if marginal, role by sharing or clarifying information, providing a forum for collective security consultations, and offering concrete proposals to prevent unwanted war.

In short, a world of several known nuclear powers, nuclear alliances, near-nuclear powers, potential terrorist groups, and large-scale regional conflicts is, at worst, a volatile political situation and, at best, a precarious peace. Because of the dangers of rapid unintended escalation from a regional conflict or isolated act of terrorism to a great-power confrontation, it makes simple sense to practice preventive politics by preparing now for any eventuality. Yet, currently no international institutions or organizations, including the UN Security Council, can adequately address the emergent threats of a multinuclear world.

COLLECTIVE SECURITY CONSULTATIONS: INTERDEPENDENT INTERESTS

Managing multilateral threats to the peace will work, within the context of the United Nations, only if the Security Council is involved. Unfortunately, Council members rarely seem to cooperate or even come to a consensus concerning issues affecting international peace and security. Even so, the realities of mutual military vulnerability and a shared concern about sheer survival create an interdependency of interests among permanent powers that sit on the Security Council.[7] Interdependent interests, such as strategic stability, are national interests that can achieve their full realization only through international cooperation.

These interests do not disappear when tension or hostility increases. On the contrary, the greater the danger and distrust, the greater the shared interest in security and survival. To deny this self-interest is to deny the fundamental will to self-preservation.

MANAGING MULTILATERAL THREATS

In view of these interdependent interests, the five permanent powers on the UN Security Council have a special role in maintaining international peace and security. They are the major nuclear powers of the world; they are also potential victims of a nuclear war.

Yet, currently no institutional mechanism, within the context of the United Nations, permits the five nuclear powers on the Security Council to confer among themselves should the need arise.

In view of the potentially grave problems caused by an increasingly multinuclear world — and by the increase in the arsenals of chemical weapons by third-world states — it makes simple sense to equip at least one salient third party, such as the Secretary-General, with institutional access to senior decision makers of the major powers. Such institutional access should have a pre-established technological infrastructure and information-fusion capabilities as provided by the electronic offices linked to the Security Council. The Secretary-General could be linked, via these offices, with each diplomatic delegation's capital.

Such a system of institutional access by the Secretary-General can supplement the recently established bilateral risk reduction centers between the United States and the Soviet Union.[8] In short, institutional access by the Secretary-General, using an enhanced telecommunications infrastructure, is complementary, not competitive, with the newly established bilateral risk reduction centers.

It may well be that a system of interlocking multinational and bilateral risk reduction centers can, and should, be established to provide a marginal degree of added security in the nuclear age. In a world of increasing nuclear and conventional military capabilities — by a variety of nation-state actors and alliances — it makes simple common sense to develop a comprehensive security system consisting of bilateral, regional, and global war risk reduction centers. Each level can complement, strengthen, and support the next level, when and if needed. Such a mutually supporting and interrelated system can provide a marginal yet meaningful degree of added confidence in a world still threatened, despite the promising rapprochement between the United States and Soviet Union, by regional confrontations, military mistakes, and unwanted war.

THE 1986 ANNUAL REPORT: THE EVOLUTION OF AN IDEA

In his 1986 *Annual Report* to the United Nations, delivered in early September, UN Secretary-General Pérez de Cuéllar called for the creation of such a multilateral nuclear alert center. Specifically, he stated:

> I would suggest that consideration be given to the establishment of a multilateral nuclear alert centre to reduce the risk of fatal misinterpretation of unintentional nuclear launchings or, in the future, the chilling possibility of isolated launching by those who may clandestinely gain access to nuclear devices.[9]

The Secretary-General is apparently concerned with the possibility of multilateral nuclear alerts and the dangers of unwanted escalation posed by interactive alerts by nuclear powers. He is one of the few significant figures in international affairs that recognizes the possible future dangers created by a multinuclear world.

The Secretary-General's proposal is consistent with the recommendation made in my Carnegie Council report, *The*

Secretary-General and Satellite Diplomacy, which was personally presented to him in December 1984. The report recommends that the "Executive Office of the Secretary-General can serve as the focal point of . . . collective security consultations. In the nuclear age, it makes eminent sense to have at least one salient third party with 'institutional access' to the senior decisionmakers of the five permanent powers on the Security Council."[10]

Citing the dangers mentioned in Paul Bracken's research, the Carnegie Council report specifically recommends:

> In order to create this institutional access, there must be electronic and telecommunications links established between the capitals of the permanent powers and the Executive Office of the Secretary-General. These linkups could be dubbed "peace lines" and should include, at the very minimum, the same technical components and telecommunications capacity as the "hot line" between the superpowers. Such linkups would insure that the Secretary-General has institutional access to the leadership of *all* nuclear powers during times of intense crisis.[11]

The purpose of such a telecommunications linkup is to provide much better information fusion and management systems centered within UN Headquarters. Only with such systems can the Security Council, and especially the Secretary-General, hope to play a more effective role in international affairs.

GORBACHEV'S ENDORSEMENT

In 1987, President Gorbachev endorsed a similar idea. Gorbachev's own proposal seems to be a combination of the Secretary-General's 1986 idea concerning a multilateral nuclear alert center and the 1984 recommendation that electronic and telecommunications links be established between the capitals of the permanent powers and the Executive Office of the Secretary-General. He specifically suggests the following:

> At the same time the world community cannot stay away from interstate conflicts. Here it could be possible to begin by fulfilling the proposal made by the United Nations' Secretary-General to set up under the United Nations organization a multilateral centre for lessening the danger of war. Evidently, it would be feasible to consider the expediency of setting up a direct communication line between the United Nations Headquarters and the capitals of the countries that are permanent members of the Security Council

and the location of the chairman of the nonaligned movement.[12]

Gorbachev adds the name of the chairman of the nonaligned movement to the list. In the same speech, Gorbachev also suggests that the United Nations should have a wider role in verifying international agreements, monitoring the military situation in conflict areas, and peacekeeping. To support his proposals, the Soviet Union paid its outstanding debt to the United Nations.

Notice that President Gorbachev does not specifically endorse the idea of a multilateral nuclear alert center. He modified the Secretary-General's proposal and suggests that it is "possible to begin . . . to set up under the United Nations organization a multilateral centre for lessening the danger of war." Later statements by Gorbachev and leading Soviet policy makers continue to endorse — but do not precisely elaborate — upon this idea. Further Soviet statements, including those of Soviet Foreign Minister Eduard Shevardnadze made during the fall of 1988 at the United Nations, suggest that the Office of the Secretary-General could develop a more significant role in verification capabilities.

A MULTILATERAL WAR RISK REDUCTION CENTER

So, as matters stand now, there seems to be an unresolved vagueness concerning the various ideas proposing a multilateral nuclear alert or war risk reduction center within the framework of the United Nations. In view of this continuing uncertainty over the very definition and nature of a multilateral center, the focus of analysis should be initially shifted from a physical entity, as suggested by the term center, to the diplomatic process that is desired in order to enhance war risk reduction within the framework of the United Nations. Otherwise, the recent efforts to reform the United Nations can be easily sidetracked by semantic (and sometimes political) problems not related to the specific goal of reducing the risk of war in international affairs.

The precise diplomatic process that seems most promising in terms of war risk reduction is meaningful interactions based on real-time information, such as satellite intelligence or verification analyses, between decision makers and diplomats. These could include the representatives of allies or potential adversaries, a significant third party such as the Secretary-General, and senior policy makers, especially of the avowed nuclear-armed nations. These interactions were described in Chapter 9, especially within the context of the United Nations, as official or unofficial consultations. The United Nations is uniquely suited to facilitate such consultations because the largest diplomatic corps in the world is accredited to UN

Headquarters, including, of course, the permanent members of the Security Council.

In short, if the permanent powers on the Security Council had a way of pooling relevant information during a crisis, the danger of unwanted war — especially regional or even nuclear war — might be reduced. By providing a forum in which clarifications could be sought — and given to a third party, such as the Secretary-General — the collective security consultations within UN Headquarters would buy time in a crisis and provide an added safety valve in international affairs. For instance, according to Harlan Cleveland, Secretary-General Thant played just such a role in the 1962 Cuban crisis; Cleveland states that "the UN, through the Secretary-General, served as a middleman in crucial parts of the dialogue between President Kennedy and Chairman Khrushchev which led to a peaceful solution."[13] Dean Rusk's surprise statement in 1987 that President Kennedy considered, as a last resort, a secret initiative aided by Thant only underlines the potential importance of the third-party role of the UN Secretary-General.[14]

Yet, today's world of interlocking electronic alert systems and globe-spanning military command and control structures is much more complex than the world of the early 1960s when the Cuban crisis occurred.[15] To be an effective third party — even in a symbolic way — in such an electronically complex environment, the Secretary-General requires accurate information concerning force deployments, alert status, and other relevant data. His office can acquire the necessary information via its electronic links with the capitals of the permanent powers and then begin to identify possible escalation controls as well as help arrange acts of political and/or military restraint.

With enhanced telecommunications, the Secretary-General could arrange escalation controls, which can be defined as an implicit agreement to halt further deterioration of military or political stability during a crisis.[16] The Secretary-General might also help minimize the danger of ripple or surge effect — the escalatory effect that sweeps through the entire command and control system of military rivals during an isolated incident. During a crisis, such a surge effect could be a dangerous cause of unwanted escalation.[17] Finally, if equipped with better information management and fusion systems, the Secretary-General could help in efforts to isolate incidents involving spasmodic violence by terrorists or provocateurs. In particular, the attribution of intentionality by one side to accidental or unplanned events, which are more likely with increased military alerts, is one of the most dangerous escalatory engines during a crisis.[18] Such attribution can lead to a tit-for-tat or mirror imaging response that can quickly expand beyond control.

One way to overcome the attribution of intentionality is to encourage sharing information or intelligence concerning an isolated incident. Such sharing need not be overt. An incident can be isolated and explained in a variety of diplomatic ways and means without one side seeming to capitulate to the other. The presence of a third party, such as the Secretary-General, may be an important way to facilitate the flow of such information as well as intelligence on unplanned, and unwanted, military alerts.

As we have seen, the United Nations obviously does not possess the satellite and electronic capacity to verify independently the military maneuvers of military forces spread over the globe. Fortunately, the permanent powers do possess this capability and presumably would be able to verify, almost immediately, changes in the military alert status, including stand-downs, of the military forces of other powers, including the other Council members.

The precise problem then becomes one of arranging mutual, or multinational, acts of military restraint so that no one nation is placed in a militarily disadvantageous position by ordering unilateral military restraint.[19] In short, there must be an institutionalized means by which leaders of opposing nations caught up in a crisis can order their troops "back to the barracks" and deactivate their military forces — including, in particular, their nuclear forces — in the knowledge that the other side is simultaneously doing the same.

The collective security consultations can be used for this purpose. Specifically, the Office of the Secretary-General can become the catalyst for cooperation by offering his services as a recognized third party to help arrange mutual or multinational acts of military restraint or of stand-downs. In short, the Secretary-General can mobilize the national means of verification that are available to the permanent powers and use the resulting information provided through the electronic offices surrounding the Security Council to help arrange mutual or multinational acts of restraint. By employing the information from the satellite surveillance systems of the permanent powers for these purposes, the Secretary-General can use space-age technology to protect the peace.

CONCLUSION: SECURITY AND SURVIVAL

Political leaders and potential third-party negotiators must appreciate the extraordinary problems of command and control during a crisis and the dangers of attributing intention to unplanned or accidental events. Ultimately, the political leaders themselves must decide whether an isolated incident is spasmodic or part of a systematic pattern of violence and confrontation. Of course, hard-liners in each government involved in a crisis will always be magnifying the "test" supposedly implied in every incident, without any appreciation for the empirical problems of controlling vast globe-spanning military machines on alert.[20] Third parties such as the Secretary-General can solicit and share relevant information that can help to dampen the escalatory effects of alerts and unplanned actions during a crisis. The Secretary-General can also remind leaders of what they already know: a great power need not mindlessly react tit-for-tat to every unplanned incident; policy should be planned, not provoked. In this way, the Secretary-General can work with the permanent powers to realize their common interest in security and survival.

NOTES

1. For a review of the continuing danger of horizontal and vertical nuclear proliferation, see Gordon Thompson (ed.), *Perspectives on Proliferation* (Cambridge, MA: Institute for Resource and Security Studies, 1985). Also see Leonard Spector's series on horizontal proliferation, including his latest book *The Undeclared Bomb* (Cambridge, MA: Ballinger, 1988).

2. Connor Cruise O'Brien, a retired UN diplomat, private letter, summer 1987.

3. See Paul Leventhal and Yonah Alexander (eds), *Preventing Nuclear Terrorism* (Cambridge: Lexington Books, 1987).

4. See Paul Bracken, *The Command and Control of Nuclear Forces* (New Haven: Yale University Press, 1983).

5. Ibid.

6. Ibid.

7. I first used the term "interdependent interests" in Thomas E. Boudreau, *The Secretary-General and Satellite Diplomacy* (New York: Carnegie Council on Ethics and International Affairs, 1984).

8. On July 17, 1984, the United States and the Soviet Union signed an agreement to update the hot line between the two countries. The new hot line, using a high-speed facsimile, will be able to transmit maps, charts, and drawings that could be essential in helping to resolve a crisis peacefully. I am suggesting here that the Secretary-General should have the same telecommunications capacity linking his office with the five capitals of the five permanent members of the Council, all of whom are also nuclear powers. Such electronic linkages could be dubbed "peace lines."

9. *Report of the Secretary-General on the Work of the Organization (1986).* Published by the United Nations Department of Public Information, September 1986. Hereafter referred to as the 1986 *Annual Report.*

10. Boudreau, *The Secretary-General and Satellite Diplomacy*, p. 37. Although this specific proposal is new, the idea is not; the French, Soviets, and, in the late 1940s, the U.S. government have suggested somewhat similar arrangements.

11. Ibid., p. 37. Also see Bracken, *Command and Control.*

12. See Mikhail Gorbachev, "Realities and the Guarantees for a Secure World," an article by the General-Secretary of the SPSU Central Committee that appeared in *Pravda* and *Izvestia* on September 17, 1987, reprinted by Novost Press Agency Publishing House. Also see Bill Keller, "Russians urging UN be given greater power," New York *Times,* September 18, 1987.

13. Harlan Cleveland, "Crisis Diplomacy," *Foreign Affairs 41* (1963). Professor Cleveland was a ranking State Department Official in the Kennedy

Administration during the 1962 Cuban crisis.

14. See J. Anthony Lukas, "Class Reunion: Kennedy's Men Relive the Cuban Missile Crisis," *New York Times Magazine,* August 30, 1987. Dean Rusk did not attend this reunion, but he wrote his recollections for the group.

15. Paul Bracken states, "It is not at all clear that the United States is facing up to the problem of living in a world where there are two highly reactive nuclear command organizations. For one thing it may no longer be as safe to de-alert the forces as it was in the past because there would be no guarantee that it would be reciprocated." Of course, this problem exists for both the United States and the Soviet Union. See Bracken, *Command and Control,* p. 224. I am indebted to Bracken's insightful discussion of the dangers of military alerts, especially those of the United States and Soviet Union, as well as the dangers of a unilateral stand-down from high alert status.

16. I reviewed these possibilities in "The UN Secretary-General and Nuclear Crisis Diplomacy: The Last Stop," a research report presented to UNITAR, March 21, 1984, during a staff research seminar. Also see Bracken, *Command and Control.*

17. Boudreau, "The UN Secretary-General and Nuclear Crisis Diplomacy."

18. Ibid.

19. For an excellent discussion of the need to develop ways of arranging mutual military stand-downs, see Bracken, *Command and Control.*

20. Ibid.

12

EPILOGUE:
A PREVENTIVE PARTNERSHIP

Diplomacy must be judged by what it prevents, not
only what it achieves. Much of it is a holding action
designed to avoid explosion until the unifying forces
of history take humanity into their embrace.

— Abba Ebban
The New Diplomacy

The operating budget for the United Nations for an entire year is
less than its Member-States pay for military matters in a single day.
Despite this disparity, criticism of the United Nations has increased
in recent years especially in the United States, concerning the
organization's "crazed extravagance." While bureaucratic overlap
and abuse within the UN Secretariat undoubtedly occur, there are
simply no comparisons between the resources spent, or "wasted," on
institutions preparing for war and those spent on institutions,
however imperfect, preparing for peace. Destructive criticism of the
United Nations is like fiddle playing while Rome burns; it may soothe
the ego, but it cannot extinguish the spreading fires.

In contrast, constructive criticism of the United Nations
emphasizes the positive potential of the Organization, despite its
imperfections, to make the world a less dangerous place. Following
this tradition, this book has tried to present a critical yet constructive
analysis of the United Nations' current ability to prevent war.

The potential of the Secretary-General's preventive role in
heading off international conflict has been emphasized. I have
argued that the constitutional options and obligations of the
Secretary-General must be defined within a global framework of
conflict prevention. Specifically, I tried to show why Article 99 of the

UN Charter obligates and entitles the Secretary-General to develop a truly global early warning and information management system that enables him to anticipate, analyze and prevent "any matter that may threaten . . . international peace and security."

At the same time, it is important not to oversell the potential power of the UN Secretary-General. His influence is limited. And he may not be able, despite his best efforts and with the most enhanced telecommunications at his disposal, to prevent a particular war.

However, as many Member-States — including the most powerful ones — have discovered, the Office of the Secretary-General is an important diplomatic and political watchman of the peace in a world of increasing international tensions. Although his influence is at times marginal, few other individuals in the world have the international standing to intervene effectively in a simmering dispute or conflict. Someday the Secretary-General's marginal influence in a brewing conflict may mean the difference between war and peace. In a world where new nuclear or chemical weapons are produced every day, such marginal influence is a priceless asset, one not to be lightly dismissed.

Yet, the Secretary-General cannot keep peace alone. In the final analysis, the United Nations is only as good as its members allow it to be. Without the political backing of its members, the United Nations will suffer from benign neglect and undergo a genteel decline. If, however, Member-States renew their commitment to the organization and work with the Secretary-General in a preventive partnership, the United Nations — and its members — may withstand the threat of highly combustible conflicts and live on into the twenty-first century. Thus it ultimately rests with every Member-State, large or small, whether the United Nations is to have a political and moral rebirth.

APPENDIX I:
CHAPTER XV OF THE
UN CHARTER

THE SECRETARIAT

Article 97

The Secretariat shall comprise a Secretary-General and such staff as the Organization may require. The Secretary-General shall be appointed by the General Assembly upon the recommendation of the Security Council. He shall be the chief administrative officer of the Organization.

Article 98

The Secretary-General shall act in that capacity in all meetings of the General Assembly, of the Security Council, of the Economic and Social Council, and of the Trusteeship Council, and shall perform such other functions as are entrusted to him by these organs. The Secretary-General shall make an annual report to the General Assembly on the work of the Organization.

Article 99

The Secretary-General may bring to the attention of the Security Council any matter which in his opinion may threaten the maintenance of international peace and security.

Article 100

1. In the performance of their duties the Secretary-General and the staff shall not seek or receive instructions from any government

or from any other authority external to the Organization. They shall refrain from any action which might reflect on their position as international officials responsible only to the Organization.

2. Each Member of the United Nations undertakes to respect the exclusively international character of the responsibilities of the Secretary-General and the staff and not to seek to influence them in the discharge of their responsibilities.

Article 101

1. The staff shall be appointed by the Secretary-General under regulations established by the General Assembly.

2. Appropriate staffs shall be permanently assigned to the Economic and Social Council, the Trusteeship Council, and, as required, to other organs of the United Nations. These staffs shall form a part of the Secretariat.

3. The paramount consideration in the employment of the staff and in the determination of the conditions of service shall be the necessity of securing the highest standards of efficiency, competence, and integrity. Due regard shall be paid to the importance of recruiting the staff on as wide a geographical basis as possible.

APPENDIX II:
PROTECTING THE INNOCENT

In the immediate aftermath of the Falkland/Malvinas War, and during the fighting in Beirut (summer 1982), I began a crisis management research project for the Carnegie Council on Ethics and International Affairs (formerly called the Council on Religion and International Affairs). The purpose of the research project was to explore and analyze ways to enhance conflict prevention at the United Nations.

In the summer of 1983, I presented the first copy of my report *Protecting the Innocent: Enhancing the Humanitarian Role of the United Nations in Natural Disasters and Other Disaster Situations* to Secretary-General Pérez de Cuéllar.[1] Many of the recommendations in this report subsequently supported and reinforced the Secretary-General's humanitarian efforts in the Iran-Iraq War. The key recommendations — in terms of the United Nations' role in humanitarian law — follow.

HUMANITARIAN FACT-FINDING: THE METHOD

One function that might well be given to a small number of unarmed, international military observers is to monitor compliance with humanitarian law. Such a responsibility could be made explicit in the observers' mandate, especially in situations in which large numbers of civilians are caught up in a war. Resolutions 516 and 521, passed during the Beirut fighting in the 1982 Lebanon War, suggest the basic preconditions for an innovative model of humanitarian fact-finding by the Security Council. Such fact-finding can be used to provide international observation of humanitarian law in a particular conflict. The three elements of such fact-finding are

(a) the consent and cooperation of the host government in close consultation with the appropriate UN organ and the Secretary-General;

(b) uncertainty about and deep concern over the possible violation of humanitarian law, that is, reported attacks against hospitals, schools, civilian centers, cultural centers, etc. (The principle that governs most UN peacekeeping operations — namely, that before UN peacekeepers can be deployed, the consent of "all parties concerned" must be obtained — does not apply here.)

(c) the dispatch of UN military or civilian observers charged by their mandate to report to the appropriate UN organ about the welfare and safety of the host country's civilian population. (To ensure prompt reporting, these observers would be equipped with enhanced electronics and advanced communications gear, as discussed in Chapter 10 above.)

Part of an explicit mandate for UN observers would include the power to provide, in close consultation with the host government, an international accounting of civilian casualties. Such a definitive determination, which is a preeminent question of fact, serves as a possible deterrent against future attacks on civilians. (Such an accounting was actually done during the Lesotho Mission discussed below.) If an aggressive regime knows that the international community will make every effort to account for the dead, wounded, and missing among a host country's civilian population, the aggressor may be more careful to restrict its attack to military targets in the future.

Humanitarian fact-finding need not be conducted solely by UN soldiers. Depending upon the circumstances surrounding the alleged attacks against civilians, as well as upon the needs of the host government, civilian observers or diplomats may be sent on humanitarian fact-finding missions. Also, diplomats and military attachés attached to neutral or nonaligned embassies in a host country could be deputized by the international community to monitor the welfare and safety of civilians during a conflict. Despite precedents for this latter type of action, apparently it was never actively considered during the Beirut fighting.

HUMANITARIAN ENQUIRY

Humanitarian fact-finding is to be distinguished from humanitarian enquiry. Humanitarian fact-finding is a main component of a

UN initiative and usually is specifically authorized by the appropriate UN organ. Humanitarian enquiry, in contrast, receives no specific mention in a resolution by the Security Council or General Assembly but is authorized by the Secretary-General to fulfill responsibilities and tasks given him by the appropriate UN organ. Generally defined (see Chapter 2 above), enquiry by the Secretary-General is "ancillary in character and limited in its purpose. In the exercise of the Secretary-General's good offices, it usually precedes or accompanies other action designed to bring about a settlement and reinforces those actions by providing an objective basis for decisions."

Humanitarian enquiry is specifically concerned with the welfare and safety of a host government's civilian population. Humanitarian enquiry also may involve consultations among Secretariat and host government officials about the mobilization of humanitarian assistance by the United Nations and the international community. Such enquiry is part of the Secretary-General's overall responsibilities for determining whether a specific situation may threaten international peace and security. An example of humanitarian enquiry is the 1983 Mission to Lesotho of the Under-Secretary-General for Special Political Affairs, Abdubrahim A. Farah.

In the wake of the South African intrusion into Lesotho on December 9, 1982, which left 42 civilians and refugees dead, the Security Council adopted Resolution 527 that strongly condemned the South Africans. This resolution also asked Member-States to provide relief aid and requested the Secretary-General "to enter into immediate consultations with the Lesotho Government . . . to ensure the welfare of the refugees in Lesotho in a manner consistent with their security."

To carry out this mandate, the Secretary-General dispatched a mission headed by Under-Secretary-General Farah to consult with the government of Lesotho on ways to ensure the welfare and safety of the refugees in Lesotho. The mission visited Lesotho for several days in mid-January and then returned to UN Headquarters in New York. The mission issued its report in early February 1983.

The four main aspects of the report issued by the Lesotho Mission are a review of the mission's consultations with the Lesotho government; a discussion in great detail of "Matters Affecting the Legal Protection, Security, and Welfare of Refugees in Lesotho"; an outline of the economic assistance needed by Lesotho to enhance the country's capacity to receive and maintain refugees from apartheid; and an accounting of the civilian casualties resulting from the South African attack, including a list of the names and residential status of those killed or wounded.

These four sections provide an analytic framework for humanitarian enquiry. First, it is important to note that the Lesotho Mission was ancillary in character because it was just one aspect of the

Secretary-General's overall consultations with the Lesotho government. Second, in the section entitled "The Legal Protection, Security, and Welfare of the Refugees in Lesotho," the mission provided a brief account of the international protections given to refugees, thus providing an objective legal basis for future decisions by both the Secretary-General and the Security Council. Concern for the legal protection of refugees and other civilians is a preeminent characteristic of humanitarian enquiry. Third, the report discusses the economic assistance needed to help Lesotho's refugees and then discusses international efforts to mobilize this aid. This emphasis on positive steps to improve the living situations of the refugees clearly distinguishes this type of enquiry from purely punitive or blame-seeking missions. Finally, the Lesotho Mission gives a human face to the tragic statistics of civilian casualties by listing the victims of the South African attack by name. In doing this, the report focuses international attention on the poignant human suffering caused by indiscriminate attacks against civilians. Publishing the plight of civilians caught up in war can also create a basis for further negotiations between combatants.

NOTE

1. For complete text, see: Thomas E. Boudreau, *Protecting the Innocent: Enhancing the Humanitarian Role of the United Nations in Natural Disasters and Other Disaster Situations* (New York: Council on Religion and International Affairs, 1983). The Carnegie Council has since changed its name to the Carnegie Council on Ethics and International Affairs; it is still located at 170 East 64th Street in New York City.

PRISM PROJECT

The Project on Policy Review in International Security and Multilateralism (PRISM) seeks to examine present and potential public policies that have a direct bearing on international stability and security. There is a special emphasis within the project on examining negotiations — especially in a multilateral context, such as the ongoing efforts to build effective international organizations and security regimes. The project uses peace and international security in a much broader sense than customarily defined and, thus, includes global, environmental, humanitarian, economic, and developmental issues — as well as more traditional military and political concerns. There is a special concern in the project on the control of nuclear weapons and reform of the nonproliferation regime.

The core group of the PRISM Project is a small group of scholars and students committed to interdisciplinary research and to making educational materials concerning public policy options available to political leaders, the media, and the public. The project is jointly coordinated by Gordon Thompson, Ph.D. (Oxford), Director of the Institute for Resource and Security, and Thomas Boudreau, Ph.D., Project Director. Inquiries can be sent to

PRISM Project
Institute for Resource and Security Studies
27 Ellsworth Avenue
Cambridge, MA 02139

SELECTED BIBLIOGRAPHY

Allison, Graham. *Essence of Decision: Explaining the Cuban Missile Crisis.* Boston: Little, Brown, 1971.

Bailey, Sydney D. *The Procedure of the UN Security Council.* Oxford: Clarendon Press, 1975.

Berridge, G. R., and Jennings, A., eds. *Diplomacy at the United Nations.* New York: St. Martin's Press, 1985.

Bingham, June. *U Thant: The Search for Peace.* New York: Alfred A. Knopf, 1970.

Boudreau, Thomas. *A New International Diplomatic Order.* Muscatine, Iowa: The Stanley Foundation, 1980.

_____. *Protecting the Innocent: Enhancing the Humanitarian Role of the United Nations in Natural Disasters and Other Disaster Situations.* New York: Council on Religion and International Affairs, 1983.

_____. "Buying Time in a Crisis." *WORLDVIEW,* November 1983.

_____. *The Secretary-General and Satellite Diplomacy.* New York: Carnegie Council on Ethics and International Affairs, 1984.

_____. *Watchman of the Peace: The Preventive Role of the UN Secretary-General.* Ph.D. Dissertation prepared for Social Science Program, the Maxwell School, Syracuse University, 1985.

Bracken, Paul. *The Command and Control of Nuclear Forces.* New Haven: Yale University Press, 1983.

Chai, F. Y. *Consultations and Consensus in the Security Council.* New York: UNITAR, 1971.

Claude, Inis L., Jr. *Swords into Plowshares: The Problems and Progress of International Organization.* 4th ed. New York: Random House, 1971.

Cuéllar, Javier Pérez de. *Report of the Secretary-General on the Work of the Organization, 1982.* New York: The United Nations.

De Bono, Edward. *Conflicts: A Better Way to Solve Them.* London: Harrap Limited, 1985.

Deudney, Daniel. "Whole Earth Security: A Geopolitics of Peace." Washington, D.C.: Worldwatch Institute, 1983, Worldwatch paper No. 55.

Fascell, Dante B., and Yatron, Gus. "Congress and the United Nations." *Proteus,* spring 1988.

Finger, Seymour Maxwell. Joseph R. Harbert, ed. *U.S. Policy in International Institutions.* Boulder: Westview Press, 1982.

Foote, Wilder, ed. *Servant of Peace: A Selection of the Speeches and Statements of Dag Hammarskjöld.* New York: Harper & Row, 1962.

Franck, Thomas M. *Nation against Nation: What Happened to the UN Dream and What the U.S. Can Do about It.* Oxford: Oxford University Press, 1985.

Frei, Daniel, ed. *International Crisis and Crisis Management.* Hampshire, England: Saxon House, 1978.

Goodrich, Leland M., and Hambro, Eduard, eds. *Charter of the United Nations: Commentary and Documents.* Boston: World Peace Foundation, 1946.

Gordenker, Leon. "Development in the UN System." Toby T. Gati, ed. *The U.S., the UN, and the Management of Global Change.* New York: New York University Press, 1983.

_____. *The UN Secretary-General and the Maintenance of Peace.* New York: Columbia University Press, 1967.

Gottlieb, Gideon. "The United Nations and Emergency Humanitarian Assistance in India-Pakistan." *The American Journal of International Law 66.*

Jackson, William D. "The Political Role of the Secretary-General under U Thant and Kurt Waldheim: Development or Decline?" *World Affairs 140* (winter 1978), 230–44.

Kalb, Madeleine G. "The UN's Embattled Peacekeeper." *New York Times Magazine.* December 19, 1982.

Kennedy, Robert F. *Thirteen Days: A Memoir of the Cuban Missile Crisis.* New York: W. W. Norton, 1969.

Lash, Joseph P. *Dag Hammarskjöld.* Garden City, NY: Doubleday, 1961.

_____. "Dag Hammarskjöld's Conception of His Office." *International Organization 16* (1962).

LeBow, Richard Ned. "The Cuban Missile Crisis: Reading the Lessons Correctly." *Political Science Quarterly 98* (fall 1983).

_____. *Nuclear Crisis Management: A Dangerous Illustration.* Ithaca: Cornell University Press, 1987.

Mitchell, C. R. *Peacemaking and the Consultant's Role.* London: Gower Press, 1981.

Morgenthau, Hans. *Politics among Nations.* 4th ed. New York: Alfred A. Knopf, 1967.

Nicol, Davidson, Croke, Margaret, and Adenivan, Babtunde. *The United Nations Security Council: Towards Greater Effectiveness.* New York: UNITAR, 1982.

O'Brien, Connor Cruise. *To Katanga and Back.* New York: Simon and Schuster, 1962.

_____. *The United Nations: A Sacred Drama.* New York: Simon and Schuster, 1968.

Pachter, Henry M. *Collision Course: The Cuban Missile Crisis and Coexistence.* New York: Praeger, 1963.

Parsons, Sir Anthony. "The Falkland Crisis in the United Nations, 31 March—14 June, 1982." *International Affairs 59,* 2 (spring 1983).

Pechota, Vratislav. *Complementary Structures of Third-Party Settlement of International Disputes.* New York: UNITAR, 1971.

_____. *The Quiet Approach: A Study of the Good Offices Exercised by the United Nations Secretary-General in the Cause of Peace.* New York: UNITAR, 1972.

Pope, Ronald. *Soviet Views on the Cuban Missile Crisis.* Washington, D.C.: University Press of America, 1982.

Ramcharan, B. G. *Humanitarian Good Offices in International Law: The Good Offices of the United Nations Secretary-General in the Field of Human Rights.* Dordrecht: Martinus Nijhoff, 1983.

Roberts, Adam, and Kingsbury, Benedict. *United Nations, Divided World.* Oxford: Clarendon Press, 1988.

Russett, Bruce, and Starr, Harvey. *World Politics: The Menu for Choice.* 2d ed. New York: W. H. Freeman, 1985.

Schlesinger, Arthur M. *A Thousand Days.* New York: Houghton Mifflin, 1965.

Schwebel, Stephen M. "The Origins and Development of Article 99 of the Charter." *The British Year-Book of International Law, 1951.*

_____. *The Secretary-General of the United Nations: His Political Power and Practice.* New York: Greenwood Press, 1952.

Singer, David. "The Level of Analysis Problem in International Relations." James Rosenau, ed. *International Politics and Foreign Policy*. New York: The Free Press, 1969.

Smelser, Neil J. *Essays in Sociological Explanation*. Englewood Cliffs, NJ: Prentice-Hall, 1968.

UNITAR. *The United Nations and the Maintenance of International Peace and Security*. Dordrecht: Martinus Nijhoff, 1987.

Urquhart, Brian. *Hammarskjöld*. New York: Alfred A. Knopf, 1973.

_____. *A Life in War and Peace*. New York: Harper & Row, 1987.

Walton, Richard J. *Cold War and Counterrevolution: The Foreign Policy of John F. Kennedy*. New York: Viking Press, 1971.

Young, Oran R. *The Intermediaries: Third Parties in International Crises*. Princeton: Princeton University Press, 1967.

Zacher, Mark W. *Dag Hammarskjöld's United Nations*. New York: Columbia University Press, 1970.

_____. *International Conflicts and Collective Security*. New York: Praeger, 1979.

INDEX

ABOUT THE AUTHOR

Although a U.S. citizen, Thomas E. Boudreau, Ph.D., started his educational career in an English day school. He has subsequently lived three years overseas in England, Ireland, and Sweden. He graduated Phi Beta Kappa, summa cum laude, from Boston College. Boudreau completed his Ph.D. in social sciences at the Maxwell School at Syracuse University in 1985. He has worked at the Carnegie Council in New York as Project Director of the Crisis Management and UN research projects. Boudreau has taught and lectured in the United States and Europe. He also served as Executive Director of the Irish Peace Institute at Limerick University in Ireland. He is currently director of the PRISM Project (Policy Review in International Security and Multilateralism) and a research fellow at the Institute for Resource and Security Studies at Cambridge, Massachusetts. He is also Professor of Peace Studies at St. John's University, Collegeville, Minnesota.